Somber Lust

SUNY Series in Modern Jewish Literature and Culture
Sarah Blacher Cohen, Editor

Somber Lust

The Art of Amos Oz

YAIR MAZOR

Translated by
Marganit Weinberger-Rotman

STATE UNIVERSITY OF NEW YORK PRESS

Published by
State University of New York Press, Albany

For information, address State University of New York Press, 90 State Street, Suite 700, Albany, NY 12207

Production by Judith Block
Marketing by Anne Valentine

Library of Congress Control Number

Mazor, Yair, 1950–
    [Lituf ba-afelah. English]
    Somber lust : the art of Amos Oz / by Yair Mazor ; translated by Marganit Weinberger-Rotman.
        p. cm. — (SUNY series in modern Jewish literature and culture)
    Includes bibliographical references and index.
    ISBN 0-7914-5307-3 (alk. paper) — ISBN 0-7914-5308-1 (pbk. : alk. paper)
    1. Oz, Amos—Criticism and interpretation. I. Title. II. Series.
PJ5054.O9 Z7813 2002
892.4'36—dc21
                                                            2001032203

10 9 8 7 6 5 4 3 2 1

Oh, those words of mine,
The sad and sunny nails of my life.
—Yehuda Amichai, Poem no. 10, in *Time*
(trans. Yair Mazor)

To Yael and Bilha

to my late parents
Rachel and Itzhak

and

to Sarah Rosentzweig

I do love you all very dearly,
and I find comfort in your love.

The Sonnet of the Sleeve of the Landscape

The sleeve of the landscape
Was folded over the arm of the shore.
The cheekbones of the ocean rose in the storm,
Your face burnt in the dark.

You had tickets for Hollywood and Sodom,
A velvet curtain covered the dream.
With a rusty needle you sewed a starlet's dress
And dead birds adorned your hair like a ribbon.

You wrapped the moon in blue paper
You could only fall down from the cotton clouds.
The mist pierced

The remnants of the light
And when you were gone, you left behind a souvenir: a hair
In the sink.

(Ronny Someck, trans. Marganit Weinberger-Rotman)

Contents

And if it is necessary to focus one's gaze and remain on the lookout for hours and days, perhaps even for years, well, there is nothing better to do anyway. Hoping for a recurrence of one of those rare, unexpected moments when the darkness is momentarily lifted, and there comes a flicker, a fleeting glimmer, which one must not miss, one must not be caught off guard. Because it may signify something that makes us ask ourselves what else is there. Besides rapture and humility.

—Amos Oz, *To Know a Woman*
(trans. Yair Mazor)

Acknowledgments

A day for toil, an hour for sport but for a friend a life is too short.
—Emerson, *Considerations by the Way*

I am grateful to the following people whose help and support have sustained me throughout the writing of this book and beyond: Dr. Sarah Blacher-Cohen, professor of English, gifted playwright, and editor of State University of New York Press's series in Modern Jewish Literature and Culture, for her continuous encouragement, generous friendship, and outstanding dedication; Dr. James Peltz, editor-in-chief of State University of New York Press, for his enthusiastic support, amicable cooperation, and unstinting kindness; Ms. Judith Block, senior production editor at State University of New York Press, for her incredibly devoted work, formidably extended help, and precious friendly attitude; Ms. Marganit Weinberger-Rotman, for skillfully translating the book from the original Hebrew, taking special pains to preserve its spirit, style, and aesthetic quality; Dr. Daniel Weber, president of the Wisconsin Society for Jewish Learning (WSJL), and Ms. Kathleen Jendusa, executive director of *WSJL*, for their highly valued friendship and personal support, as well as for their admirable dedication to the UWM (University of Wisconsin Milwaukee) Center for Jewish Studies and Hebrew Studies Program. Hearty gratitude is also extended to Ms. Mary Lineberger, rights and reproductions coordinator of the Cleveland Museum of Art, for her graciously granted help.

I also am particularly indebted to the Wisconsin Society for Jewish Learning for its continued support of my research and scholarship, as well as for its remarkable support of the UWM Center for Jewish Studies and the UWM Hebrew Studies program.

CHAPTER 1

Introduction: Mapping Poetics, Documenting Ideology, and Above All, Being Motivated by Love

A true artist sees in a stone the incipient shape trapped inside, and thus does not force the material, but rather sets the concealed shape free.
—Amos Oz, *Elsewhere, Perhaps*

Amos Oz once wrote:

> Reading two or three paragraphs will suffice to convince the reader that the author is not a thinker possessing a systematic theory, but rather an easily excitable person, who tends to react emotionally to various subjects; one of those ardent fellows who, when they don't contradict themselves, then they repeat themselves, and when they neither repeat nor contradict themselves—then they trip over their own line of thinking, and approach untheoretically topics that perhaps require a definite theoretical approach.

Introduction to *Under This Blazing Light*

Anyone reading Amos Oz's polemical and some what philosophical essays, in particular, his political, social texts, will easily observe that this is not emotional, sentimental writing, not a sweeping, gushing reaction to events that require restraint, filtering, and sorting out. Amos Oz's polemical theoretical writing is not an outpouring of emotion calling for control and restraint. Quite the reverse. Oz's polemical theoretical writing, dealing mostly with political and social issues, gives a distinct impression of very controlled, disciplined, succinct thinking, of highly methodical observations of reality, its processes, patterns, and manifestations. In sum, his writing shows a crystalline logic, sharply honed, polished, and precise.

Amos Oz approaches the reality under examination like a careful scientist in a laboratory, one eye closed and the other screwed to a sterile microscope, a sharp scalpel in hand. With great concentration and lucidity, he cuts, dissects, separates, sifts, delimits, and defines. He is always disciplined, meticulous, unerring. With economical, sure, and fluent motions of his pen, he formulates decisive, well-founded observations and draws clear, accurate, and perfectly logical conclusions.

And yet, there is not a single short story, novella, or novel by Amos Oz in which the loud, plaintive, scorching shrieks of naked desire and consuming eroticism do not erupt from the lower depths, making themselves heard and reverberating. Those desires that fill Amos Oz's literary work, those currents of libido and eroticism that course through his writings, are always somber, sinister, untamed, and defiant of the dictates of reason and restraint. This dark aspect manifests itself only within the confines of Oz's aesthetic, poetic territory, never beyond them, never in his polemical theoretical essays. Even in the literary texts, where the insistent erotic cries of desire emanate *de profundis*, there is an attempt, albeit skeptical and hesitant, to contain and restrain the gushing overwhelming sentiment, to throttle the shout and trap it inside the gaping throat.

Here we touch on the most profound, most fundamental poetic nerve of Amos Oz's fiction; the most pervasive and permanent element that recurs again and again in his writing is a state of rivalry and animosity, struggle and strife between two extremes that are irreconcilably hostile and antagonistic to each other. On the one hand, Oz's world is one founded on logic, discipline, pure reason and solid, cogent rationality; on the other hand, it is a dark, demonic world of unbridled desire, echoing with the hoarse shrill shrieks of passion and lust. The turbulent, murky world of gushing, untamed emotions threatens to invade the sober, well-lighted world of rationality and spread its deadly venom there. It seeks to undermine and destroy its order, balance, and serenity; to instill a sinister and evil spirit of malignancy and nightmare that will rob the other domain of its happiness and tranquility. Or, to paraphrase Oz's own terminology, it is a gangster out in a night of long swords, malicious, deadly, infernally clever; a highjacker conspiring to invade the cockpit, take over the helm and steer the craft off its straight and even course and eventually hurl it to perdition.

And yet, the two inveterate antagonists do not always stay barricaded behind their mutual enmity. At times there is a discernable step toward cessation of hostility and detente. There are subtle, hesitant steps toward moderation and accommodation found at the conclusion of some of Oz's stories and novels; a simultaneous attempt, in both territories, for the warring sides to inch their way toward the middle ground, to steer away from the path of perpetual strife and hatred and to accept the idea of coexistence. The dark, demonic fire begins to abate, and reconciliation, however fragile and tenuous, is given a chance. True, the power struggle between the two rivals is far from terminated, and probably will never cease, but a soft, placating, almost caressing breeze is suddenly felt on the frantic, sweaty neck.

Moreover, there are exchanges between the two sides: characteristics and properties that traditionally belong in one camp begin to migrate to the opposite side. It is not a sweeping trend, just a minor, marginal phenomenon, a modicum of assimilation. A true, complete reconciliation between the opposing poles will never be achieved, let there be no illusion. Any hope of a future truce is bound to be hollow, but something has changed, a tiny crack in the dike, a chink between stones in the wall.

Perhaps one can see an analogy here to the slow, moderate change that Amos Oz himself has wrought in his public image. He is no longer the "medicine man," the "Sage of the tribe," conjurer and exorcist of evil spirits, stirring the boiling cauldron of overflowing emotions. From now on, he redefines his function to become the watchmaker of the tribe. He is the one, cautiously, guardedly, who points out errors, time lags, and minute dislocations of the hands on the dial, and perhaps he dares to suggest ways to rectify, repair, and improve matters because, by now, he knows that one cannot subjugate the evil spirits, silence their howls, nor stifle their raucous, hoarse shrieks. What, then, can one do? At best, one can try, gingerly, tenderly, to minimize the burning, to contain the scorching flame, to tone down the noise, perhaps to quell the fury of the evil spirits. But there is no hope of silencing their malicious howling, their fiendish din. One can only try to appease their hysterical fury or, at least, to seek shelter from their venomous hissing, if only for a fleeting moment.

I shall expound on this in subsequent chapters, since this is the recurrent motif of this book: to describe the conflict between opposing poles in Amos Oz's fiction, to document the seething animosity that exists between the two antagonistic sides and, from time to time, to trace and map the guarded, tenuous, yet clearly discernible attempts at appeasement, to expose the fundamental positions of the opposing sides, and to map the poetics that impels both the struggle and the conciliation—in other words, to try to trace coordinates of the aesthetic strategy that governs Amos Oz's fiction.

My analysis of the texture of Oz's fiction in the subsequent chapters will be done from a formalistic-structuralist perspective, that is, treating the literary text as a cumulative continuum of signs but at the same time as a reservoir, a woven tapestry of simultaneous signs. In other words, perceiving the novel or novella as a two-sided textual structure: synchronic and diachronic. The synchronic side is simultaneous, comprising the spatial aspect of the text, in which the text is perceived as one unit, as if observed from an Olympian viewpoint, whereas the diachronic side is the dynamic aspect of the text, which serves as a skylight from which to view the cumulative development across the text. The literary analysis employed here attempts to identify and describe the signs and patterns that populate the textual system from both the diachronic-dynamic standpoint, on the one hand, and the synchronic-simultaneous, on the other hand.[1]

The following aspects will be examined by the two above-mentioned criteria: thematic materials, linear plots, motifs, structures, patterns, textual sequencing, depiction of characters and their motivation, the mapping of landscapes and their metaphoric and/or metonymic function, rhetorical registers, types of narrators and their points of view, the position of the implied author, and so on, in short, seeing the text as an intricate structure of signs and patterns that come together to form global systems of organization through the continual interaction of its components. This "negotiation" between all of the elements, patterns, and constituent parts of the system has a poetic, aesthetic function as well as conceptual and ideological ones, comprising all of the messages that are formulated in the literary text and corresponding with the reader through the poetic mechanism. Thus the structuralist approach to literary study focuses on the multilayered structure of the text, seeing it, on the one hand, as an integrated unit, and on the other hand, as a dynamic mechanism, perpetually moving, yet ever mindful of the poetic and ideological messages embedded in it. One might describe the structuralist approach to literary analysis as a relentless, exhaustive quest for the aesthetic and conceptual DNA encoded in the literary text and, for the task at hand, the one detectable in the narrative oeuvre of Amos Oz.

Language, doubtlessly, is one of the most salient elements in Amos Oz's fiction, a dependable, unerring watermark and one of its most attractive attributes. His style, the inner rhythm that manifests itself in syntactical patterns and idiosyncratic phrases, the captivating fluency that is not lost even when Oz imposes on it a "verbal diet," that is, restrains and streamlines it and lowers its registers—this unique, peculiar Ozian handwriting is always present, detectable, inescapable. How is one to define Oz's writing style?

The secret of his fascinating, colorful style is in its distinctive scent, in the aromatic bouquet that makes it uniquely and inimitably his. One cannot make a mistake: a single line suffices to recognize Oz's peerless, enticing style.

It is this unique verbal quality that prompted the subtitle of this chapter, "motivated by love." My aim is not merely to map Oz's poetics and document his ideas but to express love. It is not only the linguistic attributes that evoke this love. Amos Oz's writing contains more than one stratum; the worlds that he creates, evokes, molds, and shapes with so much yearning and longing must have found an echo in me and touched my innermost soul. It is as though a very clear, sharp voice, a hidden, subtle sound, emanates from Amos Oz's writing and finds resonance and response in me. And I do not mean to elaborate on this. Not here nor anywhere else, as Oz himself once remarked. But at the same time, there is something less personal that I have no problem discussing. And again, it is Oz's language, the linguistic aspect. The language of the sage, the witch doctor, the verbal magician, the skillful exorcist, the one sitting at the center of the circle, captivating and fascinating listeners with his silver tongue. As has been noted before, the seductive quality of Oz's language makes his prose practically irresistible.

Hence this joint effort to conduct a dialogue with Amos Oz and to produce a collaborative book. But there is more, much more, to it. It is not only the personal aspect of cooperating with Oz in the same literary forum; there is crucial importance, perhaps a unique one, to the correspondence between the author and the literary critic when it is gathered in one volume. It forms a crossroad for two opposing points of view to meet and complement each other, to negotiate, to exchange views, to shed light on each other, and to expose new angles of observing the texts in focus. In the process of comparison, materials are wrenched from their native context and implanted in a new one, the "host" context. Being compared and contrasted in an unnatural, nonautomatic context, each gains new dimensions and perspectives. In the process, new layers of meaning and interpretation are unearthed.

In an address delivered at a conference on S. Y. Agnon's fiction, Amos Oz spoke of a hidden, clandestine vein that exists in Agnon's fiction, a "vegetative" vein, he called it, dark, savage, untamed, undomesticated, a sinister, nightmarish current that wends its way in tenebrous depths. Perhaps he did not phrase it in these exact terms, but this was what he meant, and he was absolutely right. There is such a primeval, feral, irrational, sometimes demonic strain in Agnon's narratives, but it also is evident that such a sinister, diabolical, nightmarish strain lurks in the deepest regions of Amos Oz's own fiction.

Small wonder, then, that Oz cherishes Agnon's fiction so much and is such an excellent interpreter of his work. For, when Oz reads Agnon, he does not just read Agnon, he revisits his own fiction. But let me hasten to explain that this similarity between Agnon's and Oz's bedrock veins does not in any way diminish the latter's originality. Far from it. The affinity between Agnon and Oz is merely an additional poetic attribute that only enhances Oz's fiction and further elevates it.[2]

There is a children's Hanukkah song in Hebrew that begins, "We've come to drive away the darkness." But in Agnon's and Oz's fiction, there is no intention to drive away the darkness; quite the reverse; there is a tendency to listen to the darkness, to indulge in it, and to succumb to its savage, sinister, often venomous, ever-fascinating charm.

True, Agnon sometimes pretends to try to drive away the darkness, to defeat it or at least to camouflage it. He goes through the motions of trying to emasculate it, to curb its destructive force, to contain the erupting impulses. Oz, too, pretends to do so, but to a lesser degree. He allows the mass of darkness to float near the surface layer of the text and to peek through the chinks of the seemingly serene reality that it depicts. Agnon, on the other hand, presses down on the dark mass and pushes it back, away from the surface and into the bottom of the text. And he always covers the murky, demonic mass with one mask on top of another of sardonic, derisive, mischievous irony. His technique is reminiscent of Tchernichovsky's *Idylls* in that a tragic core is always found at the bottom of a beguiling, deceptively tranquil reality.[3] It is like the fairy-tale pea, lodged underneath a pile of mattresses and downy quilts, whose existence is persistently felt.

Yet in both Agnon's and Oz's fiction, no one attempts to drive away the darkness, no one sings light-drenched optimistic Hanukkah songs. In the deepest regions of Agnon's and Oz's fiction, darkness reigns, savagery rages furiously, and unbridled desires shriek hoarsely like baleful banshees. The demonic vein never ceases to pulsate with violence and hostility.

Amos Oz concluded his lecture on Agnon saying, "Forgive me if I did not tell you anything new. I wasn't invited here to deliver newfangled ideas. I came to tell you about suffering, love, and agony in Agnon, this Ecclesiastes who disguises himself in pretty costumes. I spoke about him the way I did out of love, love alone" ("The Profane Heart and the Way Back," *Under This Blazing Sun*). I, on the other hand, certainly intend to bring you new ideas, and I take the liberty to claim that I have, indeed, presented here a number of new interpretations. But, above all, I too came to tell you about suffering, love, and agony in Amos Oz's stories. I spoke about him the way I did out of love, love alone.

A final prefatory note:

Here and there throughout the book, one may come across some repetitions; comments in one chapter may recur in another. This was done deliberately, to render each chapter a self-contained unit, while at the same time to preserve the progression of the book as a unified whole, a panoramic map of the poetics of Amos Oz's fiction. The few repetitions, then, are meant as a convenience for the reader.

CHAPTER 2

Since the Jackals' Lament Carries the Sound of Yearning: Intertextuality and Deconstruction in "Nomads and Viper"

Somewhere in the world you are seized
By longing, like a sudden fever.
Oh, the girl in the moving train and the woman
On an empty, lighted platform.
   —Yehuda Amichai, "Sudden Longing,"
        in *An Hour of Grace*

Amos Oz wrote the story "Nomads and Viper" twice. Or more precisely, he wrote it once (in *Where the Jackals Howl*, 1965), and then he rewrote it (in *Where the Jackals Howl*, 1976).

One notices a certain duality here, but it is by no means a simple, technical duality. It stems from an attempt to effect a significant semantic, linguistic, and stylistic change, at least in the margin of the text, and possibly beyond it.

I regard this duality as a metaphor, since duality is indeed the name of the game in the aesthetics of Amos Oz's fiction. It is a complex kind of duality that begins with similarity and ends in opposition, with many shades in between. Many before me have commented on contrasts and antitheses in Amos Oz's fiction: light versus dark, order, sanity, and logic versus seething, unbridled desires, and so on.

Not only are the two poles antithetical and inimical to each other, but there is a constant attempt on the part of the untamed, sinister side to attack its sane, logical, and lucid opponent, to undermine its serenity, and to destroy its balanced existence. It is a marauding jackal raiding the chicken coop in order to wreak havoc on its denizens. Yet this dichotomy between two warring blocs is not a simple crude one either: their interaction is not restricted to conflict and rivalry but includes also analogy, similarity, an exchange of properties, and a blurring of borders. Make no mistake, then, the howling of the jackals harbors not only hatred but also a plaint, longing, and yearning.

In the short story "Nomads and Viper," the duality and the intricate pattern of opposites are a function of three fundamental approaches to literary texts: intertextuality, structuralism, and deconstruction, as will be further elucidated. While the intertextuality in the story is much more complex than at first meets the eye, and the structuralist element is likewise elaborate and ramified, the deconstructive examination is only partially applicable, although its presence is very conscious and calculated.

The term *intertextuality* was first coined by Julia Kristeva in 1966.[1] She defined intertextuality as "a theory of the text as a network of sign systems situated in relation to other systems of signifying practices . . . in a culture."[2]

The intertextual approach to literary texts is rooted in Marxist literary criticism and is a rejection and refutation of the Russian formalists' approach that emphasizes, strongly and categorically, the aesthetic mechanism of the literary text and seeks to map and catalog it as an independent entity, ignoring its potential relationship with other extratextual systems such as semiotic, social, cultural, ideological, or political (an approach later adopted by the school of New Criticism in the United States). In other words, intertextuality seeks to rescue the literary text from itself, from its separate aesthetic milieu, by emphasizing the ongoing dialogue between a given text and semiotic, sociological, historical, ideological, and other systems. No literary text, it is claimed, is an autonomous, self-contained product, unaffected by other literary and extraliterary systems. The presence of those systems contributes to the shaping of the literary text and invests it with more complete signification. Even though the original formula of intertextuality does not limit itself specifically to literary influences, stressing the role of the text as a crossroads of semiotic and semantic systems going beyond the poetic territory, many scholars tend to view intertextuality as a meeting point and a convergence of different literary texts within the framework of a given text.

The intertextual approach to literary texts is indirectly and at least partially co-opted by the deconstructive approach, since the latter focuses on incomplete, unstable relations between the signifier and the signified, between formulation and semantics. The relations between the linguistic-aesthetic signifier and the semantic signified are at the basis of intertextuality, whose purpose is to examine and explicate the hub of connections existing between the given textual system of signs and other semantic and semiotic systems that exist outside of the text. At any rate, the approach to intertextuality employed here hovers somewhere between the two extremes, emphasizing the meeting points of the given text with other texts while at the same time focusing on how the given text absorbs and reflects ideological and cultural contextual systems that are anchored outside of its boundaries and aesthetic radius.

A similar approach is used here regarding deconstruction. On the one hand, two of the basic assumptions of literary deconstruction will be used here, but on the other hand, there will be no absolute adherence to the philosophical conclusions drawn from these assumptions. In other words, only partial application will be effected, because deconstruction, though impressively cogent on a philosophical, theoretical level, is often weaker, less conclusive, and debatable when it comes to applying it to a given text in an interpretative process.

Deconstruction does not seek to take apart or dismantle a text to destroy it. It basically conceives of the text as a cumulative, perhaps infinite, continuum of contradictory, mutually exclusive significances, none of which are more valid or conclusive than the others.

In Cuddon's definition, "If anything is destroyed in a deconstructive reading, it is not the text but the claim to unequivocal domination of one mode of signifying over another."[3]

Indeed, one of the basic assumptions of Jacques Derrida, the founder of deconstruction, is that the text is nothing but a sequence of cumulative signs not possessing or projecting one absolute significance; each signifier relates to a signified, which in turn relates to another signified, and so on and so forth ad infinitum.[4] Derrida's claim is based on his observation that we are trapped in the confines of language and hence are incapable of freeing ourselves from the text (which is based on language). We lack the ability to adopt an external, objective point of view, the only point of view capable of endowing the text with a definitive, absolute truth.

As will be further demonstrated, this approach can be profitably applied to Oz's text, although, as mentioned above, only partially and very consciously so.

Another basic tenet of deconstruction theory is a function of its attack on traditional structuralism, which sees the literary text in binary terms. Thus there is a convergence in our story of the traditional structuralist approach and the postmodern, deconstructive approach. "Nomads and Viper" lends itself equally, though partially, to the textual analysis of either approach. According to structuralist theory, the binary pattern in the text is based on a solid, normative, polar hierarchy of opposites: the meaning of each arm of the polar binary structure is dictated by its semantic relation to its opposite. However, traditional structuralism (following Lévi-Strauss) defines the opposition in the binary structure in terms of stable semantic relations. Deconstruction, on the other hand, refutes the claim of stability. It maintains that the stability of semantic relations within the binary structure is both illusory and erroneous. There is no single, solid significance, either inside or outside of the binary structure, and the semantic relations are in a state of flux, forever unreliable. Nothing, in fact, is what it seems. The value system adopted and fostered by the text is refuted and undermined by the text itself.

The binary, bipolar structure, which uses pairs of contrasting opposites, is quite typical of Amos Oz's fiction. It is particularly apparent in this story.

In "Nomads and Viper," there is a clear distinction between two socio-cultural groups, as well as between individual characters: kibbutz society versus Bedouin society; tillers of the soil versus shepherds; dwellers in permanent structures, who are anchored in the land versus (seemingly) rootless nomads; Geula versus the young, one-eyed nomad; the hotheaded youngsters of the kibbutz versus Etkin, the levelheaded general secretary of the kibbutz, representative of the old guard; and the narrator himself, going back and forth between the two opposing camps, antagonizing each of them in turn.

Yet, as will be later demonstrated, the binary structure is by no means simple, crude, or inflexible. At some stage, each of the opposing groups adopts the behavior models and the moral codes that govern the other group. But, for all of the blurring of boundaries and the mutual migration from pole to pole, the two warring sides retain their dominant traits and are clearly distinguishable.

Here we reach the intertextual level at work in our story, at least in a partial meaning of the term: the dialogue between the given text and another text (i.e., the biblical story of the rivalry between Cain and Abel). And here the story itself offers an interpretation.

The reference is to the phrases used by Etkin, the kibbutz secretary and the representative of the older generation; his words clearly allude to the Genesis story of Cain and Abel. Etkin himself draws an analogy between the rivalry of the kibbutz society and the nomads, and Cain and Abel, the archetypal tiller of the soil and the shepherd. This analogy reveals not only intertextuality but an extraordinary complexity, since the biblical story is reflected in the story inversely, like the negative of a film, completely upsetting the order and balance of forces in the signified text. The formal system of norms embedded in the story emphasizes the moral and social superiority of kibbutz society over nomadic society, the supremacy of agriculturists, permanent settlers over shepherds who drive their flocks through the fields and orchards of the kibbutz, destroying crops and property. But underneath this formal system of norms exists an informal, fundamental system that has to do with the complex binary structure. The formal system of norms is based on a clear-cut distinction between "good guys" and "bad guys." The tillers of the soil are the "good guys," whereas the nomadic shepherds are the "bad guys." However, the intertextual level inverts this equation and turns it upside down; in the biblical story, Cain, the farmer, is the bad guy who rises up against his brother and slays him, whereas Abel, the shepherd, is the good guy, the innocent victim, hence the irony in the biblical punishment: Cain, the tiller of the soil, is forced to become a "fugitive and a vagabond," just like his slain brother, whose blood cried unto the Lord from the soil that Cain had tilled. There is a complete reversal here: Cain the farmer, the permanent settler, becomes a nomad, like the shepherd, while Abel, the nomadic shepherd, becomes a "permanent resident" of the same soil whence his blood cried unto the Lord.

And perhaps the irony implied in Cain's punishment is alluded to in Oz's story: carrying out his punishment, Cain assumes Abel's nomadic way of life; by the same token, the kibbutz society that sought to distinguish itself from the Bedouin society finds itself resembling it, mimicking its tribal and collective patterns of behavior.

But the reversal in Oz's story does not stop here. In Genesis, the nomadic shepherd is a victim of the tiller's aggression, whereas in our story, the reverse happens. The kibbutz society is victimized by the marauding nomads who steal from their fields and orchards and wreck their property. Moreover, in the biblical story, Cain fears vengeance and is, therefore, given "the mark of Cain," which shields him from vengeance, whereas in the story it is eventually the farmers who plan a collective punitive action and wreak vengeance on the nomads. Here there is a convergence of the intertextual and deconstructive readings. While a dialogue is conducted between the signified text and the signifying text, and during the reversal of normative forces between the texts, it becomes apparent that the binary structure is far from being clear cut or absolute. When the tillers of the soil in the story carry out their vengeful raid, they lose their moral superiority over the nomads and, in fact, adopt the behavioral model that until now had made them victims. They further upset the reversal that occurred on the intertextual level, drawing a moral line between the signified text and the signifying text; they cease to be the victims, or at least they suspend their victim status by assuming the reprehensible aggression of Cain.

We see, then, a mutual migration of behavioral models and moral norms between the two rival camps. Black is not so black, and white is not so white; whatever was considered good turns out to be capable of evil, and the binary pattern loses its shrill, sharp polarity. This is precisely what the deconstructive approach emphasizes: the lack of a definitive, incontrovertible meaning, the fluidity and instability that exist on the semantic level.

The same two-way migration between seemingly opposite poles occurs on another level of the story—in the relationship between Geula and the one-eyed nomad.

On the one hand, Geula and the one-eyed nomad stand on either side of a wall that separates normative opposites: Geula belongs to the positive, orderly, sane kibbutz society, whereas the one-eyed nomad belongs to the savage and sinister group that lurks in the dark and threatens to invade the clear, well-lighted world of the kibbutz, to rob it of its peace and undermine its foundations. This is part of the binary, polar structure of the story, identified at the outset. One also could describe the confrontation between Geula and the one-eyed nomad as a metaphor: a conflict on the personal level serving as a metaphor for the struggle between the two rival societies.

But on the other hand, we see here an exposure of the hidden, foundational level of the text, where its complex nature blunts the polarity of the binary structure. At the same time Geula is antithetical to the one-eyed nomad on the social-cultural level, she is also analogous to the nomad on the aesthetic level, because the two mirror each other. The meeting between them in the orchard underlines not only the antagonism of the two groups but also what is common to them on the personal level, their erotic attraction. They both experience erotic frustration, an unfulfilled sexual desire. They each yearn for a sexual partner that neither has yet been able to find. That partner eventually shows up in that clandestine meeting in the orchard. But even though the partner is there, the desires remain unfulfilled. No actual consummation takes place between Geula and the nomad, for although the erotic attraction between the two is undeniable, the walls of hostility and tribal abhorrence that separate them preclude any chance of sexual gratification. The one-eyed nomad leaves the orchard, and Guela, in a desperate attempt to quell her raging sexual desires, invents the rape story and eventually surrenders to the venomous, erotic bite of the viper.

The analogy between Geula and the one-eyed nomad comprises a wide web of minute details that gathers to form an undeniable reality. Their unfulfilled sexual desire is only the first detail. Geula's skill in making Arabic coffee connects her to the Bedouins. Her face, disfigured by sweat and reddish spots, brings to mind the nomad's repulsive visage. Guela hurls rocks at a "recalcitrant" bottle that refuses to shatter, and the young nomad hurls rocks at a recalcitrant goat who refuses to let go of a tree trunk. Geula lies when she makes up the story of the rape, and the nomad lies when he explains why he had entered the orchard. Geula is described as "accompanied by a sound of distant bells," while the Bedouins' camels are metonymically associated with ringing bells. Geula "puckers her lips and whistles a soft melody," and the nomads, we are told, "sing in the night," and a "long-drawn wail drifts from the Bedouin tents." The pungent odor of sweat emanating from Geula's body is reminiscent of the smell of the nomad's body. Geula asks the one-eyed nomad for a cigarette, just as he does on chance encounters with members of the kibbutz. The grimace that spreads on Geula's face when revulsion overcomes her brings to mind the unpleasant expression that spreads on the one-eyed nomad's face. Thus boundaries are blurred, opposites that seemed poles apart approach, and the rift between two warring sides becomes a complexity of antitheses and similarities.

Here the intertextuality is gaining broader scope: the negotiation is conducted not only between the given text and another text but also between the given text and a system of cultural and ethical norms that derive from a nonliterary context.

The complexity that marks this story, whereby seemingly solid, tried-and-true norms are seen as shaky and fluid, is nowhere more pronounced than in the figure of the narrator.

The narrator begins the story from an observer's position, narrating the events from a distant, detached, Olympian point of view. But, in fact, he is far from being objective; despite the external, impartial point of view he assumes at the start, his allegiance is clearly with the kibbutz society, and his attitude toward the Bedouins is one of revulsion and distrust. However, this ostensible subjectivity of the omniscient narrator soon undergoes a deliberate change: the "we" he uses at the outset ("How unlike our well-tended sheep are their scrawny sheep") soon transforms into a first-person witness account. Even though he is not actively involved in the events of the plot, he makes no attempt to dissociate himself from the other characters. Toward the end of the story, his involvement in the story gathers momentum; we find out about his intimate relations with Geula, his presence at the kibbutz debate, and his participation in the retaliatory action against the Bedouins carried out by the younger members. This dynamic of changes and transformations in the rhetorical status of the narrator functions as a metaphor reflecting and documenting the escalation in the tension and rivalry between the kibbutz and the nomads—starting with a position of appeasement and conciliation on the side of the kibbutz (dictated by Etkin, the secretary, the representative of the old guard, whom the narrator likes and supports) and ending with an aggressive, belligerent position fostered by the younger members (whom the narrator, lenient and peace loving though he is by nature, eventually joins) who rebel against Etkin's policy of restraint and propitiation.

The narrator, then, clearly embodies the flux that exists between the two seemingly inveterate opposing societies—the kibbutz and the nomads. On the one hand, like Geula, the narrator is a representative of the kibbutz community, a society facing the threats and hostility of the nomadic society. But, on the other hand, just like Geula, his allegiance to one camp is not absolute or exclusive, and he is capable of relating to the "others" and of empathizing with them.

This finds expression in his support for a policy of restraint and appeasement toward the nomads. This is true throughout most of the story until he undergoes a change of heart. But the narrator evinces not only closeness but also analogy to the nomads, particularly to the one-eyed shepherd, who also is analogous to Geula. Like the nomad, the narrator too meets Geula in the orchard, and their encounter is fraught with erotic tension. The narrator "lays a conciliatory hand" on Geula's neck, whereas the nomad extends "a caressing hand" toward her. We are told that the narrator used to sneak into Geula's room, whereas the nomad sneaks into the orchard where she walks and feels secure. And yet, at the end of the story, the narrator finds himself allied with the younger members of the kibbutz, who are the most extreme in their antagonism to the nomads. His participation in the retaliatory action against the nomads is just as pronounced as was his previous position, that of accepting Etkin's appeasement policy.

Structurally, the narrator functions as the connecting link between the two plot circles: the struggle between the kibbutz and the nomads (the outer circle) and the erotic encounter between Geula and the one-eyed nomad in the orchard (the inner circle). Due to his involvement with the main characters in both circles, the narrator serves as a point of tangency of the two circles. Moreover, his character embodies the complexity of the text: the narrator shifts from a position of omniscience to an eyewitness account, then to an involved protagonist. Formally, he is a member of the kibbutz society that is inimical to the nomads, yet he evinces sympathy and affinity for the Bedouin society and is closely analogous to one of its members. Eventually he abandons his conciliatory position toward the nomads and joins the hawkish, extremist members in a punitive raid on the nomads. Thus the narrator, by changing allegiances and rhetorical positions, reflects the constant tension that exists between the formal exterior of the text and its informal, inner tenor, as well as the fluid, blurry position of the two opposing poles.

The same imperfect duality can be discerned in another quasi-marginal analogy found in the text. The story culminates with a viper biting Geula, who languorously surrenders to its sexual venom until, presumably, she dies. This viper, however, has been adumbrated earlier in the story, when "a fat house cat killed a small snake and dragged its carcass onto the scorching concrete path to toy with it lazily." The link between the small snake killed by the cat and the fearsome deadly viper is further reinforced with the mention of the "angry snort" (or hissing sound) that comes from the kitchen when the incident with the cat occurs. This angry, snorting sound calls to mind the hissing of a viper attacking its prey. Thus we have here a double-jointed analogy based on the link between the two snakes. But these are very different snakes: one is tiny, powerless, and killed by a cat, and the other is deadly and venomous, killing a full-grown person. In other words, the same entity (a snake) is split into two discrete, conspicuously different units; the snake is both active and passive, killer and killed, attacker and attacked. Two separate, inconsistent entities converge into one image. So it is in the microcosm of the metaphor and in the macrocosm of the story; an apparently divided structure, but in fact a blurring and a merging of opposites. The little snake slain by the cat is still a snake, possessing the deadly potential of the aggressor viper. The very title of the story, "Nomads and Viper," exemplifies the same dubious duality. In keeping with the formal nature of the story, the title too presents a binary pattern (comprising two elements: nomads and viper). But this is deceptive: despite the formal binary structure, in reality the title focuses only on one side of the struggle. The nomads and the viper belong to the savage and sinister camp that lurks in the dark and threatens to invade and destroy the bright, orderly, sane camp. The title, in fact, "does not deliver the goods." The reader's expectation that the formal, binary nature of the title will reflect the formal, binary nature of the story is not fulfilled. The story's own reservations about the formal binary structure are thus intimated in its very title, even before the first line is read.

One of the definitions of deconstruction begins thus:

"Deconstruction can begin when we locate the moment when a text transgresses the laws it appears to set up for itself."[5] Ergo: we can start discussing deconstruction from the point where the text begins to subvert and undermine its own laws.

This is what happens in our story: it refuses to obey the formal, binary, rigidly divided structure that it so blatantly posits at the outset. Instead of fostering that formal structure, the story turns its back on its "sterile" pedestrian nature and offers instead another, more complex semantic structure, where the characteristics of one camp migrate, blend, and blur with those of the opposite camp. The complexity does not negate the fundamental, binary formality of the structure, but it increasingly and undeniably asserts its presence. Yet the story does not begin with a formal structure and then proceed to undermine and replace it with an alternative structure: it is based on two, contradictory, rival elements. The fact that one structure is undermined by its counterpart does not mean that the story denies its own logic; it is part of the infrastructure on which the story was based to begin with.

It is commonly held that deconstruction documents a state of perennial instability on the semantic level of the text. Every signifier is a signified of another signifier, and so on ad infinitum. Consequently, no significance can ever be construed as final or absolute; it is only there to be contradicted by another significance that will, in turn, be contradicted. Although I maintain that the validity of this claim on the philosophical level is no guarantee for its application on an interpretative level, I am aware of its fundamental merit; the refusal to take anything for granted, the insistence on a continual investigation, even after the final conclusion has been drawn. It is an approach that hones the interpretive skills, insists on the complexity of the literary text, and seeks new layers of meaning. The contradictory meanings it reveals in the text do not undermine it but rather underscore its elasticity, its manifold layers, its ability to benefit from the tension between those simultaneously conflicting semantic strata.

In "Nomads and Viper," such tension arises from a convergence of contradictory semantic levels in one aesthetic locus, as it is translated into a multilayered terminology: ideological, moral, and political. Here I deviate from the deconstructive approach, because I maintain that the simultaneous convergence of various semantic levels creates a super meaning that can be located and formulated. To wit: that there are no absolute, irreconcilable extremes, that there is no sterile, watertight buffer separating two warring camps; there is no absolute justice confronting absolute injustice; there is no "either/or" with a yawning vacuum separating extremes. Certainly opposing poles exist, but there also are intermediate stages and a complex reality where the differences between victory and defeat are not clear cut; right and wrong are not etched in stone. Even the purest of notes occasionally grates. There are no absolute states and no absolute truths. As Amos Oz once phrased it, in his wonted succinct and poignant style, "A perfect, rounded justice is a pernicious, lethal justice."[6] For justice does not stay perennially fresh on the shelf, and the lack of absolute justice is what makes reality complex; it is this complexity that demands solutions based on compromise. Compromise is indeed a far cry from the desired maximum, but it is the optimal minimum one can live with, without compromising the other's right to exist.

And let us not forget what Abu-Ziad, the editor of the Arabic newspaper *Al-Fajer (Dawn)*, said to Amos Oz in the fall of 1982: "There is this justice and that justice, but above this or that justice there is always reality."[7]

CHAPTER 3

The Father, the Son, and the Blowing of the Ill Wind, or Writing Strindberg from Right to Left

The combat deepens. Oh, ye brave,
Who rush to glory, or the grave!
—Campbell, *Hohenlinden*, St. 7

Out of the depth of your terror, lift up your eyes and look at the tops of the pine trees. A halo of pale purple light adorns the treetops. A luminous seren-ity hovers above the purified treetops, soothes them with its caresses. Only the barren rocks, the barren rocks are parched to death. Give them a sign.
—Amos Oz, *Strange Fire*

A Journey to Father: A Beginning which Is an End

Identifying the father motif in Amos Oz's works does not require very attentive reading. It certainly does not require special perspicuity, for the presence of the father motif in Oz's fiction is both obvious and prevalent, like the incessant blowing of a warm wind on the back of one's neck. The father image in Oz's work can be found on the high roads, in back alleys, in front and in back, and in the parlor as well as in the pantry. Its representation is both prominent and poetically complex, since it reflects and underscores the fundamental meaning of the work.

The father motif in *My Michael* is one of the most conspicuous and important motifs in that novel. Hannah, the heroine, is very ambivalent to-ward her father's memory; she is forever oscillating between two conflicting attitudes: nostalgic longing for her late father, and angry, resentful rejection of him. Her father's personality, at least as perceived by his daughter, is one of meekness, self-effacement, and gentleness that borders on feebleness; he has an almost compulsive need to apologize and kowtow to people around him who project a sense of power and self-confidence. The aura of submis-sion, acquiescence, and self-abnegation that emanates from her father arouses in Hannah conflicting feelings: pity tinged with revulsion and loathing but

17

also loving kindness and compassion. And then Hannah takes a decisive step; she marries Michael, who, in many respects, is reminiscent of her late father—his attentiveness and diligence, his innate docility and willingness to comply and ingratiate himself with others. Michael does not have a prepossessing, charismatic personality but rather a gray, some might say, boring one, very much like her father's.

And yet, to do him justice, Michael may be gray and a little boring, but he is not feeble. He possesses inner strength, a firm backbone and self-control. Still, on one level at least, the analogy between Michael and Hannah's father is explicit and deliberate. The novel is replete with allusions to the two conflicting attitudes of Hannah toward her father and his memory. The same ambivalence and complexity characterizes her attitude toward her husband Michael. On the one hand, his lackluster, uncharismatic personality provokes her reticence. He is too quiet, thorough, and devoted, devoid of mystery and excitement, and out of touch with his wife's romantic proclivities and her complex and many-faceted personality. He is a gray man, with a gray hat and a gray raincoat.

On the other hand, Hannah is attracted to (and dependent on) Michael's stability, solidity, restraint, self-confidence, and inner peace. The simultaneous attraction and aversion characterizing her relations with Michael become, for her, a metaphor for the forces that dominate her life—the conjunction of two contradictory elements in her torn, tormented, and restless soul. They are the source of Hannah's misfortune but, by the same token, they also are her survival and salvation.

The motif of the father in *My Michael* gathers momentum precisely because of the analogy between Michael and Hannah's father. This analogy is present in the first stages of the plot and comes to the fore in the description of Hannah's and Michael's wedding:

> Our canopy stood on the roof of the old rabbinate building on Jaffa Road. . . . Michael and his father both wore black suits with a white handkerchief in the breastpocket. They looked so much alike that I twice mistook them one for the other. I addressed my husband Michael as Yehezkel. (p. 37)

This description underscores Michael's function as the heir and surrogate of her late father in Hannah's present and future life. The mistaken identity emphasizes the thematic-metaphoric link between husband and father, which is further reinforced by the allusion to Agnon's story "In the Prime of Her Life," which evidently was a major source of influence on *My Michael*. The heroines of both stories, Tirtza Mazal and Hannah Gonen, as narrators, address the reader by written memoirs describing their unfulfilled lives, their painful frustrations, and their alienation from their husbands. Tirtza, daughter of the late Leah, chose her husband as a substitute for her mother's life, which was cut short in her youth (she lost her beloved who, correspondingly, became her daughter's "lost father"), just as Hannah chose her husband as a substitute for her father, who died young. This is how Tirtza phrases it: "Both my father and my husband have been kind to me; in their love and compassion they resembled each other."[1]

The complexity of the father motif in *My Michael* has other manifestations based on references to well-known literary texts that the reader is expected to recognize and whose thematic relevance should be appreciated. Remember Yardena? She is Michael's schoolmate, whose uninhibited, cheerful, and fearless personality serves as a foil to Hannah's restrained, repressed and dour temperament. (By the way, this same Yardena surfaces, thirty years later, in, Oz's *A Panther in the Basement*.) Yardena, then, visits Michael and Hannah on several occasions, and Michael helps her write a thesis in geology, a subject they both study:

> He lit his pipe and invited Yardena into his study. For half an hour or an hour, they sat together at his desk. His voice sounded deep and stern; hers, constantly stifling little giggles. Their heads, one yellow, the other graying, were revealed to me as if floating on clouds of smoke when I rolled in the tea cart and offered them coffee and cakes. (pp. 127–28)

Surprisingly, or perhaps not so surprisingly, one discerns in this seemingly innocent description an allusion to the famous poem *My Father* by Bialik: "Behind barrels of mulled wine, over a yellow parchment/My father's head was revealed to me, a martyred skull/As if severed from his shoulders, floating on clouds of smoke." Thus the yellow color figures in both texts, as does the rhetorical device of observing the scene from a remote observation point ("their heads were revealed to me" in Oz, and "my father's head was revealed to me" in Bialik), as well as the similarity in sounds (in Hebrew) between "rolled in" (*gilgalti*) in Oz and "skull" in Bialik (*gulgolet*). The fact that the situations in both texts (Bialik's father serving wine to his customers and Hannah offering coffee and cakes to Michael and Yardena) are analogous further underscores the affinity between the two texts. In addition, in *My Michael*, Hannah's father is described as offering his services to people:

> He used to talk to people as if he had to appease them and elicit sympathy that he did not deserve. He had a radio and electric appliance store—sales and simple repairs. (p. 10)

My Michael evokes the image of the humble, submissive father from Bialik's poem, not only to highlight the motif of the father in general but to emphasize the close resemblance between Michael and Hannah's late father and the fact that, for Hannah, Michael is a substitute for her lost father. Yet for all of his restraint and humbleness, Michael possesses a certain robust, muscular inner strength that apparently was lacking in Hannah's father. This granite-like strength serves as a ballast to Hannah's volatile, turbulent spirit, providing her with a protective shell and preventing her from crashing. Yet in the passage quoted above, the implied narrator—to use Booth's serviceable terminology—by subtly alluding to Bialik's poem *My Father*, underlines the humble, submissive qualities that both Michael and Hannah's father have in common.

In Bialik's entire oeuvre, the father's image is split, Janus-like, into two contradictory, sharply delineated sides. Whereas in the poem *My Father* the father comes across as meek and mild, resigned and defeated, pitiful in his suffering and shame, the father in the novella *Aftergrowth* is a harsh, insensitive, almost brutal man who rejects and abandons his son. Thus while the father in the poem arouses the reader's unqualified sympathy, the father in *Aftergrowth* elicits only revulsion and contempt. I have written elsewhere about a similar duality in the image of the father in Dahlia Ravikovitch's poetry and fiction: the strict, almost abusive father, in the poem *Mean Hand* (in *Love of an Orange*), who is oblivious to his daughter's sensitivity and vulnerability, compared to the warm, soft, compassionate father in the short story "Twenty Five Years," in *Death in the Family*.[2] A similar phenomenon occurs in Amos Oz's fiction; two kinds of fathers populate his stories—an implacable, demanding one versus a meek, attentive one. Admittedly, this is a generalization that may not apply in all cases, but its validity has been proven in the texts under discussion. The "soft," attentive, sensitive fathers in Oz's fiction include, among others, Hans Kipniss in *The Hill of the Evil Council*, Reuven Harish in *Elsewhere, Perhaps*, Yossef Yarden in "Strange Fire," Michael Gonen and Hannah's father in *My Michael*, and Herbert Segal, the kibbutz general secretary in *Elsewhere, Perhaps*, who, even though he is not a father, certainly functions as an attentive, compassionate father to Rami Rimmon, who has lost his own father (probably a "soft," merciful one, as is Yehezkel, Michael's father in *My Michael*). The harsh, demanding fathers who terrorize their sons, include, among others, Shimshon Sheinbaum, in "The Way of the Wind," to some extent, Yoel Raviv, in *To Know a Woman*, certainly Yolek Lifshitz, in *A Perfect Peace*, and again, partially and to a limited extent, the father in *A Panther in the Basement*, as well as the father in *Soumchi*, a novel for young adults.

This section, "A Journey to Father," is a journey toward both the "soft," compassionate fathers and the "hard," demanding ones who populate Amos Oz's fiction. This differentiation between fathers characterizes all of Oz's fiction. Its metaphoric function reflects the more fundamental dichotomy between opposing poles—the dark and sinister versus the bright and sane—that lies at the core of all of Oz's fiction.

Tender Is the Father

Softness and hardness are not absolute attributes. The tender, attentive, sensitive fathers (especially those coupled with demanding women) who populate Oz's fiction are certainly not of one piece. The attentiveness and vulnerability they display are of varying degrees. Where one exhibits helplessness, another may show strength. Yet there are several common denominators that connect them and that at times make them seem like clones of one another. One such quality is the fact that the "tender" fathers are all "tainted" with mediocrity: they all possess a lackluster, dull personality, devoid of brilliance and dazzle. There is industry but no spark. For instance, Reuven Harish, in Oz's *Elsewhere, Perhaps*, possesses a poetic sensitivity that is totally absent in the gray, somewhat vapid personality of Oz's Michael in *My Michael*. On the other hand, Michael's personality harbors restrained powers, a kind of pent-up, tight, sinewy strength. In this respect, Michael's gray, monkish aspect, with the unprepossessing, lean physique, is, to a certain extent, misleading. Conversely, behind Reuven Harish's poetic sensitivity and rich, introverted, aesthetic psyche (albeit devoid of brilliance or wit) resides, in fact, a rather weak spine, not totally limp and ineffectual but far from the robustness observed in Michael. As elsewhere in Oz's fiction, where opposing poles often "migrate" from one side to the other, in the binary equation of the fathers, the divisions are not always clear cut. A case in point is the strict and demanding father in *A Panther in the Basement*, who projects a gray, insipid, almost boring image, making him, at least ostensibly, part of the soft and gentle fathers, which he definitely is not. But the basic common denominators are still there. Reuven Harish, in *Elsewhere, Perhaps*, is described thus: "What a pity that Reuven Harish is not sharp witted and quick in repartee" (p. 24), and then the narrator adds, somewhat ironically, "But one must say in his defense that he is diligent" (op. cit.). And the same applies to *My Michael's* Michael Gonen. "He did not come up with an answer, because he is not by nature quick witted" (p. 7). And later, "A hard-working, stable young man will not get lost; he'll end up as a Teaching

Assistant" (p. 67). Here, incidentally, the stylistic influence of Agnon on Oz is evident.

The innate mediocrity of the gentle fathers is reflected also in their professions. The father in "Mr. Levi" works in a printing shop (unlike the poet, Mr. Nehemkin), which is considered a disadvantage. The father in *A Panther in the Basement* is a librarian, not a writer. His nocturnal efforts to write a book about the history of Polish Jews do not smack of inspired creativity. There also is an ironic allusion here to Manfred Herbst in Agnon's novel *Shira*, who is hard at work on a historical opus on Byzantium, a book he will never finish. Perhaps there also is an allusion here to Akavia Mazal in Agnon's story "In the Prime of Her Life," who digs up old graves in an attempt to write the history of Jews in his town. Here too the impression is of an uninspired, prosy, jejune enterprise, devoid of spark or creativity. Thus Michael Gonen, in *My Michael*, is "an intelligent, unassuming young man, perhaps not brilliant, but certainly stable" (p. 32). When Michael gets a scholarship, it is "second class" (p. 67), underscoring his mediocrity, rather than his academic excellence. Hans Kipniss, in the novella *The Hill of the Evil Council*, is indeed a doctor, but only a veterinarian. The boy-narrator emphasizes, "Father was not a real doctor, he was a horse doctor" (p. 9). (Note the derogatory tone, reminiscent of the low status of the pharmacist, compared to the physician in Hassidic literature who seeks to denigrate the Enlightenment.) When that father reaches the height of his career, it is only a "teaching assistant's position at the Hebrew University" (p. 54). Michael Gonen also does not become a professor, a lecturer, or a teacher. He does not rise above the rank of an assistant.

The limited status of Hans Kipniss and Michael Gonen is further underscored by the great achievements of other members of their families who have excelled in science and education. Michael's grandfather was a "celebrated teacher" (p. 9), and Hans' uncle was a "celebrated geographer" (p. 9). Moreover, their lackluster, mediocre personalities find expression in the feeble, ludicrous way they vent their anger. When Michael is angry, his voice sounds "thin and tremulous" (p. 25). As for Hans, "father noticed me, and burst out in thin anger" (p. 109). Even the venting of anger, normally an occasion for powerful eruption, in feeble men such as Hans and Michael, assumes the guise of something derisive and pathetic.

The gentle fathers do not become more robust when they change roles from fathers to husbands. They are typically married to impressive, overpowering women, driven by strong, repressed urges, women fueled by strange fires, "black demonic fires," in Oz's phrase, women whose deep-seated sexual frustrations and undisclosed romantic yearnings lend them a kind of acerbic, invidious intensity that overshadows and dwarfs the figures of the introverted, gentle husband-father. Put differently, the woman's tempestuous, dominant presence serves only to emphasize the pitiful stature of the husband-father. This is how Michael Gonen is depicted in one of the scenes from his married life in *My Michael*:

> He put on an apron and went back to the sink . . . stood bending over the sink, as if his neck was broken, and his movements were very tired. (pp. 68–69)

And similarly, in the story "Mr. Levi": "Dad will put on Mom's apron and wash the dishes with soap" (p. 77). In both cases, we see husbands whose prosaic grayness prevents them from satisfying their wives' turbulent sexual yearnings. In each case, the wife cheats on her husband in her own particular way, one with frenzied fantasies, in which she (Hannah Gonen) abandons herself to twin Arab boys, the other, (in "Mr. Levi") by taunting her husband and dropping hints that she has admitted Ephraim into her bedroom:

> Ephraim came in and installed a night lamp by her bed. . . . At noon, Dad came up from the print shop in the basement and, his nostrils twitching, said feebly, "Who was here this morning? Whose smell is this?" Mom laughed. (p. 81)

One is reminded of the erotic connotation that laughter has in the Bible (see the story of Joseph and Potiphar's wife, Ishmael's laughter at Isaac, proving his sexual maturation and thereby threatening Isaac's birthright, and Samson entertaining the jeering Philistines who laugh at his impotence). Perhaps it is not politically correct to claim that a husband bending over a kitchen sink projects a feeble, emasculated image, but when we see Michael Gonen in *My Michael* and the father in "Mr. Levi" almost effaced by their wives' exuberant temperaments and gushing sexuality, it is hard not to see the description of the tired, apron-clad husbands, washing dishes in the kitchen sink, as a metaphor underscoring their weakness and ineffectuality. Because the women, fascinating, seething with burning emotions, and consumed as they are by erotic yearnings, are tied, almost against their will, to the tame, much simpler husbands. The women have more complex, "wintry" personalities; they long for enchanted, moonlit European landscapes and spurn the scorching blazing light of their surroundings. They dream of lush green pastures, of thick woods on sloping mountains, of darkening lakes and russet autumn leaves. These women despise the thorny, torrid, scowling land of

Israel and are therefore trapped in their resentment and frustration. They resent both the tropical country and their feeble, ineffectual husbands who are too simple minded and too rational to understand the demonic, destructive fire that rages in their hearts. The women march to the beat of a different, distant drummer; they respond to foreign sounds and odors. Some of them end up following those distant calls, while others remain. Eva Harish, in *Elsewhere, Perhaps*, and Ruth Kipniss, in *The Hill of the Evil Council*, leave. Those who do not leave find substitutes: they escape into a dreamlike reality, indulge in fantasies, give in to searing, gnawing sadness, cheat on the dull, uninspired husbands, and succumb to sickness and even madness.

Hannah Gonen, in *My Michael*, employs several of these methods of escape. The fact is, though Michael may be *her Michael*, she is certainly not *his Hannah*. She is analogous to Tirtza, in Agnon's "In the Prime of her Life," who, fleeing oppressive reality, finds refuge in sickness. On the other hand, Hannah also is analogous to her neighbor, Duba Glick, whose insanity reflects Hannah's own incursions into the realm of madness. In "Mr. Levi," Oz introduces a female character, Helena Grill, whose mental derangement and aggressive sexuality are quite explicit. That story also contains the figure of the mother, Mrs. Kolodny, who, like Hannah Gonen, is an attractive, intriguing, yet desperate woman, whose powerful sexuality is wasted on a taciturn, stodgy husband. It is implied that Mrs. Kolodny cheats on her husband, thus daring to act out what Hannah Gonen does only in her fantasies, where she imagines herself ravished by the twin Arab boys she conjures up from her childhood memories. This is the "hairy, panting element," as Doctor Nussbaum calls it, in the short story "Longing." The pensive, wintry women who populate Oz's fiction yearn to give themselves up to the "hairy, panting element," to respond to the savage and dangerous drumbeat that, like the jackals' plaintive howl, lures them from the darkness. In a similar vein, Rami Rimmon, in *Elsewhere, Perhaps,* observes soberly, "Women actually live in a different world, a more colorful world. Even when they're with you, they are not really with you" (p. 115). Thus Proffy's mother, in *A Panther in the Basement*, is described as sitting in an armchair by the window, with an open book face down on her lap, her eyes shut in great concentration as she listens attentively to a sound emanating from somewhere far away, a sound that no one but herself can recognize or even hear (p. 27). Needless to say, the husband—who also is the father in the story—is totally incapable of responding to her desperate plea, of satisfying her needs. His passive, unsophisticated personality cannot bring solace to her yearnings, cannot quell the turbulence in her soul.

Thus the desperate, frustrated women begin to harbor bitter feelings of resentment and hate, first toward themselves, for not being able to extricate themselves from the constricting bonds of marriage to feeble, boring husbands, and second, anger toward the husbands whose lack of imagination and mental resources prevents them from reaching the innermost souls of their wives and responding to the black, demonic urges that rage in their bellies. This festering anger is then translated into a virulent, defiant attack. The women lash out against their husbands and taunt them with bitter mockery. "You will die as you were born, a miserable wretch, Micha Ganz. Period," Hannah says to her Michael in *My Michael*. And Ruth Kipniss, in *TheHill of the Evil Council*, has this to say to Hans:

> Don't look at me this way. I want you to realize, once and for all, that I detest, detest! your Wertheimer and Buber and Shertock. I wish the National Military Organization and the Stern Gang would blow them all to smithereens. I hate them with every fiber in my body. And stop looking at me like that. (p. 30)

When, to his great chagrin, Michael, in *My Michael*, finds out that a British scientist has disproved the theory he had advanced in his doctoral thesis, Hannah chastises her husband, thus:

> "Great," I cried, "here's your chance, Michael Gonen! Fight the Englishman, demolish him, don't give in without a struggle, Michael. I'd like to see you fight and win. Then I would be very proud of you." (p. 184)

Michael's reply to Hannah's challenge underscores not only the cold rationality that drives his behavior but also his inability to match his wife's tempestuous, vibrant temperament. "'I can't,' Michael said sheepishly. "It isn't possible. He's right. I'm convinced of it'" (p. 184). She was not looking for a rational, docile answer. But the point is, Michael will never come up with another response. He will never fully understand the resentment, the desperation, the defiance that is implied in her plaint. A similar exhortation is directed by Noga Harish, in *Elsewhere, Perhaps*, at her man. "Lift up your head, Rami, don't flinch, fight back. I want to see you fight!" (p. 121).

Despite the profound difference between the reserved, refined, intellectual Michael Gonen and the somewhat boorish, clumsy, inarticulate peasant Rami Rimmon, the two have this in common—they both stand helpless, flaccid, and shamefaced in front of their implacable women. What weapon do these men have in their arsenal against the black, demonic fire confronting them? Only awkward heavy silence and submission, at most a bashful smile. In *My Michael*, "Michael, of course, responded with a smile. And silence" (p. 167). Or the father in "Mr. Levi," "The wonted 'pedagogical' smile appeared on his lips" (p. 81). Or Hans Kipniss, in *TheHill of the Evil Council*, "'There, you remembered to smile. Finally. Why are you smiling?' Father kept silent."

One common denominator that these unfulfilled women have is a subtle, seemingly marginal motif that weaves itself, barely noticed, throughout the stories. It is the motif of the color blue, which is associated with many of these yearning, aching women. This fact is, in itself, rather perplexing, since blue usually has the connotation of cold, sober rationality, the opposite of the gushing, uncontrolled eroticism that typifies Oz's women.[3]

But this is a putative contradiction, since all colors carry inconsistent connotations, whose significance derives from the context in which they are couched. For example, green implies, on the one hand, venom, poison, and seething rage and, on the other hand, fresh growth and renewal. When the poet Nathan Alterman writes of "greenish evil" (in conjunction with "black suspicion"), he invokes the negative connotations of green, suspending the positive ones. Or take, for instance, the color yellow. In Gnessin's fiction, yellow invariably denotes negative qualities such as aridity, desiccation, sterility, and alienation, whereas in works by Knut Hamsun (who had a certain influence on Gnessin), yellow is associated with the exact opposite; it is the color of the radiant, bountiful sun, hence, implying creativity, inspiration, and artistic activity.[4] The color red, in contrast, is fraught with negative connotations: it is the color of blood and thus is associated with death. Yet blood also can evoke life, bloom, fruition, youthful blush. White connotes pristine, virginal purity, namely, positive qualities, and yet in different contexts it evokes images of desolate barrenness, a frigid, lifeless existence, as demonstrated by Hemingway's famous story, "Hills Like White Elephants." It should be noted that this oxymoronic nature of white also is a cultural matter. Thus, for example, in Oriental cultures, white is associated with mourning, whereas in the West, it is customary to wear white on solemn, mostly happy occasions. However, when it comes to literary texts, it is the context in which a color appears that determines the specific connotation, to the exclusion of the other potential connotations.

Let us return then to the color blue and its association with the fascinating, sensual, soulful women of Amos Oz's fiction, those women who yearn to be swept away by the "panting, hairy element" yet remain frustrated and thwarted in their attempts. Here it is not cool, lucid rationality that is associated with blue, but rather the blue of the sky, which evokes yearning for far away, imaginary, unknown places. These connotations underscore the women's longings, their desperate attempts to break away from the monotonous reality around them, toward the promising blue light that beckons to them from afar. Thus the mother in *A Panther in the Basement* "would sometimes raise her half empty glass of tea and stare through it at the blue light in the window" (p. 10), or Hannah, in *My Michael*: "I went to the kitchen. Blue drapes hung over the window" (p.128). The promising blue in the distance and the wondrous mystical shores of faraway regions send ripples of longing in her soul, echoing her own intense emotions. The blue, then, functions as a metaphor reflecting the yearnings of Oz's women and heightens their desire to get up and act, to dare, to rebel, and to extricate themselves from the confines of a dull, oppressive existence. The same symbolic function attaches to the "broken pale blue shutter" that Proffy's mother sent down a stream when she was a little girl:

It seemed that the stream which came out of the forest and vanished into it again had more bends inside the forest that completed a circle. So she sat there for two or three hours, waiting for her shutter to complete the circle and reappear. But only ducks came back. The following day she went back to the stream, but the blue shutter had not returned. (p. 68)

Thus the color blue is associated with wanderlust, with the lure of distant places, with the urge to spread one's wings and soar to the blue horizon, but also with the sharp pain of disappointment, of shattered expectations, and of the bitter taste of missed opportunities.

All of the women in Oz's fiction, who are trapped in the confines of a prosaic existence, are in some way associated with the color blue. For the most part, it is an article of clothing: a blue robe or a blue dress that assumes symbolic sexual significance and betokens fascination and longing as well as dejection and frustration.

The husbands of these sensuous, passionate women also play the role of fathers, for the most part, to young children: Yair Gonen, in *My Michael*, Guy and Nogah Harish, in *Elsewhere, Perhaps*, Hillel Kipniss, in *The Hill of the Evil Council*, Uri Kolodny in "Mr. Levi." The tender age of the children determines their limited role in the family setting, where the father is a humble, apologetic, faded figure. Such fathers are, by definition, soft and gentle; they are harried, henpecked husbands who suffer indignities in a married life that they find oppressive and painful, which does not, however, preclude a certain inner strength and determination from their personalities. Michael Gonen and Hans Kipniss are by no means ineffectual, spineless people. But in their relationships with their frustrated, demanding wives, these males are reduced to astonishing weakness. They are emasculated by the destructive, tyrannical sexuality which their women exude and which they are incapable of satisfying. When the children in these families are young and relatively uninvolved, the figure of the gentle father is for the most part presented as a castrated, henpecked husband, crushed by a sexually starved wife. And so the gentle father in this kind of familial setup is relegated to the margins, his role as father is underplayed, and he is portrayed as a dysfunctional, crestfallen, suffering spouse.

When we examine the demanding fathers in Amos Oz's fiction, we encounter a different set of relationships between father and son and between husband and wife. For the most part, the children in these stories are grown up: Yonatan Lifshitz, in *A Perfect Peace*, is the son of Yolek, a difficult, demanding father who serves as secretary of the kibbutz and is a scion to larger-than-life pioneers, whose zeal and ardor helped realize the Zionist dream but who also were overly ambitious and power hungry; Gideon Shenhav, in "The Way of the Wind," is the son of Shimshon Sheinebaum, Yolek's clone, an implacable, ideological leader who is compared to a knotty, gnarled oak tree, ancient yet mighty; Boaz Gideon-Brandstetter, in *Black Box*, is the son of Professor Alexander Gideon, a tyrannical, cynical man, seething with hatred and venom; and then there is Netta, in *To Know a Woman*, whose father is secret agent Yoel Ravid, a rigid, aloof man, masking his emotional frigidity and aversion of personal contact behind a facade of good manners and civility. It would seem, then, that when the children in the stories are of a tender age, the fathers tend to be gentle, meek, and almost sheepish. But when the children are grown up, the fathers tend to be harsh, demanding, and often devoid of feelings. This transformation of the fathers' personality entails a change in their place and function within the family setting. As a spouse, the father seems to recede and shrink, while at the same time the domineering, castrating figure of the wife is obscured and sometimes disappears altogether.

Instead of a young child with a gentle, mild father, we now have an adult son engaged in a tense, bitter power struggle with a demanding, implacable, curmudgeonly father. And this relationship now occupies center stage in the story.

Thus with the banishment of the woman from a dominant, oppressive position, Oz's fiction acquires a new center of gravity: the father transforms from the "husband" avatar into the "father" avatar. He shifts from a position of submission, inferiority, and meekness to a new one of muscular, bristling, aggressive potency.

Darkling and Bristling

Thus we remained, I and the mole,
Darkling and Bristling, facing him.
—Nathan Alterman, "The Mole,"
in *Poor People's Joy*

To you your father should be as a god . . .
To whom you are but as form in wax.
Shakespeare, *King Lear*,
Act II, Scene 4

The gap that separates the harsh fathers from their adolescent/grown-up children is a rift fraught with tension, agonizing contradictions, and often unbridgeable differences. In addition to the natural conflict that exists between parents and adolescent/grown-up children, there is an ideological discrepancy arising from the expectations of the father (usually a member of the founders' generation) and the son's refusal to follow in the father's footsteps.

The son's reaction often is blunt refusal, disgust, or truculent rejection of the path blazed by the previous generation, which makes him feel like a helpless pawn on a chess board (in fact, chess is a metaphor frequently used by Oz to describe struggle and rivalry). The more the fathers insist on the righteousness of their paths, the more the sons rebel and try to assert themselves and fashion their own individual ways. Shimshon Sheinbaum, in "The Way of the Wind," derisively refers to his son's choice as "shallow despair," and Yolek Lifshitz, in *Elsewhere, Perhaps*, haughtily brands his son's way "vulgar herd behavior," a sterile, cowardly evasion of responsibility; "scythians," "tartars," a hollow, effete generation that cannot hold a candle to its elders, those heroic founding fathers who planted the pioneers' flag at the top of the hill. To his great chagrin, Yolek realizes that there is nobody to pass the flag to. The sons turn their noses at it, consign it to oblivion, and toss it on the junk pile of history. Small wonder, then, that the elders view their sons' hesitant attempts to find paths of their own as a dead end, as proof of moral degeneration, and as a national disaster. The sons' rebellion against their elders' ideology marks a parting of the roads; the younger generation seeks to redefine itself, to assert its own individuality, which is a necessary step in the

evolution of a viable, healthy society. This is a primeval, titanic power struggle between the fathers who fear usurpation and the sons who threaten to
supplant them (cf. Freud's *Totem and Taboo* and Northrop Frye's *Anatomy of
Criticism*, in which he discerns in the generational power struggle between
fathers and sons the emergence of comedy ending with the triumph of the
sons over the tyrannical, domineering fathers).[5]

But there is another aspect to the conflict between the harsh, demanding fathers and their adolescent/grown-up sons in Oz's fiction. The younger
generation feels that the fathers' ideology has become obsolete, frayed, and
corrupt; it has lost its idealistic innocence and degenerated into lust for
power, clout, and domination, a cynical exploitation of the old slogans that
are no longer adhered to.[6] Perhaps the fathers are not aware of the moral
decay that has spread through their ideology and do not recognize the degra-
dation of their movement, but the fact is, their ideals are tarnished and de-
valued, and their sons do rebel against them. In this respect, Amos Oz's own
ideological protest seeps into his poetic writing and lodges itself in the fictional sphere. The social, philosophical critique is poetically transformed into
plot, characters, and metaphor. However, the literary analysis focuses on the
text alone and does not deal with the man behind the lines.

Thus there are three levels on which the power struggle between father
and son is played out: the ideological conflict, the need of the younger generation to free itself from the tyranny of its elders (thus ensuring the healthy
evolution of society), and the primordial, perennial tensions between father
and son, inveterate antagonists in the human drama. The struggle between
an adolescent/grown-up son and a despotic, authoritarian father is particularly prominent in the story "The Way of the Wind" and in the novel *A
Perfect Peace*, which will be discussed in this chapter. The analysis I propose
here is hitherto not encountered in the study of Oz's fiction. It draws attention not only to the ideological background of the father-son conflict but to
the deep-seated, primeval antagonism that has bedeviled the human race
from time immemorial.

Not Like the Wind and with No Perfect Peace: The Father and His Sons in "The Way of the Wind"

"The Way of the Wind" offers two critiques, from two points of view,
of the generation of pioneers and founding fathers that paved the way to the
establishment of the state. The plot reaches its peak with the death/suicide of
Gideon Shenhav, the young paratrooper, son of Shimshon Sheinbaum, the

most prominent representative of the founders' generation. It is precisely the "demeaning," "unheroic" death of Gideon, with its somewhat ridiculous aspects, so glaringly contrasted to the heroic deaths of Moshe Shamir's protagonists, Uri and Elik, who embody the ethos of the Palmach (pre-state military striking force) generation, that expresses the author's values and morals implicit in the story. No longer does one hear the call for the individual to sacrifice everything on the altar of the collective and the national interest. From now on, it is the voice of heresy, denial, and refutation of the principles of the collective that is sounded, a rebellion against the pain and deprivation that those principles inflicted on dissenting individuals. Queries and doubts about the justness of the old ideology are coupled with resentment at the price the individual had to pay for it. Thus Gideon Shenhav's unheroic death is the author's veiled protest against the ethos and myth of the glorified, curly-haired Sabra; it is the author's identification with the Other, the different, the socially inferior misfit who does not conform to the national, collective model. Inspired by French existentialism (Sartre and Camus) and by the alienation and bewilderment of the individual in Kafka's work, a new ethos has evolved, one that refuses to espouse the Sabra myth and bow to the conventions of the collective. This new ethos rejects the norm that made the individual subservient to the national in all considerations. For the first time (at least since the post–enlightenment fiction of Berdyczewski, Feierberg, Gnessin, Brenner, and Agnon) the heroic protagonist, who believes in the perfectability of society, the restoration of order, and the supremacy of logic, is rejected and superseded. He is replaced by an anti-hero, a character related to the disenfranchised and the lepers in human society (like Fima in *Fima The Third Condition*), or the forest ranger in A. B. Yehoshua's famous story "Facing the Forests," and many others), someone who inhabits the back alleys and the dusty, seamy margins of society.

"The Way of the Wind" seeks to undermine not only the image of the national hero but also the collective image of those who fostered him, the "larger-than-life" leaders of the Labor movement whose ultimate representative is Shimshon Sheinbaum, the harsh, demanding, castigating father. It was those Zionist founders who crowned the prickly Sabra, with his curly shock of hair, unbuttoned shirt, and Sten at the ready, while, at the same time, banishing from the arena the shy, modest, unassuming ones, reviling and alienating them, branding them the Others. With sharp, scathing irony, the author lashes out at the demanding, autocratic fathers, alluding to the biblical story of the Binding of Isaac. Gideon Shenhav's death/suicide, for all of its anti-heroic overtones, should not obscure the fact that the youth has volunteered for service as a paratrooper. Thus his death conforms to the ethos

(by now transformed into a myth) that is the father's *raison d'etre*: his collec-
tive-social image. It should be noted that Gideon's last name, Shenhav, a
Hebraized version of the foreign-sounding Sheinbaum, means "ivory," thus
adding an ironic touch to the son's character, since Gideon lacks both the
strength and brilliance implied by his adopted name. The death of his para-
chutist son endows the father with the venerated, much-desired halo of a
bereaved parent. The son's death—a form of martyrdom, in a way—gives the
father a new life, grants him higher status and social privilege. By dying/
committing suicide, the son sacrifices himself on the altar that the founding
fathers have erected for him before his birth.[7] This observation has not
eluded other critics: (cf., in particular, Hillel Barzel's detailed analysis in *Six
Authors*).[8] Barzel dwells mostly on Shimshon Sheinbaum's dream, offering a
convincing interpretation of its symbolism and exposing its archetypal significance: Gideon's death (which occurs when his ugly, rejected half-brother
Zaki pops up in front of him brandishing a knife) is an allusion to the fatal
rivalry between Cain and Abel. The biblical reference relates to the ideological message of the story. "The father's hypocricy . . ." Barzel concludes,
"when it becomes an ideology, leads to fratricide (ibid, p. 218). In other
words, Shimshon Sheinbaum's rejection and repudiation of his neglected bas-
tard give rise to murderous circumstances when the rejected, despised, underprivileged brother turns against the preferred and cherished son. Let us not
forget: Shimshon Sheinbaum does not turn his back on his neglected son for
ideological reasons but out of sheer bigotry. The presence of an "illegitimate"
son is a mark of Cain, a blot on his escutcheon, an ugly stain on the lily-
white gown he purports to wear as an ideologue of the movement and as a
leader of the kibbutz society.

    Following Barzel's mythic and archetypal interpretation, I offer my
analysis of Shimshon Sheinbaum's dream, which is a blatantly sexual one.
"Without consulting anyone, the gardeners dug a pond in the middle of the
lawn. . . . A tall boy was filling the pond with water from a black rubber hose
that emerged from between his tightly clasped knees. I suggested that he go
and get a chessboard so I could teach him a clever move. It seemed that my
intention was to distract him from what he was doing. The boy responded
with a lewd wink . . . and, smirking, said that when Gideon falls into the
pond, we'll have to fit him with gills. I started walking along the hose in
order to find the faucet and cut off the water" (p. 243). This dream assumes
particular importance, because it is so markedly different from the other thematic elements that make up the story, which are all firmly anchored in
reality and possess no dreamlike qualities. Of no less importance is the fact
that the dream is presented at the beginning of the story, and its recollection

perturbs Shimshon Sheinbaum's spirit. He makes an effort to recapture the dream and piece together its scattered elements. Eventually, he is able to recover the dream in its proper sequence, and it is an unpleasant, murky dream that continues to haunt him and disturb his peace of mind. The dream is crucial to the interpretation of the story; it is a *mise en abime* that encapsulates the core idea of the story and conveys the message of the implied author. The key to deciphering the dream is found in its relationship to the other thematic elements in the story.

The boy in the dream, with a black hose protruding from between his knees, is in all probability Zaki, Shimshon Sheinbaum's rejected illegitimate son, whom he wishes to blot out of the official, public biography he so assiduously and hypocritically cultivates. The depiction of Zaki in a blatantly sexual position in the dream is surely not a coincidence. Zaki is the product of Sheinbaum's much-vaunted potency. In his youth—but also later in life—Sheinbaum was known for his conquests in the "backyard" of the kibbutz (i.e., out of wedlock). It is natural for the father to feel threatened by his offspring, who might one day take advantage of his growing feebleness, usurp him, and use his own sexual prowess in the conquest of females. Freud's *Totem and Taboo* offers a perceptive and convincing analysis of the fear and anxiety that grip the old father's heart as he watches the minatory sexual development of his son. This aspect is even more pronounced with Zaki, who is presented in the story as possessing sinister, unbridled urges, dark savagery, and malicious cunning.

Both in the dream and in reality, since Zaki's sexuality casts a menacing shadow over the aging father, the father tries to divert and remove Zaki from the erotic arena, steering him toward a more intellectual domain, where his weakness and inferiority are guaranteed. "I suggested that he go and get a chessboard so I could teach him a clever move. It seems that my intention was to distract him from what he was doing" (p. 243). But the crafty boy does not fall into the trap. "The boy responded with a lewd wink" (p. 243). Both in the dream and in reality, the rejected son knows that not only does his father want to trip him and get him out of the way, but so does his elder brother, the preferred one, whose very presence constitutes a stumbling block on the rejected son's road to recognition. Thus he yearns for his brother's downfall, which in Sheinbaum's dream takes the following form: "Smirking, he said that when Gideon falls into the pond, we'll have to fit him with gills" (p.). In this context, we should note the relevance of the father's name, Shimshon (Samson), evoking the biblical figure that comprises both fabulous strength and a capacity for error and defeat.

But it is not only the rejected son who threatens the aging father, whose fears and anxieties are reflected in his dream, as in an ominous mirror. His eldest son, too, the golden boy, is perceived as a threat to him, despite the fact that Gideon is a source of disappointment to his father because of his sensitivity, which the old man interprets as a weakness. Gideon's threat to his father comes from another direction. "How he has improved in chess. Soon he'll be able to defeat his old father," thus thinks the father who has serious doubts about his "disappointing" son (p. 246). But in contrast to his intellectual achievements, Gideon proves deficient in the erotic arena, in which Zaki, his savage, sinister brother, excels. "He [Gideon] has to learn how to be more assertive with women; shyness and sentimentality are not proper qualities in a man" (muses the father, p. 246). Thus the old father, feeling threatened in both areas, the intellectual and the erotic, gears himself up to defeat his sons, to emasculate them before they turn on him to depose and supplant him. Shimshon Sheinbaum, the lion in winter, driven by fear and anxiety, seeks to banish his sons and to ensure their defeat. Differently put, he tries to sacrifice them on the altar of the future, to trip them up, to foil their attempt to triumph over their aged progenitor.

The father is intent on retaining his power and superiority over his two sons. Thus in his tormented dream, Shimshon Sheinbaum devises devious strategies to eliminate the sons' threat to his life. Zaki, who excels in the erotic domain (being the fruit of his father's vaunted sexual prowess), is lured to "migrate" to the intellectual domain, symbolized by the chess game. Even in the dream, the father acknowledges that his blandishment is nothing but a ploy to distract the boy and remove the erotic threat he poses. On the other hand, his favorite son, Gideon, who threatens him in the intellectual domain, is to be neutralized by diverting him to the erotic arena, where his failure is ensured ("As long as he doesn't marry the first girl who gives herself to him. He ought to break two or three of them first," p. 246). The dream concludes with a similar sentiment on the father's part. "I walked along the hose to find the faucet and cut off the water" (p. 243). The erotic connotation here is unmistakable, as is the father's wish to stem the flow of life from a source that is beyond his control. In the dream, as in life, the father seeks to cut off the flow of sexual potency with which his rejected son, Zaki, threatens him, as well as the flow of spirit and intellect, with which his chosen, yet disappointing, son, Gideon, threatens him. He is like Uranus, god of the sky in Greek mythology, who tried to annihilate his sons for fear that they might rise against him and depose him. Or, like Uranus' son Chronos, who sought to destroy his own son Zeus out of the same primordial, atavistic fear of an old father threatened by his son. Or Laius, in Sophocles' *Oedipus Tyrannus*, who, obsessed by the same fear, tried to get rid of his son Oedipus. In all of these mythological instances, the father's fear was justified: the son deposed the father and usurped his power. Shimshon Sheinbaum's story, then, is as old as the world.[9]

Driven by these ancient fears and anxieties, Shimshon Sheinbaum regards the flower beds of the kibbutz "with utter contempt" (p. 247) and, angry and disappointed, thinks of "the boy, his young successor, who let the garden grow to seed" (p. 247). In his dream, too, Shimshon Sheinbaum is furious at the gardeners. They are the ones who usurped his throne, banished him from his kingdom, and dug a pond in the middle of the lawn, without asking his permission. "The scandal was indeed terrible. Without consulting anybody, the gardeners built an ornamental pond in the center of the lawn" (p. 247). Here too he bemoans his removal from office, his loss of power and status due to his advancing age. It is highly ironic, therefore, that at the end of the story, Shimshon Sheinbaum collapses in the flower beds (p. 256). The domain where he used to reign supreme now becomes his grave. Shimshon Sheinbaum's tormented, nightmarish dream confirms Freud's famous dictum about dreams taking the place of action.[10] In this case, the dream does not prove false. The ideological gap between the old tyrant and the young son who refuses to tread in his path (which is foisted on him, sometimes by coercion, sometimes by wily blandishments) is a real, unbridgeable chasm. But beyond the ideological gap lurks the primeval, archetypal rivalry between fathers and sons, a confrontation fraught with hatred, suspicion, and guilt, which harks back to the dawn of civilization and cannot be resolved.

Without Peace or Solace: Fathers and Sons in A Perfect Peace

The novel *A Perfect Peace* was written several years after the publication of "The Way of the Wind," hence, one may use the term *migration* or an avatar of a motif from the earlier to the later text.

The motif in question is the yawning gap that divides fathers and sons, the rift between a harsh, demanding parent, representing the pioneers and trailblazers, and the son, now a young man, who refuses to follow in his old man's footsteps, rejects the old ideology, and tries to forge an independent way of life. Apart from the ideological gap, we noted in "The Way of the Wind" the existence of another, more archetypal chasm separating father and son. The same chasm reappears in *A Perfect Peace*, pitting one against the other: an energetic, authoritarian, relentless father, who has absolute confidence in his ideological doctrine, and a sensitive, hesitant, inarticulate son, who is uncertain and ambivalent about his way.

This was the conflict between Shimshon Sheinbaum and his son Gideon Shenhav in "The Way of the Wind," and it resurfaces in the relations between Yolek Lifshitz and his grown son Yonatan. Both sons feel oppressed and crushed by the towering figures of their fathers and try, unsuccessfully, to break away. Since they cannot stand up to the adamantine fathers, they choose the only route left to them: escape. Gideon Shenhav opts for suicide, death. Yonatan Lifshitz sneaks out at night, leaving his native kibbutz for the dusty, sweltering expanses of the Sinai desert in search of peace, solace, warmth, and acceptance.

Yonatan Lifshitz has dreamed of other escapes: to some strange, wintry city, with spiraling high-rises of cement and glass that twinkle in the dark as a million points of light, where elegant men in dark woolen suits and tall women in fur coats and delicate perfumes disappear in the lobbies of posh hotels, past discreet doormen and liveried bellhops, all intent on their own affairs, executing their duties efficiently and meticulously, as people who know the real meaning and purpose of life and act upon it gracefully and effortlessly. Yonatan yearns to disappear into this enticing, promising milieu, but these faraway shores remain unattainable to him. He is not imaginative or daring enough to answer their call and sail away. The farthest he can get is an army base in Sinai. His conventional Israeli kibbutz upbringing (undistinguished high school education, hikes across the country, minor league basketball, military service in one of the elite combat units, and then a return to the kibbutz to work in the garage, animal feed, or crops) has apparently conditioned him to not realize dreams that are outside of his immediate grasp. So he hitchhikes south, stopping along the way at dusty, dilapidated kiosks that smell of scorched thornbushes and stale urine, until he reaches the sweltering, steaming Sinai desert that stretches to the gray horizon. At nightfall he sneaks into an army base and passes the night on a rickety bed under a coarse army issue blanket, a folded khaki towel in lieu of a pillow, and over his head a naked bulb throwing feeble light. At first light, in the cool air of a pale dawn, he walks briskly along a parched wadi, his soles grinding the pebbles underfoot. He consults his map and compass, contemplates a hike to Petra, then gingerly, dubiously retreats to the army camp with its rusty iron bed and last week's newspapers gathering dust underneath. Yonatan's escape is not as extreme and terminal as Gideon's. Eventually he goes back home, and there is some kind of reconciliation.

Yonatan returns to the kibbutz, to his home, even to his wife, although from now on he will have to share her with another man, with Azaria, who has become a second husband to her. The escape ends with a compromise, with resignation, with self-awareness: this is what I am; this is how far I can go with my delusion. Like it or not, that is all there is to it, and it is time to go home.

But for all the difference in degree between the two escapes, they are similar in kind, and there are many affinities between the two texts. Both sons, the sensitive, introvert Gideon and the awkward, ascetic, inarticulate Yonatan, try to rebel against their dominant fathers, and both lack the requisite spiritual resources to do so, so they resort to escape instead.

There are other similarities and overlapping details that connect the two texts. For example, the erotically symbolic hose in Shimshon Sheinbaum's dream reappears in *A Perfect Peace*, where it carries a similar connotation of invidious sexual frustration: "Once, on a sweltering summer day, one of the neighbors volunteered to take out a rubber hose and washed her [Yonatan's wife, Rimona] naked feet with the flowing water" (pp. 32–33). Yonatan, the betrayed husband, looks on the scene with seething anger and frustration (cf. Knut Hamsun's novels *Pan* and *Victoria*, where a jilted lover observes a similar scene of betrayal). The garden hose from Shimshon Sheinbaum's dream recurs here with the repetition of the word "*zerem*" (flow), evoking an association with ejaculation, and focusing on the woman's feet, which in world literary tradition have long had erotic connotations (cf. *Song of Solomon*, ch. 7, 1, "How beautiful are thy feet with shoes, O prince's daughter! The joints of thy thighs are like jewels, the work of the hands of a cunning workman").[11] As Yonatan watches the erotic encounter, he is gripped by fierce jealousy. "He stood at a distance . . . gritting his teeth and grinning" (p. 33). The intense emotion of the cuckolded husband is not without a certain sexual gratification.

A more significant analogy between the short story and the novel centers on the conflict between the authoritarian father and the "feeble," "effete" son. In *A Perfect Peace*, Yolek Lifshitz, the aging general secretary of the kibbutz, representative of the pioneers' generation, writes to Prime Minister Levi Eshkol, his longtime friend and ideological rival, to complain about his son. "With sons like mine, one certainly can't found a dynasty" (p. 166), echoing Shimshon Sheinbaum's disparaging remark about his chosen, yet disappointing, son. "With a boy like Gideon, you can't found a dynasty" (p. 243). Similarly, the motif of the sacrifice, or the binding of the son, appears in both narratives. The rebellious son in *A Perfect Peace* refuses to fulfill the expectations of a father who tries to "bind" him at the altar of his ideology. "Lay not thy hand upon the lad!" Yolek Lifshitz writes to Trotsky, who emigrated to America and became a hotel tycoon. This is Benya Trotsky who, many years earlier, was Yolek's bitter rival, the lover of his wife, Hava, and perhaps Yonatan's biological father. The ancient resentment, never really dead, now surfaces as Yolek warns Trotsky to keep his hands off the boy, echoing the angel's call to Abraham when he was about to sacrifice his beloved son Isaac (Genesis 22:12). But, ironically, it is not Trotsky who lays his hands on him, but Yolek, who binds Yonatan to sacrifice him on the altar of the founders' ideology. Both Gideon and Yonatan are victims of tyrannical fathers who would sacrifice their sons' happiness to gratify their selfish desires to immortalize their own images. And what is more infuriating is the cloak of self-righteousness and hypocritical cant in which they wrap themselves, insisting that the sacrifice is for their sons' sake. No wonder, then, that Yonatan is haunted by the refrain of an old song, "What else will you demand of us, Oh motherland?" (p. 344), because here the motherland looms like a monstrous ancient mother with a hungry, gaping mouth waiting for her sons to leap, to sacrifice themselves, to satisfy the demanding, voracious maw.

As mentioned earlier, one of the recurrent motifs in Amos Oz's fiction is chess. Its function is always symbolic: it reflects a conflict between two opposing forces vying for supremacy (quite often in an erotic context, but not exclusively): man against man, father against son, woman against man, raging fury against raging fury.

But the chess game is not always a metaphor for rivalry and strife: in *My Michael*, for instance, the chess game between Michael and Mr. Kadishman (p. 68) is relaxed and innocent, free of any power struggle. It is carried out in an atmosphere of serenity and conciliation, without threat or confrontation, in marked contrast to the stained, acrimonious relations that later develop between Michael and his restless wife Hannah. Equally peaceful and pleasant is the chess game between Joseph Yarden and Dr. Kleinberger, in the story "Strange Fire," in *Where the Jackals Howl*. But these are exceptions to the rule. Chess, in Oz's oeuvre, is, for the most part, a metaphor for unresolved tensions, for a rivalry that would brook no compromise. In *A Perfect Peace* alone, there are at least twenty-four references to chess, all in the same metaphoric vein (pp. 14, 31, 65, 67, 80, 94, 107–09, 112, 114, 142–43, 149, 160, 169, 206, 271, 277, 346, 377, 380).

The scuffle between Azaria, the stranger who blew in from the benighted Diaspora, and Yonatan, the native son, over the woman Rimona, is symbolically expressed by many chess games in which the two rivals engage. On the very first evening that Azaria spends in Rimona's and Yonatan's humble, pleasant room, a tempestuous game of chess is waged between the two men, ending with Yonatan's triumph. But the victory is short lived; this is only the opening battle, and at the end of the war, it is the scrawny, scorned, ghetto type that triumphs over the tanned, robust, army veteran and scion of the kibbutz founders. Yonatan, who at first adopts Azaria as a kind of clown or court jester, whom he can patronize, despise, and deride, eventually has to accept the fact that Azaria has invaded his family and his bedroom, becoming in fact his wife's second—if not first—husband. Azaria's deposal of Yonatan and his invasion of his household often are couched in terms of a chess game. "They often played chess, with Azaria having the upper hand" (p. 377). Earlier in the novel, the persistent, resourceful Azaria succeeds in repairing a broken, "recalcitrant" tractor that has stood in the dusty garage like some petrified ancient monster, which Yonatan has been trying in vain to bring to life. This triumph, too, is presented as a chess metaphor. "He presided over the operation from afar, like one of those famous grandmasters Yonatan had read about in his chess magazines, who could play blind chess, without pieces or a board" (pp. 94–95). The rivalry between the two men is not just for power and control, as between two males fighting over territory, but also for the conquest of the female of the species. This use of chess as a metaphor is found in other works by Oz.

Thus in the novella "Mr. Levi," the mother flaunts her mockery and defiance at the husband who struggles to contain his jealousy. "At noon, father came up from the printshop in the basement and, with his nostrils twitching, asked feebly, 'Who was here this morning? Whose smell is this?' Mother laughed. She said, 'Ephraim Nehemkin came here this morning to play chess with me, and why not? He also installed a lovely night lamp by my bed'" (p. 81).

A chess game, indeed. The mother heaps scorn on her cuckolded husband, pretending there is nothing untoward in a young neighbor coming to play chess with her while her husband is at work. Her laughter in this context has obvious sexual connotations, recalling similar uses of the verb in the Bible (Cf. Genesis 21, where Sarah sees Ishmael "laughing" (playing, mocking), that is, displaying sexual maturity, and demands his expulsion, lest he threaten the status of her son Isaac, the designated heir. In "Mr. Levi," the betrayed husband and Ephraim often engage in turbulent chess games where they confront each other and act out their sexual rivalry. "Ephraim was a sharp but impatient player. Father was able to beat him quite often because he refrained from taking risks and used patient defensive tactics" (p. 67).

The cuckolded husband often wins the game, but this hardly ensures his final victory. Quite the reverse. A similar pattern is seen in the intermittent games between Azaria and Yonatan. "Yonatan played patiently. . . . Azaria, on the other hand, kept throwing away brilliantly gained advantages, because after each brilliant move, he would get impatient" (p. 108). The husband who is defeated in the sexual arena is the one displaying patience and calculation in the metaphorical chess battles, while the successful lover, who invades the husband's territory and replaces him in his bed, is the one throwing caution to the wind, often displaying flair and panache when playing the game. Their respective attitudes toward the game help explain the lover's triumph over the husband; the hesitant, calculating, restrained husband lacks the daring, the brilliance, the excitement that the lover evinces. The lover's personality may be lacking in stability and dependability, but this apparently becomes an advantage where sexual attraction is concerned.

In *A Perfect Peace*, the chess metaphor also is used to shed light on the conflict between the authoritarian father and the hesitant, recalcitrant son. This is how Yonatan describes his frustration vis-à-vis his implacable father: "It's like being checkmated by someone who's playing both sides of the board, because you have no pieces of your own, just your psychological problems and hangups. At the end they tell you that you have a lot to learn yet and you're not mature" (p. 149). Here too the function of the chess game, on a symbolic level, is to highlight the antagonism and animosity between two rival sides.

In the title of this chapter, I took the liberty to use August Strindberg's terminology. Writing at the turn of the previous century, this Swedish playwright and novelist set the tone in the depiction of the power struggle between the sexes. The battle usually is pitched between an unassuming, feeble, defeated, man and an attractive, seductive, domineering woman. Typically, the Strindbergian woman finds the man wanting and incapable of answering her overflowing, overpowering desires. But constrained by social norms and economic necessity, the woman is dependent on the man and thus feels frustrated, humiliated, and hopelessly entrapped. The ensuing war between the sexes is, therefore, predictable and understandable. All of the following Strindberg plays focus on the male-female conflict: *The Father* (Fadern, 1887), *Miss Julia* (Froken Julia, 1888), *Creditors* (Fordinsagare, 1887), *The Stronger One* (Den Starkare, 1888), *The Bond* (Bandet, 1892), *Easter* (Paask, 1900), Dance Macabre (Dodsdansen, 1901), *Friends* (Kamaraterna, 1886, formerly titled *Marauders*, Marodorer).[12]

The struggle between rationality and desire in Amos Oz's fiction is transformed into a clash between a tyrannical father and a rebellious son who refuses to follow in his father's footsteps, then into a scuffle between a peace-loving, indulgent man and a voracious, sexually frustrated woman. This protean struggle is strongly reminiscent of the nightmarish battle that rages in Strindberg's plays as well as in his fiction (cf. *A Bondswoman's Son*, Tjanstekvinnan's son, 1986–1987).

It is not my intention to prove that Strindberg exerted influence on Oz's fiction, although such "correspondence" between their texts exists, but this is not the place to expand on it. Suffice it to say that when we encounter in Oz's fiction the acrimonious confrontation between two antagonistic sides, the gap that separates father and son, and the mortal battle between sensuous, yearning women and humble, lackluster men, we can feel Strindberg looking over our shoulder, reaching out from the depths of dark, lugubrious, turn-of-the-century Scandinavian literature.

In "The Way of the Wind," we saw how the father's dream reflects his fear of usurpation by his sons and how he tries to forestall his downfall by banishing the sons, by steering them toward failure and defeat. *A Perfect Peace* contains more than one dream, and those dreams too reflect the bitter struggle between father and son, but in reverse. Here, in the dreams, the father's fear that the son may one day rise against him and supplant him actually materializes. This is what Yonatan's dream betokens, and to some extent, Yolek Lifshitz's own dream as well. In Yonatan's dream, "They came . . . to tell him that the police had finally found his father's body" (p. 20). The son, then, harbors a secret wish to defeat the father, ultimately to eliminate him. In a subsequent dream, Yonatan tries unsuccessfully to kill his father with a gun that shoots wet cotton bullets (p. 26). The symbolic image of the phallus-like gun spewing wet bullets highlights the archetypal stratum of the dream. Freud, in *Totem and Taboo*, states that the father's desperate struggle against his son stems not only from fear of being overthrown and usurped but from fear that the son will inherit the father's women. It is interesting to note that there is another erotic "smoking gun" in *A Perfect Peace*: the one fired by Trotsky, Yolek Lifshtz's rival, and Hava's admirer— perhaps her lover. Those shots that miss their target are certainly symbolic of defeated sexuality.

Yonatan's dream opens with his father, Yolek, urging him "to undertake a dangerous journey . . . on behalf of the security forces" (p. 26). In other words, fearing that the son will remove him from his position of power, the father preempts him and, using King David's stratagem against Uriah the Hittite, sends him on a dangerous mission that will guarantee his death. But, as noted earlier, Yonatan is not the only one who has dreams. In Yolek's dream, "Ben Gurion, red-faced and terrible, sprang at him . . . and roared: 'This is out of the question! You will kill, if you have to . . . just as King Saul killed his own son'" (p. 130). Well, King Saul did not kill his son Jonathan, but he certainly meant to. The reference is to I Samuel 14, where Jonathan, unwittingly, disobeys Saul's injunction to the troops to not eat any food until victory is ensured. Jonathan, not having heard the oath, tastes some honey in the field. When Saul hears about it, he orders his son's execution. Only the active, almost violent intervention of the people saves Jonathan's life. True, Saul could not have foreseen his son's disobedience, but the fact remains that an authoritarian, implacable father is about to kill his son. The same happens with Jephthah the Giladite; the fact that he could not foresee that his daughter would be the first to greet him on his return from battle does not attenuate his guilt: Jephthah sacrificed his own daughter, an act that clearly echoes the motif of the Binding of Isaac.

In Yolek's dream, the legendary figure of Ben-Gurion (another father, "the father of the nation," whose authoritarianism reached mythic proportions) orders Yolek to kill his son, his only son, whom he loves, Yonatan. And note the similarity in names (Jonathan is, in Hebrew, Yonatan). Indeed, in *A Perfect Peace*, the biblical figures of Saul and Jonathan are constantly on the mind of the father and son who are engaged in a brutal power struggle. This is how Yonatan perceives it:

> Just like that crappy son of King Saul in the Bible who wasn't good enough to be king . . . only to get killed in battle so that others may live. . . . Hats off to you, good old Jonathan, slain upon the high places." (p. 279)

The motif of sacrificing a son on the altar of ideology, which harks back to the Binding of Isaac, is here reiterated: Yonatan, exhausted and exasperated by the old pioneers' tyranny, seems to give up the fight, to prostrate himself on the altar, as his unforgiving father looms behind, brandishing the knife.

In a similar vein, Yonatan's mother, Hava, accuses Yolek of trying to kill his son, because the boy's awkwardness, hesitation, and refusal to toe the line are a blot on Yolek's "lily-white mantle," the mantle of chief ideologue of Zionism and the kibbutz movement. Yolek craves to leave behind a living monument to his achievements, to immortalize his spirit, and this desire overshadows his love for his son from whom he demands total obedience and self-abnegation.

And yet, for all of Yonatan's resentment and subconscious desire to eliminate his father, upon leaving the kibbutz, he stoops and "carefully picks up his father's woolen sock and hangs it on the line to dry" (p. 223). Despite the bitter antagonism and the wrenching frustration, he harbors a measure of compassion and loving kindness toward his father, and these covert, barely acknowledged feelings are of particular significance here. In fact, they mark the transition from the story "The Way of the Wind" to the novel *A Perfect Peace*. This is not merely a chronological transition, but rather a conceptual, aesthetic shift, an evolutionary stage in Oz's fiction. True, several elements from the story, those relating to the bitter conflict separating father and son, have seeped into the novel. They are the water hose that betokens sexual menace, the allusion to the Binding of Isaac, the father's scathing criticism of the son disqualifying him as heir to the dynasty, the chess motif as a metaphor for rivalry, and the string of symbolic, proleptic dreams. The affinity between the two narratives is obvious and undeniable, and yet it seems that in the transition from the short story to the novel, a perceptible change has occurred: a certain moderation has set in, an abatement of the clash between the warring sides, an unmistakable rapprochement.

"The Way of the Wind" ends with the tragic death of Gideon Shenhav, immediately followed by his father hypocritically assuming the halo of the bereaved parent. It is a harsh denouement that leaves no room for reconciliation. *A Perfect Peace* concludes on a different note: with a hesitant attempt at appeasement. Yolek, the demanding, disapproving father, has grown old, and he no longer occupies the authoritarian position of secretary general of the kibbutz. He is replaced by Srulik, member of the intermediate generation, whose personality is marked by moderation, patience, and reason. Yonatan, who fled the constricting, provincial kibbutz society, his father's unreasonable expectations, and the stifling atmosphere of the family unit, eventually comes back home, to the kibbutz, to his father, and to the same family unit. And yet they are not the same kibbutz, father, and family unit: his father has been removed from his influential position and can no longer exert the same power over his son's life; his family also has been transformed in the meantime: Azaria Gitlin, the stranger who came in from the darkest Diaspora, has invaded his home and installed himself there as part of a triangle.

Perhaps this last, extraordinary fact, so atypical of the conservative kibbutz society, underlines the conciliatory note on which the novel concludes. One realizes that there is room for compromise, that there is no need to take sides, to triumph absolutely. Gradually, perhaps with time and maturity, one accepts the middle road, the golden mean, the existence of a reality that can accommodate opposing extremes. If not perfect peace, this is at least a truce, a temporary coexistence, an acceptance of a more complex reality. Yet even when the ideological tension is somewhat relaxed, the ancient, archetypal, primordial conflict will never disappear from the scene. That same "wind that drifts among the cypress trees giving them strength to withstand the heat wave" ("The Way of the Wind," p. 58) perhaps will not bring us peace on its wings, but yet it is a good wind that may spread some comfort and solace.

There Is a Thing Called Love, They Say: A Comment on Black Box

We discussed extensively the father, the son, and the ill wind that blows them apart. We also elaborated on the Strindbergian war between the sexes. We analyzed the domineering, tempestuous woman, beset by yearnings and desires, forever dreaming of distant horizons, yet doomed to stay in her constricting surroundings, with a feeble, crestfallen husband, unable to respond to her emotional needs and wholly possess her. These are generalities and, as such, are liable to miss the point. But in Oz's fiction the struggle, the conflict, and the clash between opposing poles merely suggest the outline, the general formula into which each work fits its own particular content. This applies also to the novel *Black Box*.

The male facing Ilana, the central female character in *Black Box*, is actually split into two figures that are deliberately and blatantly contrasted. On the one hand, Michel Sommo, a Sephardic version of the Ashkenazi Azaria Gitlin in *A Perfect Peace*, comes across as an obnoxious, risible personality whose words sound unctuous and sanctimonious. Like Zacharia Siegfried Berger in *Elsewhere, Perhaps*, beneath the thin veneer of civility, one senses uncouthness and vulgarity.

At the beginning of the novel, certain positive qualities, such as honesty and probity, are associated with Michel Sommo. Later on, however, his other attributes, the ugly, evil, despicable aspects of his personality, come to the fore: typical "exilic" deviousness, cynical exploitation, self-righteousness, pietistic sanctimony, and smarmy cant. Gradually his character assumes a most odious, loathsome aspect that envelops him like a noxious miasma. The other man confronting the sensuous, vivacious Ilana is Professor Alex Gideon, a dour, tormented, angry man, who is emotionally sterile and given to bouts of malice and vindictiveness. Intellectually, he is bright, witty, and resourceful, but at the same time, he is coldly rational, cynical, suspicious, and supercilious. His personality possesses a certain sinister charisma, and he is very sharp and precise when attacking an antagonist. In some respects, Alex Gideon is reminiscent of Shimshon Sheinbaum, the despotic patriarch in "The Way of the Wind," with his aggressive masculinity, crass authoritarian attitudes, and ascetic, truculent approach to life. The very thought of Shimshon Sheinbaum evokes the generational struggle. *Black Box* centers on the rivalry between Boaz and his stepfather, Michel Sommo, on the one hand,

and between Boaz and his biological father, Professor Alex Gideon, on the other hand.

Boaz, from early childhood, has the physical dimensions of a Titan; muscular, broad shouldered, hulking, he stalks the earth like an angry yet innocent Gulliver; or like the colossal Samson, he is about to bring down the temple walls and emerge from the ruins unscathed. Boaz is depicted on such a large scale as to almost turn him into a mythological figure. This magnitude renders the struggle between his two fathers particularly intense. Boaz could easily crush his stepfather, but the latter, to his credit, is not intimidated. He chastises and browbeats the youth, often deriding and ridiculing him. As for Boaz's biological father, the physical estrangement between father and son minimizes somewhat the intensity of the struggle between them. But even across oceans and continents, sparks fly when the two men, the dour, vindictive father and the muscular and savage son, lash out at each other, verbally abuse each other, and try to settle an ancient account. But the real showdown is yet to come.

And the woman? Ilana's character harks back to all those earlier sensuous, desperate yearning women in Oz's fiction, the women who heed the call of mystic, faraway places yet are tethered, confined, and imprisoned in their frustrations. They hear the call but cannot go, except for very few. Ruth Kipniss in *The Hill of the Evil Council* left; and, in a different manner, so did Steffa Pomerantz in *Touch the Water, Touch the Wind*, as did Eva Harish, who heard the call and answered it.

But the other ones did not leave: Hannah Gonen in *My Michael*, the mother in "Mr. Levi," Rimona in *A Perfect Peace* and Ilana in *Black Box*. There is a poem by Yehuda Amichai that captures this sentiment of the woman who hears the siren's call but does not follow it:

> *I remember telling you many years ago,*
> *Come to me, be mine, I love you so.*
> *You cried and said, "You come at the wrong time,*
> *I am bound, body and soul,*
> *To this handsome, evil man."*
> *So I left you, with a broken heart.*
> ("A Man's Life Is Very Long," *An Hour of Grace*)

To her misfortune, Ilana is bound, body and soul, to a handsome, evil man who harrows and torments her. She cannot extricate herself from the trap that she has set for herself. What, then, is left for these women who are doomed to live with their thwarted desires, with longings that will never be satisfied, confined in a prison of their own making? Escape is their only choice. But only a partial escape that will afford them momentary respite. Hannah Gonen chooses two escape routes, illness and writing, like her kindred soul Tirtza Mazal in Agnon's "In the Prime of Her Life"; she escapes to childhood memories, to wild sexual fantasies about the twin Arabs she conjures up from her distant past. Those partial escapes afford her a modicum of revenge, without compromising her existential and economic security. Lily Danenberg, in "Strange Fire," goes even farther in her escape: first she leaves her pleasant yet boring husband, Joseph Yarden, and then, not content with rapturous erotic fantasies, she dares to initiate a forbidden liaison with her future son-in-law. And yet her escape, too, is incomplete. There is a clear indication that the mother-in-law's sexual indiscretion is not going to jeopardize the union of the wayward groom and the unsuspecting bride. Similarly, Noa, in *Do Not Call It a Night*, plunges herself in a flurry of social activities, constantly running around town under the blazing sun of the desert. Noga Harish, in *Elsewhere, Perhaps*, is not ready to go as far as her mother Eva did; she stays in the kibbutz, despite her yearning to be elsewhere. But she does not give up escape altogether: her form of partial escape is to carry on an affair with Ezra Berger, an aging, heavy-set, uncouth truck driver who could easily be her father, if not her grandfather.

And where does Ivria, in *To Know a Woman*, run away? Ivria locks herself up in her study, where she is surrounded by monastic bizarreness (cf. the pictures of Byzantine monasteries on the walls and the spare, ascetic furniture). She immerses herself in writing a master's thesis entitled "Shame in the Attic," based on the Bronte sisters' novels. But this is not her only escape. Ivria engages in an illicit love affair with an aging neighbor, a guitar-playing truck driver who is strongly reminiscent of two earlier Oz lovers: Ezra Berger in *Elsewhere, Perhaps*, who, like Ivria's neighbor, is fond of quoting Scripture, and Azaria Giltin, in *A Perfect Peace*, the stranger who hails from afar with a guitar. Then there is Ivria's death, perhaps the ultimate escape to the beyond. From the outset, there are intimations that Ivria's death is an act of choice (i.e., suicide), and her demise is a pervasive and insistent presence throughout the novel.

Ivria's daughter, Netta, has her own escape route too. Her epilepsy (the "lunar malady," as her father called it) that has afflicted her from early childhood serves as a shelter from the deathly frigidity and alienation that characterize her parents' relationship. Netta does not belong to the category of Oz women who are forever pining and yearning for another place, another reality. And yet she too has found an escape route.

Rimona, in *A Perfect Peace*, is another escapee. She indulges in reveries about Chad in darkest Africa, a sun-baked, sweltering land where a raging ram, feral and sweaty, is gored by hunters' spears. Rimona withdraws into her inner world, where isolated, muted, and tormented she waits for a sign from afar.

The mother in *A Panther in the Basement* also is in a state of perpetual expectation for a loud and clear voice that will break the silence. Her palms hug a cup of tea, as though trying to draw warmth and consolation from it (p. 66) (cf. Rimona in *A Perfect Peace*, p. 97). As she withdraws inwardly, her face turns to the window, toward the blue horizon. Her mind often harks back to her childhood memories, to distant regions replete with meadows, sylvan cottages, long-drawn dusks, and the peal of church bells. This is how her son, Proffy, describes her. "My mother would sit on the other side of the room, in her rocking chair, reading, or, with her open book face down on her lap, listening attentively to some sound that I could not hear" (pp. 26–27). It is a sound no one, except her, can hear. She is one of several women populating Oz's fiction, who writhe in their frustration and agony, who yearn for other places, other smells, and other horizons.

In *Black Box*, however, the heroine's escape takes on a different guise. Not an introspective, isolated contemplation, nor erotic fantasies that blur the boundaries between humdrum reality and dizzying ecstasy—her escape is more connected to the here and now.

Ilana Brandstetter-Gideon-Sommo's escape takes the form of innumerable extramarital affairs, random, opportunistic, hastily concocted, insipid, and sometimes demeaning, sleazy love affairs, motivated by anger, frustration, spite, and loneliness, affairs that fester and rankle like cancer; they reflect her distress, desperation, humiliation and defeat, a last-ditch effort to regain the love of the only man she cares about, a man whose cold disdain and alienating aloofness have driven her to the cycle of betrayals. She harbors a vain hope to reunite with her husband, Alex Gideon, to open a new leaf. Eventually, Ilana tears herself away from this tortuous escape route by allying herself with Michel Sommo. But she has to run the entire course first. Ilana does not despair, does not throw in the towel. Her marriage to Michel Sommo asserts her struggle for life and happiness. Sommo, at least in his first avatar, is presented as rather likable and sympathetic, albeit a paltry "consolation prize" for the loss of the charismatic and fascinating Alex Gideon. The sensitive attentiveness of which Michel is capable serves as a poultice that heals the wounds and scars Ilana has suffered during her excruciating marriage to Alex.

Ilana's relationship with her first husband brings to mind Hannah Gonen in *My Michael*. While, in one respect, Michael is her protector and defender (as his name, Gonen, indicates in Hebrew), he also besieges, be-leaguers, and destroys her. His strength and solidity sustain her physically and prevent her from descending into the abyss that lies at the bottom of her turbulent, tormented psyche.

The novel opens with a metaphoric description of their first encounter: "This is how we met: one winter day, at nine o'clock in the morning, I slipped on the stairs. A strange young man caught me by the elbow. His hand was strong and full of restraint" (p. 5). Here is their story in a nutshell: Michael's solidity and his restraint save Hannah from tripping and falling. But Michael is not only her stay and support, he also is the source of her misfortune, because his shallow, insipid, lackluster personality and inability to respond to her urges and yearnings doom Hannah to a spiritual death, to an emotional paralysis. There is an old children's song that haunts Hannah's mind relentlessly: "Little clown, little clown, won't you dance with me?/ Pretty little clown will dance with everyone." Hannah herself is able to crack the code: "I would like to note that there is a reply in the second verse of this rhyme to the question posed in the first, but the reply is a disappointing one" (p. 59). Indeed, it is a disappointing reply from Hannah's point of view. The cute little clown will dance with everybody; there is no uniqueness or dis-crimination to his gift, which makes it tedious and boring. Thus the clown will miss the uniqueness of Hannah's personality. The metaphor extends its application to include Michael, who also is indiscriminate, tedious, and bor-ing—at least in the eyes of Hannah, his wife, who is never really his. Like the little clown, Michael is bound to frustrate Hannah's expectations to lead an exciting, passionate life, full of fascination and mystery. Like biblical Eve, she desires to taste of the tree of knowledge, to give in to temptation, but instead she finds herself locked up in a prison bearing the name of Michael Gonen. Thus while his stability and solidity prevent her from descending into insanity (and note the analogy with Duba Glick, who lost her mind trying to endure life with her gray, boring husband), his dull personality imposes on her emotional death, or at any rate, causes her derangement. Paradoxically, Hannah cannot live without him, and she cannot live with him.

This also is true of Ilana and her first husband, Alex Gideon, in *Black Box*. Alex's sinister charm and his savage, venomous demeanor exert irresist-ible fascination on her, almost hypnotizes her. But it also is inimical and destructive. There is contradiction and duality in the relationship.

There is an affinity as well between Ilana and Rimona in *A Perfect Peace*. Here too a woman essentially belongs to two men. Thus Ilana, in *Black Box*, writes to her ex-husband:

But you were and you remain my lord and master. Forever. And in the life after life, Michel will hold my arm and lead me to the bridal canopy to my marriage ceremony with you. (p. 43)

Similarly, *A Perfect Peace* concludes with a domestic triangle when Rimona and her two husbands, Yonatan and Azaria, settle down together. The powerful, violent intensity that marks Yonatan has something in common with the malevolence and ruthlessness displayed by Alex. The analogy between the two should not be overlooked. Yonatan forces himself on Rimona with naked savagery that almost constitutes a rape: "And Yoni grabbed me by the shoulders and took me and threw me on the bed like a sack and did it to me in a nasty, mean, and hurtful way" (p. 182), while Alex seems repeatedly to violate Ilana by remote control, through letters suffused with savage, vitriolic cruelty, by the corrupting influence of his money, and by the hypnotic lethal web he weaves from afar. There also is a noticeable similarity between Azaria and Michel, the two "secondary" husbands who join the existing marital units. Azaria Gitlin, the Ashkenazi, and Michel Sommo, the Sephardi, both represent Diaspora Jews with their concomitant unsavory traits of baseness, deviousness, moral turpitude, and sycophancy. These two emissaries of "benighted" Jewry insinuate themselves into the heart of sunlit Israeli society, and like invidious worms gnawing at a ripe fruit, they undermine, corrupt, dispossess, and destroy it from within. As in the case of Zacharia Siegfried Berger in *Elsewhere, Perhaps*, here too a veneer of excessive, mealy mouthed civility and fulsome manners masks vulgarity and baseness. The emerging picture is almost an anti-Semitic caricature: hideous distortion, revolting degeneration, and vile underhandedness, all contrasted with the "Sabra" solidity, with the suntanned, robust, curly haired natives Alex and Yonatan, models of probity, straightforwardness, and integrity.

The analogy between Azaria and Michel is further reinforced by descriptions of their lovemaking. Here is Ilana's account: "There are times when I call him child, and hug his thin, warm body as though I were his mother" (p. 42), and Rimona's, talking about Azaria: "With Zaro it's mother and child" (p. 180). Ilana says about Michel, "I finally managed to teach him . . . how to wean himself from behaving like a bicycle thief whenever we made love" (p. 79), echoing Rimona, "From the first caress to the last little shriek, I'll teach him not to hurry like a little thief" (p. 180).

As for the chess metaphor, just as the game between Yonatan and Azaria reflects the erotic power struggle between them, in *Black Box*, too, Alex couches the struggle between him and his ex-wife in terms of chess: "It's all over, Ilana. Checkmate" (p. 85). I discussed earlier the function of the color blue as a metonymy for the exotic, dreamy quality of the spirited women who yearn for distant places: Ruth Kipniss's blue dress with the low-cut décolletage in *The Hill of the Evil Council*, Noga Harish's "thin, light-blue robe" in *Elsewhere, Perhaps*, Rimona Vogel's "blue house gown" in *A Perfect Peace*, Noa's blue house gown in *Do Not Call it a Night*, and above all, Hannah's "blue woolen dress" in *My Michael*, which is a deliberate allusion to the folktale of Hannale's Sabbath dress that was stained by coal dust. Hannah Gonen's blue woolen dress seems to have migrated to Ilana's closet in *Black Box*: "After breakfast I would put on my blue woolen dress" (p. 73).

There are strong similarities between *My Michael* and *Black Box*. The former opens as a letter, or a journal that Hannah writes for herself, to alleviate her distress and misery. "I am writing this because people I loved have died. I am writing this because when I was young I had the power to love, and now that power is dying. I do not want to die" (p. 5; cf. Agnon's "In the Prime of Her Life," which is a recorded memoir of Tirtza, its frustrated, distraught narrator-protagonist.

Structurally, *Black Box* is a series of correspondences between various people who use their writing not only to squabble, spar, and lash out, but also to alleviate their mental anguish and to channel their distress and suffering into other avenues. In some respect, *Black Box* is a continuation and development of themes and trends first introduced in *My Michael*. The heaviness that characterized the child Yair Gonen in *My Michael* seems to have increased and transmogrified into the mythological dimensions of Boaz Gideon. On the other hand, Professor Alex Gideon seems to have made up for some of the deficiencies observed in Dr. Michael Gonen (at least by his disappointed wife); whereas Michael is restrained, introverted, humble, and socially awkward, Alex Gideon is dashing and daring, astute, quick-witted, and seductive, and he exudes virility. Moreover, Michael's inarticulateness, which elicits his wife's disdain and condescension, is transformed into refined linguistic mastery and acerbic, vitriolic verbalism in Alex Gideon. Michael's muted, hesitant personality stands in sharp contrast to Alex's proud and aggressive masculinity, in his take-no-prisoners tactics and dangerous charm. In sum, everything that Hannah Gonen looked for in vain in her husband has materialized in Alex Gideon with a vengeance.

The disappointment, therefore, is evident. Dreams and wishes whispered in the dark in *My Michael* have sprouted and mushroomed in *Black Box* to frightening and malignant proportions. Something must have gone wrong in the mechanism of the wish fulfillment, and the modest request metamorphosed into something monstrous and nefarious.

What is left then? Only pain, disgrace, and disappointment; a sense of loss and deprivation, an ancient, hideous hatred, because all hopes and expectations have been dashed, leaving a sour taste of missed opportunities. A venomous cloud, like a malevolent entity, hovers above. The memory of past disappointments gathers mold and mildew and "ever turning blows the wind/ On its round the wind returns" (Ecclesiates, 1; 6). Only the box remains unchanged: black and barren, cold and empty.

CHAPTER 4

The Spy Who May Never Come in from the Cold:
A Discussion of *To Know a Woman*

Love is still incomprehensible to me. I wonder if I'll ever have the oppor-
tunity to learn. Pain, however, is a proven fact. But despite all this, I'm
positive we can accomplish a few things here.
                                              —Amos Oz, *A Perfect Peace*

When Cool, Cynical Rationality begins with Abnegation
of Feelings and Ends in Betrayal

How does the novel *To Know a Woman* fit into the binary structure that characterizes Oz's fiction? The basic concept of two rival entities perennially at war with each other determines not only the depiction of the central characters but also the plotline. The main characters in the novel are Yoel, his wife Ivria, and their daughter Netta, who is apparently epileptic—afflicted with "a lunar malady," as Yoel found it described in an encyclopedia. Ivria tries very hard to deny that the disease exists; she calls it "theater," a drama that Netta acts out in order to draw attention. Ivria cannot accept the fact that her daughter has a "defect." She drags the child to numerous holistic healers—"witch doctors," Yoel calls them—seeking confirmation for her denial of the disease. But Ivria dies at the beginning of the novel, perhaps in an accident, perhaps as a suicide, along with an elderly neighbor, Mr. Eviatar Vitkin, who rushed to help when she was electrocuted, and thus died with her. Throughout the novel, a suspicion lingers: was the aging neighbor Itamar Vitkin, in fact, Ivria's lover, while Yoel, the secret agent, was abroad? This point is deliberately never made clear. And similarly, there is a deliberate confusion of names: is it Eviatar or Itamar, as an obituary erroneously refers to the neighbor? The theme of duplicate names and dual identities is central to the novel, whose protagonist is a secret agent, leading a double life which, incidentally, calls to mind Oz's own description of himself as "a double agent of two superpowers," a point on which I will elaborate later. This Eviatar Vitkin, then, the aging, eccentric (presumed) lover, a truck driver

53

given to playing doleful melodies on his guitar and to quoting Scripture, is a recognizable figure from Oz's earlier fiction. He calls to mind Azaria Gitlin in *A Perfect Peace*—another lover of a married woman, Rimona Lifshitz, whose husband Yonatan, like Yoel, leaves home and goes away to lead a double life, assuming another identity. Azaria, too, is a "strange bird" who plays the guitar. Eviatar Vitkin also is reminiscent of Ezra Berger in *Elsewhere, Perhaps*, who is an elderly lover and a truck driver fond of quoting the Bible. Themes and characters recur. As Oz himself says at the conclusion of *A Panther in the Basement*: "Such is our story: it comes from darkness, wanders around a little, then returns to darkness."

Even though the novel opens with Ivria's somewhat enigmatic demise—an enigma that her husband, the secret agent, inured to cracking riddles and solving mysteries, fails to decipher—her physical absence from the scene does not diminish her presence in the novel.

The three main characters who dominate the plot—Yoel, Ivria, and Netta—all do their utmost to restrain and eviscerate their feelings and sentiments. They relegate and atrophy every emotion to deprive themselves of desire, leaving room for only cool, sane, sober rationality. Ivria adopts a cold, austere, almost ascetic existence. The white clothes she insists on wearing at all times call to mind Leah, the heroine of Agnon's "In the Prime of Her Life," whose white, shroud-like garb symbolizes the denial of feelings, since she has buried her love, turned her back on passion, and imposed emotional abstinence on herself, all of which lead to her death in the prime of her life. Ivria, too, entombs herself in her bare, monastic room, enveloped in melancholy airs and excessive modesty, avoiding real contact with the outside world. Her master's thesis is entitled "The Shame in the Attic," hinting at her deliberate effort to suppress and eradicate all emotion. This is how Ivria's room is described:

> The floor was bare. There was also an office desk made of metal, two metal chairs, and some metal bookshelves. Over the desk she had hung three small black-and-white photos of ruined Romanesque abbeys of the ninth or tenth century. . . . It was here that she had decided to barricade herself. (p. 11)

The cold, bare floor, the metal furniture, and the bookcases all give off an aura of monastic asceticism, of minimalism and utilitarianism, which rejects all considerations of aesthetics, intimacy, or comfort. The black-and-white photos of ruined abbeys reinforce the monastic association, seclusion, and deliberate withdrawal. The use of the verb "barricade" clinches the image of self-denial. The coldness and sterility of Ivria's character are further heightened by her white clothes that call to mind winding sheets. Later in the novel, Ivria is described wearing a white sweater that makes her look like "a sailor whose fleet has set sail without her" (p. 51), another image of seclusion and distance from life. Similarly, Hannah Gonen, in *My Michael*, describes herself as a "captain of the navy," relinquishing her part in the flow of life, preferring to document her life rather than live it. Just as Hannah mistakes her father-in-law for her husband, we are told that Ivria and Netta " were so alike, the mother and daughter, engulfed by music . . . that on one occasion Yoel . . . mistook her for Ivria" (p. 79). And Ivria's fair hair "falls over her right shoulder" (p.135) in a manner reminiscent of Noa in *Do Not Call It a Night*. Similarities abound, but let us return to Ivria's monastic study and its reverberations throughout the novel. It is not unlike the spare room that Yoel chooses to occupy in the rented house in Ramat Lotan. The monastic quality, with its attendant attributes of austerity, asceticism, and Christian humility, will later gather momentum and become one of the major motifs in the novel, the figure on the cross, in the same way that the statuette of the blind predator coalesces with the figure of the handicapped man in Helsinki:

> The source of torment, after all, is not in the point of fusion between the base and the paw, but somewhere else. Just as the nails in the Byzantine crucifixion scene were delicately crafted and there was not a drop of blood gushing from the wounds, so that it was clear to the observer that it was not a matter of liberating the body from its attachment to the cross but of liberating the youth with the feminine features from the prison of the body. (pp. 87–88)

The narrative presents a confluence of motifs in this passage: the statuette of the blind predator merges with the image of the crucified Jesus, which echoes the description of Ivria's study, and that is further associated with the cripple in Helsinki who is repeatedly described as having gentle, feminine features and who, having no arms or legs, is trapped in a wheelchair. Ivria's deliberate denial of feelings and the austerity and self-abnegation that she imposes on herself, which border on self-immolation, seep and ramify into other materials and recurring motifs in the novel: the statuette of the blind predator, the cripple in Helsinki, the crucifixion—a crux of symbols and significances that will be elucidated later in the analysis. Incidentally, Ivria's almost pathological attempt at denying the "strange fire" that lurks beneath Netta's epilepsy is another example of her concerted effort to repress, block, and stop up any outlet where emotion or natural impulse may seep through. To Ivria, allowing feelings to escape is tantamount to releasing a baleful, venomous virus that threatens to bring an epidemic. Combating it requires the mobilization of every means and resource. Every manifestation of feeling must be eradicated.

Netta too is dedicated to the same pursuit of ridding the reality around her of any trace of feeling. She adopts an attitude and a mode of expression that are mordant, acerbic, and caustic, like a viper rearing its head to spray venom at anyone who attempts to approach. Netta assiduously stifles and represses any hint of femininity. She crops her hair so short that it makes her look like an ungainly porcupine; she wears frumpy, slovenly clothes that disguise any feminine curves; she pokes fun at herself—at her flat chest—cynically, sarcastically, unsentimentally.

And Yoel? He is a staunch enemy of any display of emotion. Yoel either nips sentiments in the bud or dilutes and represses them. Emotionally speaking, he is on automatic pilot; cautiously, logically, dispassionately, he examines reality and decides when to pounce, what to excise, and who to eliminate. He divests himself of feelings as though they are soiled clothes that one tosses into a hamper with distaste and revulsion.

When Yoel finds out about Ivria's sudden death, he makes a snap decision: to resign from the Secret Service. What is the connection between his wife's death and his decision to resign? Well, there is a connection, and it will be discussed later. Yoel quit his job as a secret agent, a job he had held for many years, which had become second nature to him. But it is only a putative resignation. Even in retirement, when he preoccupies himself with the trivia of everyday life, he continues to practice the routines of the secret agent, perhaps the double agent, forever detached, uninvolved, aloof, keeping the world at a safe distance. Hands in his pockets, Yoel peers through hooded eyes, straining and squinting them across the barbed wire that he has put up to protect himself.

He takes showers, washes dishes, dusts, and disinfects; he imposes order, system, discipline, and control; he changes the bedding, trims the hedges, and manicures the lawn, all the while refraining from real contact with his neighbors. The change comes later, but that too is carefully calculated, measured, and controlled. He conducts his life like a pharmacist, carefully and dispassionately weighing every step, avoiding decisions.

Yoel investigates every detail meticulously (such as the blurred spot in a photograph of one of Ivria's ruined monasteries). Focused, alert, sharp, and lethal—"like a gangster on a night of long knives," in Oz's inimitable phrase—he deconstructs reality with gloved hands, infinitely patient, methodical, thorough, and discreet. He tries to read every clue, to anticipate the result of every move. He uses words sparingly, reluctantly; he avoids touching his daughter; he never commits himself, whether to colleagues or paramours. He is the inveterate spy who does not dare to come in from the cold.

Yoel, Ivria, and Netta, each in his or her own way, seek to impose cold, sober rationality on his or her life and to ignore the decree of their feelings. Here, once more, one may discern the basic dichotomy between the rational and the emotional, the two contradictory forces perennially vying for supremacy. In these three characters, the rational, indeed, has the upper hand, roundly defeating the emotional, but not without exacting a price.

And yet despite the pyrrhic victory of sober rationality that characterizes the novel, a slight change of attitude can be detected toward the end: the extreme structuralism dictated by the clear-cut polarity loses some of its edge and gives way to a deconstuctionist mode that speaks of a constant state of flux, the merging of opposites, and the absence of a unique, absolute meaning. Toward the end of the novel, Yoel, the austere and intransigent recluse, relents a little, takes off the surgical gloves, and opens up to the world. This development will be discussed later.

The novel opens with a figurine of a blind predator (probably a big cat), which is the first object Yoel focuses on when he enters the house in Ramat Lotan, a prosperous and serene suburb of Tel Aviv: "Yoel picked the object up from the shelf and inspected it closely. His eyes ached" (p. 5). The binary structuralism that underlies all of Oz's oeuvre is apparent here— looming like an X-ray photograph—in the description of the exotic figurine:

> It was an ornament, a small figurine, the work of an amateur: a feline predator, carved in brown olive wood and coated with several layers of lacquer. Its jaws were gaping wide and the teeth were pointed. The two front paws were extended in the air in a spectacular leap; the right hind leg was also in the air, still contracted, its muscles bulging from the effort of jumping, only the left hind leg preventing the leap and grounding the beast on a stainless steel stand. The body rose at an angle of forty-five degrees, and the tension was so powerful that Yoel could almost feel in his own flesh the pain of the fastened paw and the desperation of the arrested leap. He found the figurine unnatural and unrealistic, even though the artist had succeeded in imposing on the material an excellent feline litheness. . . . Ostensibly, this was a perfect piece of carving, liberated from its woodenness and achieving a cruel, sharp, almost sexual vitality. And yet, something had not come out right. Something or other was wrong, exaggerated, either too finished, as it were, or not finished enough. What the error was, Yoel could not discover. His eyes ached.

Perhaps it was also because the figurine with its hidden flaw seemed to be flouting the laws of gravity: the weight of the predator in its hand seemed to be greater than that of the steel base that the creature was struggling to break away from, and to which it remained attached by only a tiny point of contact between the hind paw and the base. It was on this very point that Yoel now focused his attention. He discovered that the paw was sunk in an infinitesimal depression carved in the surface of the steel. But how? His vague anger intensified when he turned the object over and to his astonishment found no sign of the screw that he had supposed would have to be there, to attach the paw to the base. He turned the figurine over again; there was no sign of any screw in the beast's flesh either, between the claws of the hind paw. What was it, then, that stopped the animal's leap, that arrested its attack? . . . If the predator was heavier than the base and projected almost entirely beyond it, it ought to turn over. . . . If there was a hidden trick, what was it? . . . Delicately, with a slow caress, Yoel ran a cautious finger around the secret joint between the living and the inanimate . . . a faint recollection of a Byzantine crucifixion scene flickered in his mind: a scene that had something implausible about it and yet was filled with pain. (pp. 5–7)

Only later does Yoel find out the additional element hiding inside of the figurine of the beast of prey:

Even if there is some simple way of liberating the predator in the statuette from the torment of its trapped paw without breaking it or hurting it, there is still no answer to the question how and where an eyeless creature will leap. The source of the torment, after all, is not in the point of fusion between the base and the paw, but somewhere else. (p. 87)

One is reminded of a similar description of a wooden statue that exerts a powerful tension in *Touch the Water, Touch the Wind*:

On a chest of drawers in the study stood a figure of an African warrior carved in wood and painted in battle colors. The warrior looked as if he were about to leap. Day and night, his enormous, angry member seemed to threaten the delicate, naked pink girl in a Matisse painting that hung on the opposite wall. (p. 8)

Here too the binary structure, the savage and sinister versus the gentle and refined, is clearly distinguished; the raging, bristling element threatening to annihilate the fragile, domesticated, bashful element. Here are two novels featuring two different statues, but the symbolic-conceptual import is the same. In *To Know a Woman*, the blind predator statuette serves as a focal point for several motifs: the crucifixion scene evoked in Yoel's mind by the sight of the figure; the image of the cripple in Helsinki with the gentle, Christ-like face; the blindness motif, of which Yoel is the chief representative in the novel; and others. There is a strong affinity between the blind predator and the three main characters, Yoel, Ivria, and Netta. It has to do with the intense inner force that the figure exudes, its rootedness, its paralysis, and its arrested motion. It is not only the predator who is typified by powerful intensity and frozen emotions threatening to erupt; Yoel, Ivria, and Netta all try to tame the savage spirit, to abort the flight, to stifle the groan, and to emasculate all sentiment. They betray the primal cry of the blood, and betrayal is a recurrent motif in Amos Oz's fiction (see in particular *A Panther in the Basement*, where betrayal is the central theme). In fact, *To Know a Woman* opens with an act of betrayal—Ivria's presumed betrayal of her husband—and ends with betrayal—Yoel's betrayal of his secret agent mission, the treachery he practices on his colleagues.

The predator is blind, blind as a mole, which is a synonym for secret agent, spy, spook, undercover man. Proffy, the narrator in *A Panther in the Basement*, also defines himself as a double agent, a term Oz has applied to himself (in an interview in *Maariv*, May 2, 1980). Oz sees himself as a secret agent, a Jeruslalem undercover man in the foreign territory of Kibbutz Hulda, and vice versa. Zecharia-Siegfried Berger, in *Elsewhere, Perhaps*, describes himself as "a spy sent by a hostile superpower (an observation made by Avraham Balaban in *Between God and Beast*). By the same token, the image of a panther caged in the basement conveys the same arrested force and chained intensity as the blind predator whose flight is arrested in midair by blindness and by confinement to matter.

Thus the blind predator is a metaphor for Yoel, Ivria, and Netta, who seek to abolish feelings and deny basic human nature. But banishment of emotions exacts a price: Ivria pays with her life. Yoel pays by being a living dead. At the end of the novel, though, he experiences a kind of resurrection, like Christ, with whom he is associated through the blind predator. This is not an arbitrary revival: Yoel is capable of experiencing a resurrection only when he stops trying to repress and deprecate his emotions. What is the price Netta has to pay? She pays with her illness and with the sarcastic, vitriolic cynicism she has affected since early childhood. Eventually she realizes that the acidity has seeped into her bloodstream, has poisoned her soul and backfired. Like Yoel, she is saved in the end, or at least she finds partial salvation when she extricates herself from her father's constricting, stifling presence and goes to live with Duby Krantz. Only Ivria dies, and not just a metaphorical death, like the other two. She dies too early, in the prime of her life, like her predecessor Leah, in Agnon's story, whose shroud-like clothes symbolized her alienated, sterile soul. Since she has renounced love, Leah dwindles and fades and, finally, she is snuffed like a tallow candle.[1] Thus the image of the blind predator encapsulates Yoel's and Netta's precarious situation: the spectacular leap frozen in midair, the aborted assault, the blindness that betokens hollowness and despair and, above all, the apparent defiance of gravitation, a betrayal of the laws of physics, which all create an unbearable tension, since the figure always seems about to lose its balance, to tip over and smash to smithereens. The characters' embrace of rationality to the exclusion of feeling and human authenticity amounts to a betrayal and denial of life. Only someone emotionally blind and castrated can hope to persist in such denial with impunity.

Betrayal is a cardinal theme in the novel, and not just betrayal of the *elan vital*, the human life force. *To Know a Woman* offers a rogues' gallery of traitors. It opens with a betrayal and ends with a betrayal. It opens with Ivria's supposed betrayal of Yoel; the seemingly naive narrator scatters numerous hints about Ivria's affair with the elderly neighbor, Eviatar Vitkin, whose guitar—in Yoel's imagination—continues to produce cello-like sounds in the dark. Ivria's death in her suspected lover's arms—perhaps an accident, perhaps a suicide—only strengthens this theory. Another betrayal occurs at the end of the novel; Yoel is accused by the Patron, his superior at the agency, of having stabbed a colleague in the back, an accusation reiterated by the father of that colleague, Ostashinsky, a.k.a. Cockney, the Acrobate, Sasha Shine—there is no shortage of aliases that the secret agents assume to mask their identities. The father calls Yoel "Cain" and "Traitor," hissing the epithets venomously as a shaken Yoel hastens to retreat. Yoel has, in fact, escaped death "on the job," death by accident, which is an occupational hazard in a secret agent's line of work.

Betrayal is an oft-encountered motif in Amos Oz's fiction. In *Elsewhere, Perhaps*, Bronka cheats on Ezra Berger with Reuven Harish, while Ezra Berger retaliates by having an affair with Reuven Harish's daughter, Noga. Eva Harish betrays her husband, her country, her kibbutz, and her pioneering ideology, when she departs unexpectedly, leaving behind a stunned husband and two children. She leaves in the company of her repulsive—her word—cousin, Isaac Hamburger, for Germany, where he runs a sleazy nightclub with Zecharia-Siegfried Berger, brother of Ezra Berger, the betrayer and betrayed.

In *My Michael*, Hannah feels that she is betraying her husband when she engages in savage, torrid lovemaking with him. She betrays his placid, composed personality with his own body. She proves even more treasonous in her frenzied, delirious romps with the Arab twins. In *Touch the Water, Touch the Wind*, Steffa Pomerantz cheats on her husband when she marries the Russian spy Podoseyev while she is still legally married to Pomerantz, who incidentally "looked like a crafty spy in an American comedy" (p. 5). In the novella, *The Hill of the Evil Council*, Ruth Kipniss cheats on her husband, the stolid and uninspired veterinarian. In "Mr. Levi," gossip has it that Uri Kolodny's mother cheats on her husband (another ineffectual, wimpy male) with Ephraim, who greatly resembles Mitya, the foul-smelling, rabidly right-wing lodger in *The Hill of the Evil Council*, whom Ruth Kipniss wishes to gather to her perfumed arms. Mina (i.e., Dr. Hermina Oswald), in the story "Longing," deserts Dr. Emanuel Nussbaum, her moribund husband. Lily Danenberg, in "Strange Fire," betrays her daughter when she seduces Yair, her daughter's intended. In the novella *Unto Death*, the betrayal centers on the Jew who has surreptitiously infiltrated a crusaders' convoy. In "Late Love," the traitor is the body of the protagonist, Shraga Unger, beset by disease and pain that waste away his flesh and hasten his demise before he can fulfill his life's mission: to warn the world about the perils of an insidious, illusory communism that threatens to annihilate the Jewish people.

In *A Perfect Peace*, Rimona cheats on her husband, Yoni Lifshitz, with Azaria Gitlin, the guitar-playing, exilic Jew. In *Fima* (*The Third Condition*) at least one of Fima's lady friends cheats on her husband, as of course does Ilana in *Black Box*, who cheats on Alex Gideon with a "whole battalion of men." Even Noa, in *Do Not Call It a Night*, hovers around the edges of betrayal of her husband, Theo, when she flirts with Muky Peleg, seducing and repelling him at the same time with the charms of her mature femininity.

Betrayal, then, is a recurrent theme in Oz's fiction. In *To Know a Woman*, Ivria probably cheats on Yoel, while Yoel often dreams of cheating on Ivria with a submissive Eskimo lover. He also is accused of betraying his country and his ideology. His commanding officer, the Patron, reprimands him in an accusatory, acrimonious tone:

But you, comrade, when you were needed, when you were sent for, you did your own calculations and you got someone else sent in your place. One of them. So now just go home and live with that. (p. 150)

And this is a secret agent, a spy for whom betrayal is the greatest danger, a threat that can cost him his life. It is possible that a suspicion of betrayal changed the course of Yoel's life, because as soon as he found out that his wife had died in her lover's (?) arms, he announced his resignation from the service. Perhaps he felt guilty for the long absences from home, which were a kind of betrayal in themselves, and which may have impelled Ivria to betray him. Perhaps, by resigning from the agency and staying home exclusively, he wished not only to expiate for his supposed betrayal but also to protect his daughter Netta, who was now living with him.

Yoel's betrayal is reinforced by an oblique analogy to Judas Iscariot. Having long tried in vain to catch the paperboy in the act of throwing the paper on the sidewalk instead of putting it in the mailbox, Joel finally manages to "ambush" him—not unlike the pouncing, blind predator. Yoel offers the man a bonus of thirty shekels, plus a promise to pay the fee until Passover. Thirty shekels and Passover bring to mind Judas' betrayal of Jesus, on Passover, for thirty shekels.[2] This subtle, furtive analogy between Yoel and Judas underlines the motif of betrayal surrounding the secret agent Yoel Ravid (or is it Raviv?).

Attributes of the statuette of the blind predator crop up on many occasions throughout the novel. For instance, Yoel's car is described as "ready to leap," calling to mind the frozen leap of the predator; The Patron with a "twinkle of feline cruelty" in his eye, underneath the facade of civility; the constant preoccupation with the cat and her litter in the toolshed; Yoel waylaying the newspaper man like a beast of prey early in the morning; and Netta's room in Jerusalem containing a poster of a cute kitten snuggling in its sleep against a German Shepherd (p. 94). It is said about Yoel that "his working years and his travels had accustomed him to wake like a cat, a sort of inner leap straight from sleep to a state of alertness without any transitional stage of drowsiness" (p. 131). He often is described as "driving his car sharply" (p. 159), "darting to the telephone booth" (p. 145), "leaping from his seat" (p. 143), "bursting forth suddenly" (p. 138), "charging wildly and tearing up the right-hand lane" (p. 152), and conducting "a hawk-eyed search" (p. 158). Netta tells him, "You look like a killer" (p. 136), and Ivria hisses at him maliciously, "No, I'm clean off my rocker—for agreeing to live with a murderer" (p. 53), while Yoel tells himself, "I killed my wife . . ." (p. 154). Netta upbraids him, "Just look at yourself. You look as though you're about to kill somebody" (p. 157). The Patron tells him, "Here I fought like a tiger" (p. 78), and earlier the Patron smiles "like a drowsy cat" (p. 39), while Yoel discerns in him "a kind of gentle, drowsy cruelty, the cruelty of an overfed cat" (p. 40). There are many more allusions, both direct and metonymic, to the blind, predator figurine displayed on the shelf of the rented villa in Ramat Lotan: a motif representing the dominant theme of the novel; the struggle between rationality and emotinalism; the figurine embodying the idea of turbulent, gushing desires, aggressive energy, and sinister, lurking conspiracy, all arrested, grounded, imprisoned, and subjected to the laws of gravitation. The mouth is open wide, but no shout escapes; it remains imprisoned deep in the throat (cf. the image of the bird whose beak is wide open as if perennially thirsty in *A Perfect Peace*). The figurine is reminiscent of another historical statue, Laocoon, the Trojan priest who warned his people against the Trojan horse which he recognized as a wily stratagem. But the goddess Athena, who sided with the Greeks, sent sea serpents that coiled themselves about the limbs of the priest and his sons and suffocated them. The famous statue, displayed at the Uffizzi in Florence, shows the priest's face contorted in fear and excruciating pain, his mouth wide open but mute. The shout remains unuttered, arrested, imprisoned, reverberating in silence forever. (Cf. also Gottfried Lessing's famous book, *Laocoon*). Thus the statue of the blind predator, poised in mid-leap on a shelf in an upscale suburb of Tel Aviv, is an apt metaphor for the secret agent, the undercover spy whose personality combines tremendous intensity with calculated caution, pent-up tension with the need for restraint and camouflage.

There is another analogy between the blind predator and the secret agent. The figurine seems to contain an insoluble riddle; it defies the laws of physics, threatening to tip over at any moment, and yet it stays erect on its base, forever frozen in midair. The life of Yoel, the secret agent, is equally enigmatic, shrouded in veils of mystery, replete with masks, disguises, camouflages, and false identities. He is in constant danger of tripping and falling, yet he forges ahead in the dark. Yoel is obsessed with the riddle of the blind predator, striving persistently to puzzle out its hidden mechanism, to decipher its secret, just as he strives tirelessly to solve the riddle of life. "It would seem that I have been here for forty-some years and I still haven't so much as begun to work out what's going on" (p. 32). Blindness is a common trait of Yoel and the predator. The physical blindness of the beast is translated, in Yoel's case, into stinging, painful eyes, a metaphor for his inability to see into the hidden meaning of life. Like blind Oedipus in Sophocles' classical tragedy, who was also, in his way, a failed detective, Yoel Ravid is a secret agent, a mole as blind as the predator figurine that stands on a shelf in his house and serves as a constant reminder of his silent cry.

"Since the World Is Double and Its Lament Is Twofold" (*From Nathan Alterman's "The Mole"*)

Yoel Ravid, the secret agent, is undone by his blindness. But Ivria and Netta, who are misled to believe that one can live by rationality alone, also are afflicted by blindness and tainted by treason, by the betrayal of life itself.

To Know a Woman is replete with dualities, doubles, duplicates, multiple identities, and doppelgangers; like a spy's suitcase with a false bottom, or like Yoel's cast-iron safe where he keeps his numerous passports. Duplication is the name of the game here, and it is most apparent when it comes to names. Take, for example, the elderly neighbor, Ivria's presumed lover, Eviatar Vitkin, who is sometimes referred to as Itamar. Yoel Ravid is sometime called Raviv. Netta, if her father had his way, would have been named Rakefet (cyclamen) for her father's favorite flower. The Patron, Yoel's superior in the Secret Service, also is referred to as the Teacher and Brother, and his real name is Yirmiyahu Kordovero. Secret agent Ostashinsky is nicknamed Cockney and the Acrobat. The real estate agent, Arie Krantz, is called Arik. Yoel presents himself as Sasha Shein when he volunteers to work at the hospital. Sasha Shein is another of Ostashinsky's appellations. Ivria's brother, Nakdimon Lublin, when reciting the "Kaddish" over his sister's grave, mispronounces three ancient Aramaic words of the prayer for the dead. Yoel's mistress, his neighbor, Annemarie, is mistakenly referred to as Rosemary, and in the obituaries Ivria is called Ivria Raviv instead of Ravid. The neighbor, Vitkin, tells Yoel that "the Hebrew word *shebeshiflenu* (in our meekness), mentioned in Psalm 136, could easily be a Polish word, whereas the word *namogu* (faded away) at the end of chapter 2 of the Book of Joshua has a distinctly Russian sound to it" (p. 71). Yoel often thinks about the Urdu word for love which, when it is read backward, means hate.

There are other dualities: both Yoel and the Patron are middle-aged widowers. Yoel has two "fathers": one his biological father, who was probably a Christian Roumanian, a lean man with a gloomy face, who disappeared from Yoel's life when he was a baby; and the other "father," a crude, hefty, bald man with a bristly beard who was involved in an ugly, violent brawl with Yoel's mother on board the ship that brought them to Israel. Yoel often wonders about these two "fathers" of his. He himself lives with two grandmothers—his mother Lisa and his mother-in-law Avigail—and with two additional women, his adolescent daughter Netta, who in some respect functions as his companion—although not sexually, since their relationship is totally devoid of erotic tension—and the neighbor Annemarie, or is it Rosemary? Annemarie has her own duality: she apparently lives with two men, Yoel and her own brother, with whom she seems to have an incestuous relationship. Ivria has two men in her life, her husband Yoel and an aging lover, her neighbor, Eviatar Vitkin.

A woman living with two men is a recurrent theme in Amos Oz's fiction. In *Elsewhere, Perhaps*, Noga Harish has an affair with Ezra Berger, an old truck driver fond of quoting Scripture, yet she is married to Rami

Rimon, who helps her raise the daughter she had with Ezra Berger. In *Black Box*, Ilana tells her ex-husband, Alex Gideon, simply, "I'm married to Michel Somo, but I am also your wife, and in the life to come, on our renewed wedding day, my husband Michel will lead me to the bridal canopy and give me away to you, my husband." At the denouement of *A Perfect Peace*, Rimona becomes the wife to two men simultaneously: her husband, Yoni Lifshitz, who has come back from his travels, and her lover, Azaria Gitlin, the stranger who has latched himself on to the kibbutz community. In *Touch the Water, Touch the Wind*, Steffa Pomerantz marries "a little spy-master" while still married to Pomerantz, whose face "brings to mind a spy in an American comedy." And Ernest—the secretary of the kibbutz—is mentioned with "his two mistresses." In the short story "Late Love," Shraga Unger, the seedy, rejected, marginalized lecturer, approaches the aging singer Lyuba and her new husband with the following proposition: "From now on there will be harmony between us . . . the three of us will live together, under one roof . . . we'll establish a little kibbutz of our own." . ." And in *My Michael*, Hannah Gonen, in some respect at least, lives with two (in fact, three) men, her husband Michael and the two tempestuous Arab twins, the subjects of her fervid dreams. In *The Hill of the Evil Council*, Ruth, the wife and mother in the Kipniss household, lives with two men, her husband, the kindly and good-natured veterinarian, who evokes in her only boredom and dissatisfaction, and their lodger Mitya, a firebrand impelled by messianic and nationalistic dreams. Despite the foul smell that his body emits—or perhaps because of it—she is moved to mollify him and assuage his and her frustration by gathering him to her lap. Bronka Berger, in *Elsewhere, Perhaps*, lives with two men: her husband Ezra, the heavyset Bible lover, and Reuven Harish, the sensitive, vulnerable poet whose wife has deserted both him and the sweltering, sweaty land of Israel and emigrated to wintry, sylvan Germany, where she married her repulsive cousin, Isaac Hamburger. There also is a vicious rumor that Uri Kolodny's mother in "Mr. Levi" is cheating on her wimpy, boring husband with the unkempt, wooly electrician, Ephraim.

Oz's fiction, then, is rife in situations where married women carry on with other men and lead a dual existence. But duality, doubling, replication, and duplicity are particularly fundamental to *To Know a Woman*, due to the double life that Yoel leads as a secret agent. Yet upon learning of his wife's death (suicide?), Yoel decides to resign from the service and ceases to lead the life of a spy. But quitting his job does not rid him of his lifelong habits of cover-up, detection, and investigation. Perhaps he does not really want to be rid of those habits. The patterns of Secret Service routine are too deeply ingrained in him, and so he continues to follow, observe, stake out, examine, memorize, and map the details of his surrounding reality, in an attempt to decipher its inner code. But international intrigues and state affairs are no longer at stake; now it is the banal, humdrum, prosaic reality of day-to-day living, with its myriad details, routines, and procedures that absorb him in a desperate attempt to fathom its meaning, to crack its secret. So he looks for signs, like the movement of clouds across the sky at nighttime; like the wind rustling the drapes in the darkened parlor; like the dewdrops glistening on the mailbox at dawn, then evaporating; like the hesitant signs of withering in the foliage with the approach of autumn; and like the arrival of the old Bulgarian paper distributor who tosses the paper on the sidewalk instead of putting it in the mailbox. These minutiae are documented by Yoel's consciousness and filtered through the narrator's point of view:

> [T]he scent of burned thorns wafted from the nearby citrus grove, the chirping of the swallows before sunrise on the branches of the apple tree now rusting from autumn's touch . . . the scent of watered soil, the taste of light at dawn. (p. 101)

All of these details seem to Yoel fraught with a secret meaning: if only he could uncover it, strip it of dross, clean it of the refuse that obscures and obstructs the vision, then he would be able to penetrate the inner stratum, to expose the underlying mechanism that governs the tiny details that make up ephemeral living—and perhaps understand the riddle of his own existence and the mystery of life in general. He would find a clue, a thread to unravel the tangled skein:

> At times you can almost sense, here and there, some signs of a pattern. The trouble is that I can't figure it out and I probably never will. (p. 32)

And later:

> A slight anger arose in him at the thought that everything was so secret. But, in fact, secret was not the right word. It was not like a sealed book, but, rather, like an open book in which one could aimlessly read clear, everyday things, morning, garden, bird, newspaper, but which one could also read in other ways; combining, for example, every seventh word in reverse order. Or the fourth word of every other sentence. . . . There is no limit to the number of possibilities, and each one of them may point to a different interpretation. . . . How will you know which is the right access code? How can you discover, among the

infinite combinations, the correct prefix? The key to the inner order of
things? (pp. 71–72)

Perhaps this is a self-defeating quest. But then again, perhaps Yoel is
asking the wrong question. Is reality, indeed, such a mystery, a conundrum
requiring an access code? Or is it simply that Yoel's view of reality is skewed
and distorted due to years of involvement with espionage and intelligence,
undercover operations, and hush-hush investigation? Perhaps the minute details that make up his life are really devoid of any mystery, denuded of any
hidden meaning. Maybe there is another reason behind Yoel's distorted vision, his warped point of view. After all, we are told repeatedly that his eyes
sting and smart and squint. And as we noted earlier, being a secret agent, a
mole, Yoel is metaphorically blind. He is analogous to Oedipus, who was
able to solve the Sphinx's riddle but failed at solving the riddle of his own
life. The metaphorical blindness eventually leads to physical blindness as
Oedipus gouges his own eyes when he discovers the extent of the devastation
he has caused. The figurine of the predator also is blind, "the predator had
no eyes. The artist—an amateur after all—had forgotten to give it eyes" (p.
10). In the end, it all comes back to the statue of the blind predator. Solving
the riddle of Yoel's life and cracking the thematic code of the novel hinge
upon solving the riddle of the blind predator, which seems to defy the laws
of physics, standing erect and punching the air with its arrested leap. We
must solve its riddle in order to puzzle out Yoel's riddle and fathom the
deeper meaning of the novel.

The Figurine of the Blind Predator: The Riddle Etched on the Wall, or the Interpretation of Blindness

The blind predator weaves itself in and out of the plot. Its presence
hovers above the events and the characters, and it is never absent for long. It
functions as a metaphorical focal point for several semantic ideas and themes
explored in the novel. The blind predator encapsulates the eternal strife between two contrasting poles: clear, sober rationality that betokens symmetry,
balance, strict order, and proportion versus unbridled, subversive emotionality
that is irrational, savage, and sinister. We have noted that the three main
characters in *To Know a Woman* are all devotees of order, discipline, and cold
rationality. This aspect is captured in the predator's arrested motion, in its
contained violence, in its checked and controlled savagery. It also embodies
the concept of the betrayal of the life force, the stemming of the natural

eruption of instinct, impulse, and sentiment. In addition, the sightless, expressionless eyes of the predator underscore the theme of blindness and emphasize the irony of the secret agent who purports to investigate and decipher the data he accumulates but fails miserably. In this respect, Yoel is analogous to Oedipus Rex, the classical riddle solver who, due to spiritual blindness and refusal to stare truth in the face, fails to solve the riddle of his own identity and to discover the original sin that has wreaked havoc on Thebes and decimated its population. His blindness, willfulness, and hubris prevent him from listening to the voice of reason, and so he ends up shattering all of the expectations placed upon him. Eventually, when the blinds are removed from his eyes and the horrid truth penetrates his consciousness, he is moved to gouge his own eyes, and he blinds himself. He begins with metaphoric blindness and ends with horrendous physical blindness. Like the stony predator and like Oedipus Rex, Yoel too is blinded by his stubborn denial of emotions. In vain he tries to feel his way in the darkness. The thick armor he wears to ward off feelings blinds him, grounds him, enervates him, and cuts him off from the truth he seeks. The riddle posed by the figurine— its ability to stay erect and leap in the air in defiance of the laws of gravity— is as tantalizing and perturbing as Oedipus' riddle. Yoel fails in his attempt to solve this riddle, just as he fails to penetrate reality and puzzle out the meaning of life.

Ivria (whose name echoes the sounds of the Hebrew word for blind, *Iver*), in her denial of emotions and sentiments, is presented as blind, not only metaphorically but also physically. Her first encounter with Yoel and their hasty, impetuous lovemaking in the grove behind her parents' house in the Galilee is described in the following terms:

> They were both stunned, their bodies clung together . . . rolling in the dust, panting and burrowing into each other like a pair of blind puppies. (p. 130)

Their impaired sight is further underscored by frequent references to reading glasses. Ivria deliberately chooses "square, frameless glasses that suggested a stern family doctor of an earlier generation" (p. 22), whereas Yoel "had chosen a pair of ridiculous round black-framed glasses that made him look like an elderly Latin priest" (p. 26). The image of an elderly Latin priest will later coalesce with the motif of the crucifix and the cripple from Helsinki.

Ivria's master's thesis "The Shame in the Attic"—an examination of the Bronte sisters' works—brings to mind another recurrent concept, epitomized in the saying, "when it comes to it, we all have the same secrets," often quoted by Ivria's father, a veteran police officer who winks lewdly at Yoel when he utters it, filling him "with rage, almost with loathing, directed not at Lublin, but at Ivria" (p. 48). The connection here is quite clear: the shame in the attic is such a secret, or perhaps it is all of the secrets that people try to hide and bury. But there is mockery and ludicrousness in secrets that are shared by one and all. What is the point of trying to conceal such open secrets?

What is the shame in Yoel's attic? It is the skeleton in his closet that he tries both to repress and to investigate. Perhaps this is the source of his failure, the fact that he is trying to accomplish two contradictory things simultaneously: to seek to solve the mystery of life, while at the same time to hide and suppress the secret whose disclosure he dreads. He insists on building a protective shell around himself and then feels trapped and imprisoned, yet he is blind to the fact that the basic contradiction of his existence will inevitably lead to failure; with one eye he seeks to find the secret of life, yet the other eye is covered. His eyes always hurt, because he squints and strains them both to see better and to avoid seeing. It is his willful blindness that prevents Yoel, the secret agent, the mole, from solving the mysteries of his own life, of life in general, as well as that of the leaping predator, no matter how alert and sharp and perceptive he purports to be. Walking on tiptoe, "like a gangster on a night of long knives," he maps and etches in his mind every minute detail that crosses his path. With one hand he tries to shed light on reality, with the other he tightens the mask, leaving his face in the dark. And like in *The Emperor's New Clothes*, it is the boy, Duby Krantz, the slouching, gawky youth, the typical anti-hero, whom Yoel mocks as "not exactly James Dean," who eventually tears the veil of mystery and solves the enigma of the blind predator that seems to defy the laws of gravity:

> Don't take offense, Mr. Ravid. You're asking the wrong question. It has to do with physics. Instead of asking how come it doesn't fall over, we should simply realize that if it doesn't fall over, that proves that the center of gravity is over the base. That's all. (p. 183)

The fact that the answer to the riddle of the figurine is relatively simple emphasizes Yoel's blindness, his being mired in the morass of a contradictory existence; like Oedipus, he is incapable of regarding the realities of his life from an external point of view, and thus he repeatedly fails to solve the riddle that haunts him like a specter.

*From a Blind Predator to Blind Oedipus to the Cripple in Helsinki
and Back to Yoel, the Blind, Emotionally Crippled Secret Agent*

Apart from the motif of the blind predator, there is another highly
charged recurrent motif in the novel, the cripple in Helsinki, whom Yoel sees
fleetingly on his tryst with the Tunisian engineer. While that meeting is
taking place, in another part of the world, Yoel's wife, Ivria, finds her death
in what may be either an accident or a suicide.

What do we know about that cripple? What can we learn about him?
The details are sketchy, but they do add up to a discernable picture. This is
how the cripple in Helsinki is captured in Yoel's memory at the beginning of
the novel:

> The cripple in the wheelchair in Helsinki had been young, very pale,
> and Yoel seemed to remember that he had delicate, feminine features.
> He had no arms or legs. From birth? An accident? (p. 23)

The components that make up the image of the cripple are scattered,
in various guises, throughout the novel, and they all relate in some way to
Yoel himself, since Yoel, directly or indirectly, is connected to the cripple.
There are, for instance, repeated references to a dog, Ironside,

> perhaps named after the detective in a wheelchair in an American tele-
> vision series of a few years back, which Yoel had happened to watch by
> himself in hotel rooms in one city or another. Once he had watched an
> episode dubbed into Portuguese and had still managed to follow the
> plot. Which was a simple one. (p. 23)

The dog, Ironside, is mentioned several times, always in connection
with Yoel. We have here then an evocation of a paralyzed detective in conjunction with a legless man in a wheelchair in Helsinki. Yoel himself, we are
indirectly told, is paralyzed, because he froze or eliminated all emotions from
his life and now stands helpless in front of the riddles he vainly tries to
puzzle out. The image of the wheelchair crops up again, at the side of the
road, as Yoel makes his way to Jerusalem:

> An overturned truck, lying with its wheels still spinning by the road-
> side on the winding ascent to Jerusalem, reminded him again of the
> cripple in Helsinki. (p. 19)

And later:

Once, years before, his mother told him how, when he was three years old, she had pushed him, in a squeaking carriage, completely covered and buried under packages and bundles hastily thrown together, for hundreds of miles from Bucharest to the port of Varna. (p. 24)

There may be an indirect allusion here to the holy trinity ("when he was three"), since we noted earlier that Yoel is associated with the crucifix and with the cripple in the wheelchair. There is another reference (p. 105) to the mother's story about the "journey in the baby carriage." Here, the baby Yoel, helpless, motionless, lies in the baby buggy like the cripple in his wheelchair. The cripple's features are described as delicate and feminine, suggestive of a tender baby face (cf. also baby Jesus). Thus is reinforced the link between the cripple and Yoel in his infancy:

He imagined himself at that moment a limbless cripple, a sack of flesh from which popped a head that was neither a man's nor a woman's but of some more delicate creature, more delicate than a child even, bright and clear-sighted, as though knowing the answer and secretly delighted at its almost unbelievable simplicity, for there it was before your very eyes. (p. 80)

A similar description, precise and perceptive, centers on the cripple in Helsinki:

The invalid in Helsinki really did have the face of a girl. Or, rather, of something gentler still, gentler than a child, bright and clear-sighted, as though he knew what the answer was, and quietly delighted at its unbelievable simplicity, for there it was, before your very eyes. (p. 110)

We have here a kind of celestial fetus, perfect and mysterious, like the image at the end of the movie *2001: A Space Odyssey*, or like the gentle, willowy aliens in the movie *Close Encounters of the Third Kind*. Indeed, elsewhere in the novel, the cripple is described as "white as an angel, and smiling as if he knows" (p. 51). Thus the connection between the cripple in the wheelchair and the infant Yoel in the baby buggy is further reinforced. Add to this the dream recounted by Yoel's mother, "Inside a sort of carton they put you. Like a puppy" (p. 89), strengthening the link between the baby and the cripple and also bringing to mind the dog, Ironside, named for a paralyzed detective. The wheelchair, connecting the cripple in Helsinki and the emotionally paralyzed Yoel, is alluded to elsewhere in the novel:

Out of professional habit he noticed, from the corner of his eye, that
the Asian beauty who worked as the neighbors' maid was carrying her
shopping not in heavy baskets but in a wire cart. (p. 74)

We later see Yoel lying in wait for the Asian girl to come out of the
supermarket with her groceries. He even plans to oil the hinges of her cart.
Again, we have a cart with wheels, reminding us of the cripple in Helsinki
and of the infant Yoel.

That same Oriental girl brings to mind the attractive young woman
Yoel meets in Bangkok and almost falls for. The narrator comments that she
is the only one who never lied to him. "All the people he had ever con-
fronted had lied to him. Except in the Bangkok case" (p. 32). But even that
attractive and charming woman in Bangkok is an enigmatic figure whom
Yoel fails to decipher. On the one hand, he is convinced that she has not lied
to him, and the Patron confirms that she supplied extremely valuable
information:

If it turns out that she can offer, this time, even a quarter of what she
granted you last time, then it's worth my while to send you to her for a
romantic reunion even in a golden carriage drawn by a pair of white
horses. (p. 94)

On the other hand, this woman who gave Yoel so much and did not lie to
him now lays a deadly trap for him and conspires to kill him on their second
meeting. It was only Yoel's refusal to undertake the mission that saved him
from falling into that trap. The Acrobat is sent in his place and perishes.

The analogy between the cripple and Joel is further reinforced when it
is linked to the image of the crucifix. Surprisingly, Yoel often is associated
with Christian imagery. We noted that Yoel brings to the villa in Ramat
Lotan the photographs of "ruined Romanesque abbeys of the ninth or tenth
century" that used to hang in Ivria's study in Jerusalem, and later he focuses
obsessively on one abbey where he seems to detect a suspicious spot. He
strains his aching eyes, acquires a powerful magnifying glass, and considers
taking the photo to the Secret Service lab to be analyzed. He puts on "ridiculous round black-framed glasses that made him look like an elderly Latin
priest" (p. 26), and of all the available rooms in the house, he chooses the
smallest, the owner's den, which contains, among its sparse furnishings, "a
monastic couch" (p. 28). Yoel often ponders "the Byzantine crucifixion scenes
that contradict common sense" (p. 131) in the same way that the blind predator's position defies logic and the laws of gravity. Yoel's office at the Secret
Service is described as a "monastic cell" (p. 148). Arie Krantz urges Yoel to

"come out of his monastery" (p. 179), and Yoel, in his strange nocturnal
excursions, comes to the Trappist monastery in Latrun (p. 154). His mother,
Lisa, is described thus. "After the operation his mother's face beamed like
that of a village saint in a church mural" (p. 108). Not to mention the fact
that Yoel's biological father was, in fact, Christian.

The link between Yoel and the cripple in Helsinki is mediated through
the image of the crucifix. Here is what Yoel thinks in connection with the
cripple: "One who has lost his arms and legs could never be crucified" (p.
152), and elsewhere he ponders the affinity between the cripple and Christ
and also the figurine of the blind predator:

> Even if there is some simple way of liberating the predator in the
> figurine from the torments of its trapped paw without breaking it or
> hurting it, there is still no answer to the question how and where a
> creature will leap if it has no eyes. The source of the torment, after all,
> is not in the point of fusion between the base and the paw, but some-
> where else. Just as the nails in the Byzantine crucifixion scene were
> delicately crafted and there was not a drop of blood gushing from the
> wounds, so that it was clear to the observer that it was not a matter of
> liberating the body from its attachment to the cross but of liberating
> the youth with the feminine features from the prison of the body. (pp.
> 87–88)

All of the elements are present: the "youth with the feminine features"
is the cripple from Helsinki whose delicate features bring to mind Jesus' face
in paintings of the Crucifixion. The delicate features relate also to the image
of the infant Yoel, driven by his mother in a carriage, as well as to the blind
predator, paralyzed, grounded, and imprisoned, just like the grown Yoel, who
has become an emotional cripple.

Thus Yoel, the cripple from Helsinki, and the blind predator converge
into one point: the disability, the paralysis, and the blindness are aspects of
the same complex. In faraway Helsinki, in a back alley awash in the light of a
pale, silvery, eerie moon, the cripple with the delicate Christ-like features is
first revealed to Yoel, who glances at him briefly and then flees in horror, as a
man who has looked upon his own reflection in a sinister, surreal light. Yoel
is petrified and nauseated at the sight; he has seen a ghost, and the ghost
strikes terror in his heart and haunts him relentlessly. Wherever he goes from
there, however hard he tries to flee, the specter follows him. The wall of
alienation and cynicism that he has built around himself in a vain attempt to
put a buffer between him and reality only intensifies his disability, his emotional paralysis; he cannot extirpate from his mind the image of the cripple

with the gentle, feminine features in a distant, moonlit alley in Helsinki, and that image lurks in every recess, follows him everywhere, lays waste his life, and threatens to unhinge him.

Yoel, then, is blind and grounded like the predator, crippled and paralyzed like the invalid in Helsinki, nailed to a wheelchair like Jesus on the cross, or like a gentle-faced infant, driven by his mother in a buggy. At one point he is described as a fetus protected by the placenta in the mother's womb. His lovemaking with Annemarie is described thus: "Sometimes she seemed to be not so much making love to him as conceiving and bearing him" (p. 155).

He strives to break through the protective shell that imprisons and suffocates him and threatens to bury him alive, but to no avail. He bangs on the walls of the womb, searching in vain for a crack, for an escape route. But his blindness, his willful denial of emotion, is the source of the betrayal. His blindness leads to alienation and to a rejection of the vital, vigorous, and life-sustaining forces. The analogy between Yoel and Oedipus—who betrays his father by killing him and marrying his mother—is that they both try to solve the riddle of life while in a state of blindness. Oedipus kills his father, not knowing his identity, and proceeds to marry his own mother. His blindness and betrayal bring great affliction and devastation to his town.

When Yoel accidentally hears about the death in Bangkok of the Acrobat—who was sent in Yoel's place and thus saved his life—he stumbles and hurts his knee severely. As a consequence, he limps and hobbles and seethes furiously. This injury is another link to Oedipus, whose foot was swollen and misshapen from birth (as his name indicates). Hence, it is ironic that Oedipus declares at the opening of the play that he will stand Thebes on its two feet, while he himself limps.

Yoel hurts his leg when he realizes that he has betrayed the Secret Service, his colleagues, and his friends; he has allowed the Acrobat to go in his place on a mission that was a death trap; he refused to go to Bangkok without giving an explanation; he did not warn against the mortal danger lurking there and did not share his misgivings with the Patron. Yoel's betrayal, like Oedipus', led to calamity. Furthermore, when Yoel flees in horror from the house of the Acrobat's father—who called him "traitor" and "Cain" —he swerves his car frantically, crushing one of the taillights. The light is like an eye, and when it is broken, the car goes blind. This, again, is analogous to Oedipus, who gouges his own eyes when he realizes the magnitude of his betrayal. Similarly, Yoel and Oedipus are both killers. Oedipus kills his father, Laius (albeit unbeknownst to him). At one point, Ivria spits venomously at Yoel, "Murderer!" explaining to her stupefied daughter, "You ought to know, Netta, a murderer—that's his profession" (p. 53). This is the same accusation that Hava Lifshitz levels against her husband Yolek in *A Perfect Peace*. And Ilana, in *Black Box*, accuses her ex-husband, Alex Gideon, of murder. There are many echoes and reverberations. True, unlike Oedipus, Yoel does not physically murder anybody, but the classical tragic hero serves here as a literary prototype, as a significant analogy that, with the cripple from Helsinki and the figurine of the blind predator, hounds him and haunts him relentlessly, even in the tranquility of his rented villa in Ramat Lotan, a ten-minute drive from downtown Tel Aviv, and one minute more to the beach.

The Verbal Layer As a Boundary Line: Lovers and Haters of Verbalism

Yoel's blindness and his failure to recognize that denial of feeling leads to suffocation and death and frustrates any attempt to fathom the meaning of life find expression also on the verbal level, in Yoel's use of language. Yoel does not realize his linguistic potential; he arrests and stems the use of his tongue. Just as he barricades himself behind a wall of cold rationalism and cynicism, eschewing any display of sentiment, so does he behave in regard to language, as if giving in to verbalism might burn or scar him. Consequently, all of Yoel's pronouncements are terse, measured, laconic, as if he is shielding himself from a fist that might hit him any moment; his eyes are half closed, as if recoiling from sharp, piercing light.

Yoel's manner of expression and his attitude toward language are typical and symptomatic of a certain segment of the population of Oz's fiction, except that in Yoel's case, his reluctance to verbalize functions as a metaphor for his negation of feelings, for his denial of the forces of life.

One of the criteria for classifying and mapping the characters in Oz's fiction is their attitude toward language, phraseology, and verbal expression. There are basically two distinct categories: those who are proficient and fluent, who feel comfortable with language and revel in its verbal richness, and those who are reticent and apprehensive when it comes to using language, who see in it a crafty, treacherous enemy to be shunned and eluded. Hence, the latter try to abstain from talking, saying only the necessary minimum, sparingly, succinctly, with pursed lips and a sour facial expression. They regard speech as something redundant, repulsive, onerous.

Among those who reject language and shun it are: Rami Rimon, Guy Harish, and Oren Geva in *Elsewhere, Perhaps*; Yonatan Lifshitz in *A Perfect Peace*; Boaz Gideon in *Black Box*, and to a lesser extent, Theo in *Do Not Call it a Night*; Ben-Hur in *A Panther in the Basement*; the kibbutz youths in "Nomads and Viper"; and the Knight and the Pilgrim in *Unto Death*.

Those for whom language is a comfortable and congenial element include Reuven Harish in *Elsewhere, Perhaps*, and in a different manner, Zecharia-Siegfried Berger; Etkin, the narrator, and Geula in "Nomads and Viper"; Shimshon Sheinbaum in "The Way of the Wind"; Azaria Gitlin and Yolek Liefshitz in *A Perfect Peace*; Alex Gideon, Ilana Gideon-Somo, Michel Somo, and the lawyer, Zakheim, in *Black Box*; Shraga Unger in "Late Love"; and most emphatically, Proffy, the protagonist and narrator of *A Panther in the Basement*, for whom verbal expression is almost the essence of his life.

These characters are verbal, fluent, and loquacious; for them, language is an ally, a shelter, a sanctuary. They face reality armed with a tongue that can lash and chastise. Quite often, they believe in the power of their verbal virtuosity to change and to mold reality. Chief among these characters is Proffy, the protagonist of *A Panther in the Basement*, a "child of words," who tirelessly collects, discovers, hoards, and classifies words. It is said of him that for the sake of words, he would be willing to sell his own mother.

Other characters who display verbal facility and virtuosity are Mitya, the excitable, nationalistic lodger in *The Hill of the Evil Council*, the father in *A Panther in the Basement*, Yardena in *My Michael*, and her twin, Yardena, in *A Panther in the Basement*, Hannah Gonen in *My Michael*, and Steffa in *Touch the Water, Touch the Wind*. In a slightly different manner, Fima, the anti-hero of *Fima* (*The Third Condition*), is given to an outpouring of words that is exhausting and tiresome, and so is Muky Peleg in *Do Not Call It a Night*, who combines good-natured boorishness with typical Israeli camaraderie.

But Yoel, in *To Know a Woman*, Yoel the secret agent, the retired spy, is a different kettle of fish. He belongs in a Trappist monastery. He is part of that category of characters in Oz's fiction, mostly men, repelled and disgusted by verbal abundance. These men weigh and measure every word carefully, stingily, suspiciously. They spit words out grudgingly, through pursed lips, and they consider every verbal—as well as emotional—engagement a necessary evil. Yoel mulls over every utterance dozens of times before responding, plays out possible answers in his mind, and repeats phrases he has heard and expressions he happens to catch; eventually he concedes that "he could not find anything wrong with it." This is a phrase he repeats to himself softly many times throughout the novel. And his analytical yet tired mind latches on to banal and insignificant cliches such as "tomorrow is another day" or "the sea won't run away." His consciousness sifts through thousands of mundane, mostly insignificant details that make up his daily routine. He often thinks about Ivria's putative lover, who used to say that certain biblical words sound like Russian or Polish words, and he notes that the word "love" in Urdu, when read backwards, means "hate." He is so averse to words and uses them so frugally that when he refuses to go to Bangkok because his sensitive spy's antennae have picked up signs of danger, out of contempt for words he says nothing to his handlers, does not warn them, and does not share his insight with his colleagues. He turns down the mission with a couple of terse words, then he keeps mum.

Amos Oz once wrote a very fine phrase about the thin, delicate wind that sneaks between two silences. Yoel Ravid (Raviv?) is stubbornly silent; just as he dissociates himself from feelings and emotions, so he refuses to allow even one full sentence into the narrow space between his silences. There is a direct connection between verbal invalidity and emotional invalidity.

But Everything Is So Simple: The Secret Is So Open, the Mystery Is So Obvious

By not warning his colleagues of the danger lurking in Bangkok, Yoel commits an act of betrayal that results in death. His betrayal stems from his blindness, the same blindness that caused Oedipus' downfall, which also is connected to the invalid in Helsinki. Yoel is an emotional cripple doomed to failure in his quest to solve the riddle of the human condition.

But Yoel fails equally in his attempts to cope with life's mundane details, metaphorically summed up by the daily ambush he lays for the paper-man in a vain attempt to catch him. This symbolizes his professional failure as a secret agent and his personal failure as a human being. His eyes are blind, and his heart has turned to stone, because he has willfully excised all feelings from it. His denial of the forces of life dooms him to failure in his attempt to comprehend the meaning of life. Yoel does not know how to give of himself nor how to receive. He wonders about the nature of birds: what secret mechanism in their body enables them to migrate thousands of miles, to fly, unerring and unwavering, and to arrive precisely at their destination. So unsuccessful is Yoel in his attempt to solve the riddle of the birds that he misses the mysterious flight of the storks, "like masses of tiny white silk handkerchiefs streaming across a vast black silk screen, all bathed in a luminous silvery lunar glow." Ironically, this flight takes place on Passover night, which commemorates the release from bondage and affirms the freedom of the human spirit. But Yoel remains mired in his blindness and emotional sterility.

Most glaringly, Yoel fails to ascertain the identity of the cripple with the delicate, feminine features, even though his face looks vaguely familiar to him. Yoel finds himself as crippled and grounded spiritually as the limbless man in Helsinki is physically. Thus investigating the cripple's identity is tantamount to exploring his own identity, both the real one and the dead one, which is eerily reflected in the cripple's face in that chilly, alien alley in Helsinki. To look the cripple in the face, to dare to confront the mirror that reflects his own image back to him, is to fathom the depth of his own identity and discover the truth he has been running away from. Yoel refuses to look at his reflection for fear of discovering the chain of betrayals, large and small, for which he is responsible, starting with the Tunisian engineer and ending with his colleague, the Acrobat, who went to Bangkok in his place and got killed because Yoel would not share any information with his colleagues at the office. There is a bitter, almost painful irony in the fact that Yoel chooses the pseudonym Sasha Shein—one of the Acrobat's aliases— when he volunteers as an auxiliary at the hospital. Is this not the ultimate betrayal?

And yet the biggest betrayal that Yoel commits is turning his back on life and on the people around him. By divorcing himself from feelings and erecting a wall of rationalism and cynicism, he has distanced and alienated himself from the forces of life itself. Perhaps this is the explanation for the prevalence of birds and the theme of flight in the novel, as is evident in the following examples:

A half-frozen bird was found on the kitchen balcony. Netta took it to her bedroom and tried to warm it. . . . Towards evening, the bird recovered its strength and began to flutter around the room, emitting desperate chirps. Netta opened the window and the bird flew away. (p. 15)

All around, birds were singing in the treetops, hopping on the fences, flitting from one garden to the next as though they were flooded with joy. Even though Yoel knew that birds do not flit for joy but for other reasons. (p. 23)

Add to that the picture of a bird with an open beak seen through shadows and mist that hangs in Rimona's and Yoni's room in *A Perfect Peace*, where the evocation of the bird motif is highly significant. Compare that bird to the following description in *To Know a Woman:*

> On the lawn, amazingly close to him, Yoel suddenly noticed a little bird that had buried its beak between its wing and was standing there, frozen and silent. He moved the stream of water to the next bush and the bird-statue flew away. (p. 48)

And here are other components of the bird motif:

> [He] . . . instantly imagined that he could receive—not receive, sense—between two vertebrae at the base of his spine, the birds' African orientation sound. If only he had wings he would respond and go. (p. 70)

> . . . a small bird among the apple leaves rusting from the touch of autumn (p. 70); The storks flew away. Unless those were cranes. (p. 72)

> Was there a bird trapped in the room, fluttering and struggling to get out? (p. 81)

> Her chin had dropped at an angle on her chest, and she cried silently . . . looking like a bird with a broken neck. (p. 85)

> The sleeves of her kimono opened out like the wings of a bird in flight. (p. 87)

> [He] went out . . . to watch the migrating birds for a while. (p. 91)

> She knows . . . that you're fond of birds. (p. 94)

> . . . the chirping of the swallows before sunrise. (p. 101)

> While outside, between showers, drenched, frozen birds sometimes appeared at the window. (p. 104)

> This hypothesis could help him in his present investigations: for example, in connection with the African beam guiding the migrating birds. (p. 110)

> He found the cats on the kitchen porch playing with the stiff corpse of a small bird that had, apparently, died of the cold. (p. 121)

There's that cat . . . watching the bird on the tree with a hungry look. (p. 131)

Finally, when the sun had set and in an instant the cold set in and the bird that had survived the winter, or perhaps it was another one, suddenly started to chirp sweetly. (p. 133)

. . . flying fairly low with green and red lights flashing alternately from its wing tips. (p. 140)

No doubt to the astonishment of a couple of winter birds that were used to picking up crumbs from his breakfast when Yoel went out to shake the tablecloth out on the lawn. (p. 146)

Vast flights of storks, in broad stream, one after another, without a break, flying northward under a full spring moon, in a cloudless sky, thousands, perhaps tens of thousands, of lithe silhouettes hovering over the earth, their wings silently swishing. (pp. 168–69)

. . . following with a speculative gaze the flight of a bird whose name Yoel did not know but which thrilled him with its unique blue color. (p. 170)

There are many more such examples. *To Know a Woman* is replete with references and allusions to birds. This is not accidental. The bird imagery expresses the wish to soar, to fly away, to extricate oneself from the confines of present reality, to be rid of shackles that tie one down to the ground, and to fly to the horizon, to the stars, beyond imagination.[3] To leave and never come back, as Yoel ponders, "Why not just sneak away, without leaving any mark behind?" (p. 152). This yearning to break away, to forsake all connections, accompanies Yoel, the secret agent, who rejects and erases every sign of sentiment, because sentiment means connection. To feel means to relate to someone, to something, to a woman, a mistress, a daughter, a motherland, a principle, a memory, or an ideal. The allusions to birds underscore a basic trait of Yoel's personality. They are a metaphor for his desire to be free, to liberate himself from human sentiments he views as constricting and confining, hence, Yoel's need to barricade himself behind a thick shield of rationality and cynicism, which to him is the only chance for survival.

Both Yoel, in *To Know a Woman*, and Yoni, in *A Perfect Peace*, are associated with birds, but while Yoel represses any vestige of feeling or human sentiment, Yoni feels trapped in a cold and barren wasteland:

His loneliness. At three in the morning, on a wide and arid sheet, beneath a white arid ceiling, with everything gleaming like a skeleton in the eerie light of a dead moon in the window; he's wide awake, and yet trapped inside a white nightmare in the middle of a polar wasteland, at the heart of the snow covered tundra, you're alone, forever tied to a corpse. (*A Perfect Peace*, pp. 68–69)

The analogy between the two protagonists is only a partial one, since Yoel ensconces himself behind a buffer of cold rationality that admits no sentiment or display of emotion, whereas Yoni goes in the other directon: he struggles to break through the wall of isolation and sterility, to flee from the emotional wasteland in which he is mired. Yoel retires from the Secret Service and returns from the wide world only to immerse himself in humdrum daily trivia; Yoni, on the other hand, yearns to uproot himself from God's little acre, from the banality of daily routine, to cross the ocean and inhabit the enchanted shores that beckon him from beyond the horizon. But for all of their differences, they are both marooned in a barren, emotionally arid, and life-denying environment. And they are both men of few words, averse to verbal expression. Yoni is described as catching "her [Rimona's] child's breasts . . . in his heavy hands like two warm chicks" (*A Perfect Peace*, p. 68), while Yoel yearns "to enfold those fingers in his clumsy hands and try to warm them, like reviving a frozen chick" (*To Know a Woman*, p. 140), and earlier in the novel, "he imagined his own broad, ugly hands roughly clasping those breasts and putting an end to their convulsions, like catching warm chicks" (p. 86). For all of their differences, the two protagonists have something fundamental in common: they are wrapped in a thick, impenetrable, protective layer that cuts them off from reality and the flux of life.

Yoel remains detached, alienated, uninvolved. Even when he spends hours, patiently, obsessively cultivating a garden, it is the garden of a rented house that he can leave at will without ever looking back. He assiduously avoids committing, belonging, getting involved (except for his allegiance to his immediate family and to the Secret Service, both of which he eventually betrays). Yoel is a doleful pilgrim trudging the byways and side roads, hugging the margins, never striding the highways.

Yoel is not only stingy with words, he also is suspicious of any physical contact. Annemarie asks him, "Tell me, what's the matter with your daughter? . . . I always see you together, but I've never seen you touching one another" (p. 154). He observes life from a safe distance, contemplating each detail in his mind, like a scientist examining each particle under sterile laboratory conditions; he approaches reality equipped with a sharp scalpel, calculating, circumspect, impassive, always alert and ready to pounce like a furtive feline. His face wears a frozen expression, like a death mask. His daughter chides him, "Just look at your face. You look as though you're about to kill somebody" (p. 157).

The recurrent avian imagery also can be interpreted as freedom from commitment, connection, and emotional attachment. It also is appropriate that the components of the bird motif associated with Yoel often are frozen or clipped wings, like the bird found on the porch in Jerusalem, or the one that froze to death on the patio in Ramat Lotan, or the depiction of Annemarie as a bird with a broken neck. Those frozen, broken birds are metaphors for the frustrated desire to take off, and for Yoel's dissociation from all feelings. "If he hadn't lacked wings, he would have responded to their call" (p. 70), the narrator says. The image of Yoel as a wingless fowl is linked to the frozen birds and to the barren cage in which he imprisons himself.

Thus tending a garden that is not his, deracinated and alienated, Yoel evokes the image of the biblical Cain. Cain is what the Acrobat's father calls him, spitting out the name with hatred and venom. Cain was not just a tiller of the land, he was the first murderer, doomed to roam the earth as punishment for striking his brother, the nomadic shepherd. And Yoel is called a killer several times in the novel. He himself admits, "I murdered my wife" (p. 154); the Acrobat's father calls him "a licensed killer" (p. 175); Ivria calls him "a murderer" (p. 53); and Netta remarks that his face looks "as though you're about to kill somebody" (p. 157). The Patron, Yoel's superior in the Secret Service, who later accuses him of betrayal, is known as Yoel's brother. The biblical allusion here is pronounced and unmistakable. The analogy to Cain reinforces the theme of betrayal, of the denial of life, of the exile from the land of the living.

So all of Yoel's tireless efforts, his addiction to trivia, to the examination of minute details, his parsing and analyzing every aspect of mundane existence, his attempt to decipher the secret of life, all prove futile and vain. The garden is not his, and all of his exertion and dedication do not change the fact that he is rootless, displaced, unattached to the soil. His obsessive examination of the photo of a Byzantine monastery under a magnifying glass is equally fruitless. The spot he stubbornly frets over is just a meaningless blotch without secret or mystery.

By the same token, no examination or surgical analysis can excuse or expunge the resounding failure of Dado (David Elazar, chief of staff of the Israel Defense Force during the Yom Kippur war) who, like Yoel, should have been the guardian, the scout, the seer, but who failed ignominiously because his eyes were blind and he was unable to see the writing on the wall;

he failed to foresee the impending danger that almost caused the destruction of the State of Israel. As supreme commander, it was Dado's duty to observe and interpret reality, then take the necessary action. But he too was afflicted by blindness—typical Oedipal blindness, fueled by hubris and overconfidence—that resulted in calamity and the loss of thousands of lives.

Just as the picture of the Byzantine monastery yields no secret, there is no mystery in the history of the Yom Kippur war. In both cases, Yoel's investigation is redundant: the truth lies naked in front of him, but because of his blindness and emotional paralysis, he keeps peering and staring in vain. Likewise, no mystery surrounds the newspaper delivery that preoccupies Yoel continuously: the paper distributor happens to be an elderly Bulgarian pensioner who simply does not bother to put the paper in Yoel's mailbox. There is no secret involved, just a trivial, banal explanation. But due to his blindness and his obsessive need to cover up, camouflage, and encipher, Yoel invests everything around him with an aura of secrecy and mystery; consequently, inevitably, all of his efforts at solving these mysteries are doomed to failure.

But what is he hiding from, and what is he concealing? Is it "the shame in the attic" (the title of Ivria's master's thesis that is mentioned several times in the novel)? Perhaps Shealtiel Lublin, Ivria's father—an uncouth yet perceptive man—is right in claiming that, in the final analysis, everybody has the same secrets. We all have the same shame hidden in our attics. Some details may vary but, in principle, it is the same attic and the same shame.

Consequently, the secret that Yoel tries so hard to conceal is the most exposed and well-known secret in the world, because it is everybody's secret. And yet he does not give up: he continues to cover up, to conceal, to suppress. The people around him open up to life, refuse to stay isolated in their cage. Lisa and Avigail, Yoel's mother and mother-in-law, respectively, attend classes, lectures, and cultural events, and do volunteer work for charitable organizations. Arik Krantz works the night shift as an auxiliary in a nearby hospital (and it turns out that his motives are truly humanitarian, not just a cover-up for his philandering). Even Netta begins to emerge from her airtight shell. She decides to join the army, despite the epilepsy that has plagued her since childhood. She finally steps out of her domineering father's influence and goes to live in a rented apartment with Duby Krantz. Only Yoel persists in turning his back on life, huddled in his isolated existence, barricaded behind his obsessive preoccupation with trivia. Blind as the feline predator, crippled emotionally like the invalid in Helsinki, like Oedipus incapable of solving his life's riddle, he sinks deeper and deeper in his paralysis.

Yet All May Not Be Lost

At last, Yoel begins to open up; he lets a tenuous, hesitant ray of light penetrate his crusty armor. This happens at the very last minute, almost before the curtain falls. We will discuss shortly what brought about this salutary change. There is a certain cyclical progression in the development of the plot. The novel opens with a house and ends with a house. At the beginning, Arik Krantz arranges for Yoel to rent the house in Ramat Lotan. Toward the end, Krantz, acting in Yoel's behalf, is about to sell the two apartments in Jerusalem and buy that same house in Ramat Lotan. This cyclical movement may indicate a certain irenic trend, a more peaceful, conciliatory mood, a small step toward attaining "a perfect peace."

Perhaps it is Krantz's boisterous conviviality and joie de vivre that tears Yoel away from his sullen monastic existence and convinces him to become a volunteer at the local hospital. Here one should note a certain theme in Oz's fiction that has to do with the difference between Jerusalem and Tel Aviv. In *My Michael*, the two cities transcend their limited geographical significance and assume a metaphoric status. They represent antithetical orders of human existence. Jerusalem is somber, introverted, wintry, Chekovian in mood, ascetic, and windswept. Tel Aviv, on the other hand, is characterized by openness, levity, insouciance, spunk, and a certain in-your-face impudence. Hugging the seashore, it is a sunny, easygoing, mischievous, uncomplicated city. Hence, Yoel's departure from Jerusalem and his installation in Tel Aviv—a move epitomized by the sale of the Jerusalem apartments and the rental of the house in the Tel Aviv suburb of Ramat Lotan—mark his first step toward divesting himself of the constricting armor of the dour secret agent and opening himself up to a more positive, life-enhancing existence. True, it is only a tiny crack, a very modest beginning; volunteering at the hospital twice a week, and doing so under an assumed name—that of Sasha Shein, one of the Acrobat's aliases—is really tantamount to donning a mask on top of a mask. But this is Yoel's first attempt at giving something of himself, of breaking away from the cage, from prison, from the cross. At the hospital he does errands, makes beds, launders, cleans lavatories, and tends to patients. Undeterred by stench and filth, blood, sweat, urine, vomit, and excrement, he shows himself helpful, compassionate, understanding, and charitable.

Perhaps a new Yoel is emerging, certainly a transformed one. The curtain falls on Yoel's story when this incipient change in his personality and attitude has not yet had a chance to gather momentum. This is precisely what the implied author has in mind: to indicate a slight change in the way Yoel relates to his immediate environment. He ends the novel with a question mark, not with an exclamation mark; there is perhaps a new beginning, a new hope, a new promise. But we must not be too optimistic or raise our expectations too high. And yet, Yoel, who has been reluctant to touch his own daughter, now touches the sick and the old, giving them succor and solace. True, they strangers, and it is well known that sometimes it is easier to open up to strangers than to those close to us—the threat of excessive exposure can make us vulnerable. Still, for Yoel, getting close to complete strangers is a welcome step toward human contact after years of aloofness and shying away from intimacy. Perhaps this will lead to closer contact with his daughter, to whom, until now, he related, both physically and emotionally, only through her illness, through her disability: he would hesitantly touch her only when she had an epileptic seizure. In other words, only Netta's physical disability—and to some extent, her emotional disability—enabled Yoel to overcome his own emotional limitation and briefly get closer to his daughter. Now their relationship may be put on a healthier footing, no longer needing the mediation of physical and emotional disability. Perhaps Yoel will muster up the courage to face his own emotional paralysis and delve deep into his atrophied soul to examine his true identity.

His new, compassionate, charitable disposition also is coupled with amazing humility and self-effacement, as is evident by his reaction to the harsh and offensive words that a young doctor directs toward him. The obvious link between his dedication to the patients and the almost preternatural meekness and self-abnegation he exhibits naturally brings to mind Jesus, whose chief attributes were humility and meekness and who cured the afflicted. Christ was, of course, invoked earlier in connection to Yoel. The blind predator, which is strongly analogous to Yoel, is obliquely related to the crucifix through the idea of suffering and being nailed down:

There is still no answer to the question how and where an eyeless creature will leap. The source of the torment, after all, is not in the point of fusion between the base and the paw, but somewhere else. Just as the nails in the Byzantine crucifixion scene were delicately crafted and there was not a drop of blood gushing from the wounds, so that it was clear to the observer that it was not a matter of liberating the body from its attachment to the cross but of liberating the youth with the feminine features from the prison of the body. (pp. 87–88)

Here is a highly charged symbolic trinity: the figurine of the blind predator; Yoel, the secret agent; and the cripple from Helsinki, all conjoined and welded together, nailed to one cross; all three are paralyzed, grounded—

either physically or emotionally—weighted down by suffering and anguish. Yoel in his blindness is reminiscent of Oedipus who, at the end of Sophocles' *Oedipus in Colonus*, becomes a saint, and is thus analogous to Jesus.[4] (cf. Northrop Frye, *Anatomy of Criticism*, 4).

Yoel's Christ-like attributes at the denouement of the novel come after numerous prior allusions to Christian imagery, as noted above. This is clearly an intentional device of the implied author, who is responsible for all of the thematic, aesthetic, and conceptual elements of the literary text. It is only toward the end that Yoel is ready to remove the mask of impassivity, to return from the cold and let the reservoir of his frozen emotions thaw; only then can his salvation begin. Not salvation in the religious sense, but in a profound spiritual, emotional, and existential sense.[5]

The crack in Yoel's armor and the hesitant steps he takes toward spiritual recovery are conveyed through the theme of vision. There are frequent references to Yoel's stinging, burning eyes, to his constant squinting, to his thick glasses—all pointing to his metaphoric blindness, to his inability to fathom the truth and solve the riddle of human existence. However, toward the end of the novel, when he volunteers at the hospital and begins to shed his protective shell, at that promising and conciliatory point where the novel ends, Joel's eyes seem to open up, and he can stare ahead, free of strain and pain:

> And so Yoel Ravid began to give in. Since he was capable of observing, he preferred to observe in silence. With tired but open eyes. Into the depth of darkness. (p. 199)

This marks the turning point, the salutary change that henceforth will allow him to connect to reality, to give of himself, to share, to bestow. As in previous novels by Amos Oz—at least since the early 1980s—the denouement spells a reconciliation, perhaps a hesitant, wary, gingerly reconciliation, but an unmistaken one; a rapprochement between the two opposing poles of sober, disciplined rationality, on the one hand, and turbulent, aggressive, savage emotion, on the other hand, between the yearning for balance, moderation, and temperance and the longing for unrestrained, orgiastic excitement.

This theme was first apparent in *Elsewhere, Perhaps*, published in 1976, which ends with the rebellious and fiery Noga Harish soberly and humbly marrying Rami Rimon, who is perhaps staid, lackluster, and uninspired yet has the solid, rational, and pragmatic disposition characteristic of kibbutz life. Similarly, *A Perfect Peace* ends with Yonatan Lifshitz giving up his dream of faraway places and returning from the desert to the placidity and serenity

of the kibbutz. His wife Rimona also abandons her escapist visions of enchanted, darkest Africa, and the two of them settle on a highly unconventional compromise: a ménage à trois that includes the foreign-born Azaria
Gitlin. The two men attain harmonious living with Rimona, whose personality combines domestic ease and tranquility with the redolence of distant,
exotic regions. *Black Box*, too, ends on a partial, hesitant note of appeasement
with one woman—Ilana—becoming a convergence point for two extremely
different men. Ilana remains married to Michel Somo while still embracing
her rejected and rejecting ex-husband Alex, once disease and distance have
blunted his venom and steered him in a new direction, toward reconciliation,
perhaps even toward humility.

Even in *My Michael*, an earlier novel, this trend can be discerned:
Hannah Gonen, exhausted by anguish and frustration, finds solace and peace
of mind in writing down her memoirs. In this she follows the prescription of
Tirtza in Agnon's "In the Prime of Her Life," who poured her anguish and
frustration into her memoirs. The link between the two works is no accident,
and the influence is easy to detect (as demonstrated by, among others, Ar-
nold Band).

A cautious reconciliation also is noted at the end of *A Panther in the
Basement*, where Proffy's obsessive search becomes less demanding and hectic
and more restrained and moderate: he learns to be more attentive, patient,
and considerate.

In *To Know a Woman*, Yoel's aching, squinting eyes are opened for the
first time. The turning point seems to occur when Yoel again meets with
Duby Krantz. Something the boy says makes him stop and think, lifting a
little bit the curtain of frosty rationality and cynicism that stands between
him and the world. A new channel of communication opens up, not just
with his environment but with himself. The change triggered by Duby's
words may have been long evolving in Yoel's psyche. It may have been brew-
ing in his subconscious, slowly bringing him back from the comatose state he
was in, like a body recovering from a concussion. Yet something in Duby's
words acts as a catalyst helping to bring about the transformation in Yoel.
What was it that Yoel heard from Duby? He heard a request to stop trying
to be the perfect father to Netta, to stop following her around like a secret
agent, to give her some space, some breathing and living territory. He also
heard from Duby that there was no mystery in the blind predator figurine; it
was just a question of its center of gravity. No defiance of the laws of me-
chanics was behind its precarious position, just a simple, logical explanation.

There is a connection between the two things, Duby says; Yoel is blind
not only about the meaning of his life and life in general, he also is blind

about his relations with his daughter Netta. If only he relaxed his control over her, if only he gave her some space, she might lighten up and lose some of her sarcastic, sardonic attitude. She may emerge from the shadow of the epilepsy that has haunted her since childhood. In fact, this is what happens at the end of the novel; as soon as Yoel realizes the truth about the figurine that has bedeviled and haunted him all along, he also realizes that unless he tears down the wall of impassivity and cynicism that he has erected around himself, he stands no chance at cracking any secret, any code. Once this dawns on him, Yoel begins to relent: he no longer squints his eyes in an attempt to discern elusive details—a miniscule spot in a photograph of a monastery, a possible misjudgment on the part of the commission of inquiry set up in the wake of the Yom Kippur war, the comings and goings of the newspaper distributor—but dares to open them widely, stretching a hesitant, gingerly hand toward the deposits of suppressed emotions inside of him. It is no accident that precisely at this juncture he retrieves Virginia Woolf's *Mrs. Dalloway* and the knitted shawl that he thought he had left at the hotel in Helsinki (which brings to mind the cripple in the wheelchair, Yoel himself as a baby in a buggy, the cart of the Asian maid in the supermarket, and the woman in Bangkok who set the trap for the Acrobat who died in Yoel's place). Thus *Mrs. Dalloway* and the shawl are pieces in the same complex, carefully constructed puzzle. When the putative enigmas are exposed to the light and seen to harbor no secret or hidden ruse, they prove to be simple, concrete, and accessible. The mysterious, conniving newspaper distributor is in fact an elderly Bulgarian too lazy to get out of his old jalopy. The mystifying blur in the photograph is perhaps the shadow of some object or a trick of the camera. Equally simple and devoid of any mystery is the case of Chief of Staff Dado in the Yom Kippur war. A commission of inquiry found him responsible for the disaster and recommended relieving him of his duty. (Prime Minister Golda Meir and Defense Minister Moshe Dayan also were implicated, but the commission preferred to overlook their responsibility). No further inquiry is called for; the facts are clear and irrefutable, as was the death toll of 3,000. Dado was the supreme commander whose duty it was to watch, to warn, to prepare, but he was blinded by hubris and overconfidence and failed to see the impending danger. No mystery surrounds the disappearance of the knitted shawl; it was just a case of simple forgetfulness (perhaps Freudian). The shawl was given to him by his wife, whom he used to forget from time to time, or at least leave behind. Virginia Woolf's *Mrs. Dalloway* is written in the "stream of consciousness" technique that seeks to fathom the depth of the human psyche, something that Yoel also attempts and shies away from at the same time.

Even the mysterious cripple from Helsinki turns out to be a simple, easily solved riddle: he is none other than Yoel's double, the true reflection he has been shunning all of his life. The figurine of the blind predator is another reflection of Yoel: blind and petrified, frozen and imprisoned, frustrated in its attempt to leap and capture its prey. But when Yoel learns to lighten up and open his eyes, he begins to overcome his emotional inhibitions. He distances himself from the blind predator analogy and has a chance at solving the riddles that have haunted and eluded him. He can reach out and touch reality. Significantly, at this point, he also finds the lost book and shawl.

Thus *To Know a Woman* concludes with a tentative, hesitant attempt to reach out, a first step toward reconciliation and resolution of conflicts; a certain equilibrium is reached, a possible coexistence, a mutual acceptance by warring antagonists, if not a veritable truce or a perfect peace.

CHAPTER 5

At Last, the Secret Double Agent
Takes Off His Gloves and Removes the Mask:
A Discussion of *A Panther in the Basement*

Over the pathos of the emptied heart,
And above the ruin of foolish rationality
Our fog hangs like patchwork,
Bitter, damp and lethal.
— Meir Wieseltier,
Over the Mountains and Over the Waves

"A Window Shalt Thou Make to the Ark":
A Short Introductory Chapter Serving As a Peephole

The very short first chapter of the novel—barely a page and a half—like a quick blink of the eye or a brief snapshot, reveals the most fundamental elements of the story: its thematic import, the intricate relationships between the main characters (the father, the mother, and Proffy, their son, the narrator), the differences in their personalities, and the interaction that results from these differences.

What happens in that short first chapter? Who and what is introduced? The chapter opens with a betrayal. "I have been called a traitor many times in my life." The speaker/narrator is the protagonist, Proffy, short for Professor, "which they called me because of my obsession with checking words (I still love words: I like collecting, arranging, shuffling, reversing, combining them (p. 7). A few sentences later, the treachery allegation is further explained. "One morning, an inscription appeared on the wall of our house, painted in thick black letters, just under the kitchen window. 'Proffy is a despicable traitor'"(ibid.). The father is the first to spot the writing on the wall: "My father went out to get the newspaper at half past six that morning and saw the writing under the kitchen window" (ibid.) and his sarcastic, accusatory reaction is not long in coming. "What a pleasant surprise! And what has his highness been up to now, that we should deserve this honor?" (p. 8).

The mother, however, rises to her son's defense, berating the father for his hasty and unjust judgment, whereupon the father launches a lengthy, pedantic, academic disquisition on the word "traitor," ending with an admonition to his son to finish his egg. It is hard to miss the narrator's harsh criticism of the overbearing, condescending, slightly pathetic father, whose preachy, high-minded exhortation jars with the prosaic setting of the breakfast table laden with sliced bread, salad, eggs, and jam. The mother's reaction, however, in sharp contrast to the father's, smacks of romanticism. "Anyone who loves isn't a traitor" (p. 8). It is an emotional, sentimental expression that requires no proof or substantiation. The mother addresses these words neither to the son nor the father; "she was talking to a nail that was stuck in our kitchen wall just above the icebox, that served no particular purpose" (ibid.). The rational, academic, self-righteous imperiousness of the father is thus contrasted to the romantic sentimentality of the mother. We shall later see that the son's character combines these two contrasting qualities.

This terse opening chapter encapsulates in a nutshell the themes, ideas, and relationships that are later identified and developed in the novel. It also reflects a fundamental trait—like a conceptual DNA—of Amos Oz's fiction in general, that is, the battle between two contrasting, antagonistic poles: cool, lucid rationality versus dark, savage emotionality. The opening chapter points also to another characteristic of Oz's poetic territory, which is the mutual migration of attributes from one camp to the other. Thus the few sentences referring to Proffy, the narrator, contain the contradictory qualities that he has inherited from his rationalist father and his romantically inclined mother.

The conciseness and intensity displayed in the opening chapter gain added importance in light of the fact that this novel serves as a reservoir for all of the raw material used in Oz's work, like a quarry providing the building stones of the themes and ideas found across his fiction.

Let us start with the character of the father as it is reflected in the opening chapter. The father is very verbal; his speech is precise and meticulous, just like his short khaki pants that are always smooth, scrupulously ironed, neat and orderly. In his self-conscious, self-righteous attitude, the father seems to project a subtle message, saying, if only everyone were like me, there would be no more trouble, misery, and injustice in the world. The father parses and analyzes the meaning of every word (including the word "traitor" that was smeared on the wall under their kitchen window) and is so intent on fathoming all of the possible semantic niceties of the word that he neglects to voice anger at the damage done to the wall and totally ignores his son's pain and hurt feelings. He bawls out the boy without first ascertaining his guilt. His excessive linguistic preoccupation is coupled with a tendency to preach and pontificate, to point out deficiencies and imperfections. "Finish your egg, please. It says in the paper that people are dying of hunger in Asia," he remonstrates. Reflecting on the events from a grown-up's point of view, Proffy comments, "He had the gestures and the voice of a man who was absolutely right" (p. 8). (The rhetorical device of the adult narrator "invading" the consciousness of the formal narrator will be discussed later.)

The father is a decent, upright man (though not always fair, especially when it comes to his son), with a profound, ingrained sense of justice. However, sometimes he is so filled with a sense of justice and righteousness that he is not aware of the wrong he does his son. In the opening scene, he takes for granted the validity of the graffiti referring to his son's "treason," totally ignoring its effect on the boy. The father is so imbued with his mission of justice and correctness that, in his zeal to find them and publish them, he misses them altogether.

Thus the father's portrait, sketched in a few sentences, is one of a strict, meticulous, pedantic person, infatuated with words and carried away by their inner meaning; he is methodical, orderly, disciplined, forever seeking justice and justification to the point of being blind to the pain he inflicts on his nearest and dearest.

The manner in which the father "suddenly plunged the knife into the jam jar up to the handle . . . dredging up a thick mass of raspberry from the bottom of the jar and spreading an equal amount on both halves of his slice of bread9 (p. 8) serves as a metaphor for his personality traits: uncompromising, resolute, and unflinching in the execution of his just and righteous intent; he knows no hesitation or self-doubt and often exhibits repressed and controlled aggression. The precise and measured way in which he spreads the jam on the bread epitomizes his character.

And the mother? She is totally different, as can be easily inferred from her slim contribution to the opening scene. The mother is the exact opposite of the pedantic, meticulous father. Compared to his intensity and assertive activism (a trait he shares with his son), she is marked by pensiveness and introversion; the mother listens, deliberates, and mulls things over before she reacts. But her reaction, though soft and unassuming, is heeded and resonates with the others. It is like a small coin dropping to the floor in an empty room. Its clear sound is heard in the farthest corner. Thus it is with the mother vis-/ga-vis her husband and son: their intensive and accelerated verbalism does not drown or obscure the clarity of her silence. Her position in the margins, away from the center of activity, is not a measure of weakness but rather a conscious and deliberate decision. She has elected to withdraw into her enclosed world, to distance herself from the others. She reacts and interacts only when she sees fit to do so. Even when the mother ceases to be a passive listener and decides to react, her rhetoric is moderate and oblique; she seems not to address herself directly to her interlocutors but rather to formulate a thought to herself, as if speaking to herself in a private, internal voice, a voice that does not seem to come from her throat but from some distant repository of feelings deep inside of her, or as if responding to another voice, far away, beyond the horizon, sounds that only she can hear with closed eyes and great concentration. Then she utters a few words that often cause eyebrows to be raised and hastens to withdraw back into her inner world to barricade herself behind silence.

Unlike the father (and the son), who is always charged with energy, tense like a coiled spring and armed with a verbal response, the mother is withdrawn and introverted, shying away from the barrage of words and the hectic activity of the others. The mother has the ability to shut herself off and come out from her mental seclusion at will. As we shall see later, her strongest childhood memory involves a blue shutter, an object signifying separation, seclusion, a buffer. As mentioned earlier, the mother's position is not one of weakness. In the opening scene, when the father taunts and rebukes his son, assuming (wrongly) that the epithet "traitor" is well deserved, the mother does not hesitate to reprove him. "Don't nag him first thing in the morning. It's bad enough that the other kids nag him" (p. 8). The father does not respond directly to the rebuke but later launches a disquisition on the various semantic registers of the word "traitor." The mother has one more verbal comment in this short chapter. "Anyone who loves isn't a traitor." Compared to her husband's somewhat pompous lecture, her reaction is not only concise and succinct but emotional, not based on empirical data. Her statement can perhaps be refuted, but it possesses an almost magical power and touches the soul.

Thus within the confines of the brief introductory chapter, before the plot has even begun to unfold, we have gathered detailed information about the main characters, their fundamental differences, and the intricate relationship that evolves from them. To a great extent, those contrasting characters determine the thematic and aesthetic trajectory of the novel, which brings to mind Chekhov's famous dictum about a gun on the wall in the first act that is bound to go off in the final act. The first chapter is like a musical score for the novel as a whole, which in itself is like the score of Oz's entire oeuvre, resembling a Russian *matrushka* doll.

The binary division between antagonistic forces, clear, orderly, disciplined rationality versus dark, sinister, unbridled passion, which typified Oz's fiction in the past, also is evident here, not schematically or bluntly but rather subtly and suggestively. The mother symbolizes the passionate and sentimental aspect of human nature, its darker, more otherworldly aspect, the desire to transcend humdrum reality, the toil, sweat, and commotion of present reality, and to be transported to green pastures, sylvan brooks, and crepuscular winter scenes.

The mother in *A Panther in the Basement* (like her counterparts in many other novels and stories by Oz) is of a hibernal, dreamy, European temperament. Due to historical circumstances, naive Zionism, or biblical romanticism, these women find themselves in the land of Israel, which turns out to be not just the promised land and the fulfillment of ancestral yearnings but also an arid, thorny, aggressive country where the sun blazes mercilessly, and shrill gutteral sounds pelt one like stones. In this respect, the mother represents the emotional pole, the domain of dreams and secret longings.

These aspects of the mother's personality unfold throughout the novel, but they are incipiently, embryonically present in her brief appearance in the opening chapter. And the same applies to the father, who represents the opposite pole of realistic, practical, sober, "sane" rationality, who is anchored firmly in reality and does not seek to transcend it. The father is an ardent Zionist who centers all of his hopes and aspirations on rebuilding the ancient homeland and harbors no nostalgic yearnings for the European landscapes and the genteel culture he has left behind.

The mother, on the other hand, feels trapped and lost in the harsh reality of her adopted country. Her only escape is to indulge in dreamy, romantic visions of the past that she left behind, an indulgence that the father regards as an aberration and a betrayal, because to him there is no other reality than the immediate one. Looking back on the events, both compassionately and ironically, this is how the adult Proffy views his parents. "He was a principled, intense man, deeply committed to the concept of justice. My mother, on the other hand, liked to raise her half-empty glass of tea and stare through it at the blue light in the window" (p. 10). Purposeful practicality and unswerving determination versus the romantic inclination to leave the here and now and follow the beckoning blue light, a dichotomy that informs not only the two characters, so succinctly depicted in the opening chapter, but the basic thematic scheme of Oz's entire fiction.

And here the betrayal motif comes to the fore. It is the mother lode for all of the other themes in the novel. Every element of plot or character is either directly or indirectly related to treachery. In the first sentence of the opening chapter, the narrator declares, "I have been called a traitor many times in my life," and he proceeds to explain in detail:

> The first time was when I was twelve and a quarter and I lived in a neighborhood at the edge of Jerusalem. It was during summer vacation, less than a year before the British left the country and the State of Israel was born out of the war. One morning an inscription appeared on the wall of our house, painted in thick black letters under the kitchen window. "Proffy is a despicable traitor." The word "despicable" [Shafel] raised a question that still interests me now, as I sit and write this story. Is it possible for a traitor not to be despicable? If not, why did Cheetah Reznik (I recognized his handwriting) bother to add the word "despicable"? And if it is, under what circumstances is treachery not despicable? (pp. 7–8)

Following the mother's admonition, the father relinquishes his unfounded attack on the son, only to pick up the betrayal theme from a different angle; he launches an academic, semantic discussion of the term:

> Nowadays people use the epithet "traitor" too freely. But what is a traitor? Yes, indeed. A man without honor. A man who secretly, behind your back, for the sake of some questionable pleasure, aids and abets the enemy against his own people. Or harms his family and friends. He is more despicable than a murderer. (p. 8)

Betrayal, treachery, and treason inform every aspect and facet of the first chapter, just as they do the book as a whole. They dictate, guide, and condition every turn of the plot, every theme and idea.

In the opening chapter, betrayal is contrasted to the basic values of justice, loyalty, decency, good order, and sober rationality that the father espouses and exemplifies (albeit imperiously and self-righteously). Betrayal, being at the antipode of what the father stands for, thus allies itself with the savage, rebellious, and untamed element, the "panting, hairy element" that aims to subvert order, morals, and normative behavior.

It is important, at this point, to reiterate the fact that betrayal is a cardinal theme in all of Amos Oz's fiction: Hannah, in *My Michael*, betrays her husband in her erotic fantasies and with her flirtation with her private student; Eva Harish, in *Elsewhere, Perhaps*, betrays her husband, her children, and her country when she follows her morally corrupt cousin to Germany; Bronka Berger (ibid.) cheats on her husband Ezra with Reuven Harish, while Ezra retaliates by having an affair with Reuven's daughter, Noga; Ilana Gideon-Somo cheats on her husband Alex with a whole host of men, if she is to be believed; Elisha Pomerantz, in *Touch the Water, Touch the Wind*, is suspected of treason and investigated on charges of treason. His wife Steffa marries a Russian spy while still legally married to Pomerantz; the Crusader nobleman, in *Unto Death*, on his tortuous way to the Holy Land (which includes inflicting horrendous atrocities on local communities, especially Jews), suspects an insidious, "poisonous" infiltration of a Jewish traitor into the camp; the mother of Uri Kolodny is rumored to have an affair with Ephraim, the electrician and underground activist in the novella "Mr. Levi"; Ruth Kipniss, in *The Hill of the Evil Council*, betrays her naive husband and her adoring son in a most base, ignominious manner when she runs away with a boozing, boorish British officer. She also is attracted to the lodger, Mitya, who is emaciated and reeks of rotten teeth. Other women in Oz's fiction are attracted to the less savory physical side of sexuality: Rimona, in *A Perfect Peace*, rejects her husband Yoni, the kibbutz-born Sabra, for pathetic-looking, Diaspora-born Azaria Gitlin, who (like Michel Somo in *Black Box*) nevertheless is capable of commanding respect and appreciation. At least one of Fima's lady friends in *Fima* (*The Third Condition*) cheats on her husband with sad-sack Fima, the haggard and bedraggled philosopher who inhabits the margins of society. Fima is strongly reminiscent of the protagonist in A. B. Yehoshua's *Facing the Forests*, with whom he seems to conduct an open dialogue. We noted that in *To Know a Woman*, the theme of betrayal recurs with increased intensity throughout the novel: the betrayal there is not confined only to personal relations (although Ivria presumably has an affair with her elderly neighbor, and Yoel, on several lonely occasions, gathered strange women into his bed). Yoel also "cheats" on Ivria in his fantasy, with an Eskimo woman who is "submissive like a dog." Yoel also betrays his mission, the Secret Service, his friends, and his colleagues. But the biggest betrayal of all in that novel is Yoel's (as well as Ivria's and Netta's) betrayal of life itself, as he turns his back on feelings, emotions, and sentiments.

However prevalent the theme of betrayal is in Oz's fiction in general, in *A Panther in the Basement* it is the mainstay of the plot, the code word and the key to deciphering its meaning. The novel begins and ends with betrayal. It opens with, "I have been called a traitor many times in my life" and ends with "Have I again betrayed them all by telling their story? Or is it the other way around; would I have betrayed them if I had not told it?" And, in between, betrayals abound, weaving themselves into all levels and ramifications of the plot.

Proffy betrays his friends in the underground, or does he? Proffy betrays Yardena (by spying on her and catching sight of her naked), or does he? Proffy betrays his British friend Sergeant Dunlop, or does he? Proffy betrays his father—by almost succumbing to temptation and peeking inside of the mysterious package his father hides in his library, or does he? Proffy's friends accuse him of treason and conduct a trial in which he is found at least half guilty, perhaps more. Proffy experiences his betrayal as a huge, foul wave engulfing him. "So why did I feel once again that taste of treachery in my mouth, as though I had been chewing soap?" (p. 49). And he knows in his heart, "The fact is I knew in advance that the trial would make no difference. No explanations and no excuses would help me. As in all underground movements everywhere and at all times, anyone who is branded a traitor is a traitor and that's that. There's no use trying to defend yourself" (p. 28).

Proffy examines himself in the mirror and asks, "Is this the look of a traitor? or of a panther in the basement?" (p. 128). Again we see the same ambiguity and duality in Proffy's personality. He tries to determine his identity. "Henceforth, I am a spy. A mole. A secret agent disguised as a child seeking to master the English language. From this moment on, I would act as a chess player" (p. 47). The double agent, as we saw earlier, is also a recurrent theme in Oz's fiction. We mentioned Oz's definition of himself as a double agent, stationed simultaneously in two superpowers: Kibbutz Hulda and Jerusalem, the sane and orderly kibbutz nestled in the coastal plane versus the mystical, messianic city perched on the mountains on the edge of the desert.

On the one hand, Proffy is confident that he is not a traitor. On the contrary, he tries so hard to be just, decent, and loyal. But, on the other hand, he cannot help feeling that perhaps, after all, he is tainted with treachery. When Proffy desperately pleads with Ben Hur, "What have I done to you?" (the same words and the same tone Yoel uses with the Patron when the latter accuses him of betrayal in *To Know a Woman*), Ben Hur replies, "It's because you love the enemy, Proffy. Loving the enemy, Proffy is the height of treachery" (p. 76). Hearing this, Proffy is engulfed by a wave of nausea and revulsion, as around him "Pine trees whispered and cypresses rustled: Shut up, despicable traitor" (ibid.). The bitter taste of treachery sticks in his craw, because Proffy knows, and the trees around confirm it in their whisper, that there is truth in Ben Hur's accusation; deep down in his heart, the sensitive, amateur philologist, Proffy, is very fond of Sergeant Dunlop. Yes, he loves the eccentric, bedraggled, and disheveled Englishman, that kind-hearted policeman who loves the Jewish people and speaks quaint Hebrew redolent of the Bible. Yes, Proffy, the Hebrew boy, member of the underground, loves the naive and quirky Englishman. Despite his ungainly corpulence, protruding pot belly, limp and damp handshake, and generally unappealing appearance, Sergeant Dunlop evokes in Proffy only feelings of compassion, sympathy, and companionship, and the two form an alliance of the weak and sensitive, of the underdogs who feel oppressed and crushed by society's demands and by its contempt for those who are sensitive and vulnerable.

This, then, is the paradox that causes Proffy's misfortune; he is trapped in an inescapable duality. On the one hand, he is convinced of his justness, decency, nobility of character, and pure intentions, but, on the other hand, he feels weak, humiliated, even despicable. He has to contend with prevailing social standards that extol machismo and aggressive self-assertion but interpret any display of sensitivity as feebleness and turpitude.

But Proffy does not feel only weak and humiliated, he feels he is a traitor. His treachery lies in having succumbed to those reprehensible social standards that glorify power, aggression, and rabid masculinity. Proffy feels that he himself has adopted and internalized those standards.

Proffy is doubly traitorous: he betrays the standards of his society, since he cannot measure up to them; he knows he is doomed to failure, because his personality and mentality are incommensurate with those standards of machismo and aggression. He cannot adhere and be faithful to those values.

And here Proffy proves himself not just a double agent but a double traitor, because his second betrayal is a more harrowing and searing betrayal: it is a betrayal of himself, of the real Proffy who does not accept those standards that view sensitivity as a mark of weakness and depravity. And yet he tries to espouse these standards, or at least to placate and propitiate those who maintain them, to gain their approval. Thus, he thinks, "If Ben Hur had ordered me, say, to remove all the water in the Dead Sea to the Upper Galilee, bucket by bucket, I would have obeyed, so that when I had finished I might have a chance of hearing him say, out of the corner of his mouth, in that lazy voice of his, the words, 'You're really okay, Proffy'" (p. 29).

The opening chapter, then, encapsulates and adumbrates all of the themes, motifs, and plot elements later developed in the novel, as well as reworks the central theme (betrayal) of Oz's fiction as a whole.

The very title of the novel, *A Panther in the Basement,* contains betrayal, and a double one at that. The expression itself is a contradiction in terms, an oxymoron, a semantic paradox. "Panther" evokes mighty strength, ferocity, brute, natural force, whereas "basement," despite some romantic aura it may have, essentially connotes confinement, restraint, enclosure, perhaps torture. It is a place for storage, of mold, cobwebs, dust, and musty odors, in short, an antithesis to the pride and splendor of the jungle panther. When the panther is locked in the basement, it is subjugated and defeated, its power neutralized. The confinement renders the beast powerless, mutes its roar, and declaws and emasculates it. The basement is a betrayal of the panther's true nature. Add to this the fact that in Hebrew the words for panther (*panter*) and basement (*marteph*) are very similar in sound—they share almost the same consonants—and the betrayal is doubled: the reversal of sounds in the two words reflects, in a kind of phonic metaphor, the contrasting significance of the mighty panther and the dark restraint of the basement. The similarity in sound between *panter* and *marteph* seems to point to a likeness between words which, in fact, implies opposition.

The fundamental Ozian dichotomy we keep referring to is nowhere better exemplified than in the person of Proffy, the narrator. Like the biblical Rebecca, whose two "children struggled within her," Proffy has two opposing impulses vying for supremacy inside of him. On the one hand, Proffy follows his father's model. The father is a learned, bookish man. By profession, "father was a proofreader and a sort of editorial assistant in a small publishing house" (p. 10). Later on, an entire chapter (17) is dedicated to a detailed, scrupulous description of the father's enormous library. (Compare this to a similar description of the library in Aldo's house in *Soumchi* which, in many respects, is a twin of *A Panther in the Basement* and will be discussed later.)

Books and words fill the father's entire being, occupying him day and night:

> At night he used to sit up till two or three in the morning, surrounded by the shadows of his bookshelves, with his body immersed in darkness, and only his gray head floating in a circle of light from his desk lamp, his back bent as though he was wearily climbing the gully between the mountains of books piled up on his desk, filling slips and cards with preparatory notes for his great book on the history of the Jews in Poland. He was a principled, intense man, who was deeply committed to the concept of justice. (p. 10)

Compare this description to that of Manfred Herbst, in Agnon's *Shira*, who is hard at work on a grand opus on the history of Byzantium. Note also the allusion to Bialik's poem "My Father" (1933; to be found as an allusion in *My Michael*, p. 127): "My father's head was revealed to me, a martyred skull/ As if severed from his shoulders, floating on clouds of smoke . . . dragging at a crawling pace his wagonload of stony burden through the mud-clogged roads."[1]

The analogy between the father in the novel, who devotes his life to books and to the study of words, and Bialik's father, who slaves at the alehouse, is no coincidence. The poet's father has to give up studying holy books in order to support his family, while the father in the novel fulfills both his soul's needs and his family's by his dedication to books. This total devotion reaches almost grotesque proportions in chapter 19. During the curfew imposed by the British, an officer searches the father's library for an "incriminating object" connected with underground activity against the British rule in Palestine. The father, in his fervent eagerness to prove to the officer that he is cultured and versed in intellectual matters, leads the officer around his library and almost discloses the cache of underground contraband, jeopardizing himself, his family, and his underground connections.

Proffy inherited his father's bibliophily and devotion to words. This is how he is first introduced to us:

> I had the nickname Proffy attached to me ever since I was so high. It was short for Professor, which they called me because of my obsession with checking words (I still love words; I like collecting, arranging, shuffling, reversing, combining them. As people who love money do with coins and banknotes and people who love cards do with cards.) (p. 7)

And a moment later, when the inscription "Proffy is a despicable traitor" appears on the wall accusing him of perfidy, defaming and besmirching him, his first reaction is not anger, hurt, or frustration at being falsely accused but rather a linguistic inquiry: is the accusation hurled at him grammatically and logically sound, or is "despicable traitor" merely a tautology, thus requiring editing? Like his father, the obsessive preoccupation with words takes precedence over everything else. Later in the novel, Yardena states, "This kid . . . will sell his own mother for a pun" (p. 57).

As soon as his parents leave for work, Proffy closes the windows and the shutters, turning the house into "a shady den," as he phrases it romantically (proving he is his mother's son no less than his father's). He also has a practical reason for this. "The sun and the dust were liable to damage my father's books that lined the walls, among them some rare volumes" (p. 9). Having turned the house into a "shady den," Proffy proceeds to immerse himself in travel books and encyclopedias, emerging only at lunchtime when hunger steers him toward the kitchen. He wolfs down the food, not bothering to warm it up, because "I couldn't spare the time," (p. 15), and he returns to the magical realm of books. His inordinate fascination with books and words also is expressed in the poems he writes (p. 21; and compare this to the poems written by Soumchi) and in the fact that his attraction to Sergeant

Dunlop is based on language and words; Dunlop teaches Proffy English and, in exchange, Proffy teaches him modern, colloquial Hebrew.

Proffy takes after his father not only in his addiction to books and words but in his passion for order, discipline, and tidiness.

Here, for example:

> First of all, I cleared the table and put everything in its proper place, in the icebox, the cupboards, or the sink, because I loved not having to do anything the rest of the day. . . . I read the morning paper, then I folded it neatly and put in on the corner of the kitchen table, and I put my mother's brooch away in her drawer. I did all this not like a traitor atoning for his despicable deed but out of my love of tidiness. (p. 9)

Both tendencies, verbalism and orderliness, which the father and the son share, imply a reserved, restrained, somewhat aloof attitude toward reality, an attempt to put a buffer between oneself and the outside world. We noted earlier Proffy's unusually restrained response to the defamatory writing on the wall; instead of voicing disgust, resentment, or embarrassment, he channeled his reaction to the linguistic level. Mustering both his verbal sensitivity and his self-discipline, he is able to contend with the scathing insult. Parsing the inscription and analyzing its grammatical and logical validity is a defense mechanism Proffy activates when facing cruel and disappointing reality. Instead of venting feelings or fighting back, he focuses on pedantic, meticulous details. The same defense mechanism is at work in the opening sentence, when Proffy tells us that he was "twelve and a quarter" at the time, that he lived in "a neighborhood at the edge of Jerusalem," and the time was "the summer holidays, less than a year before the British left the country and the State of Israel was born out of the midst of war" (p. 7).

From the point of view of tone and delivery, Proffy clearly carries his father's personality DNA. On several occasions, the mother berates the father for using a pompous, dramatic, pontificating tone when talking to his son: "Instead of lecturing him, why don't you find the time to play with him a little? Or at least talk to him? A conversation; do you remember? Two people sitting down together, they both talk and they both listen? Trying to understand each other?" (p. 95). Proffy too has a tendency to grandiloquent declamation, as Yardena comments sardonically, "You sound like the Voice of Fighting Zion [the radio station of the Jewish Underground during the struggle against the British—au.]. Where are your own words? Haven't you got words of your own? Didn't you ever have any?"

But Proffy also is very much his mother's son and heir to her personality traits. The romantic tendencies displayed by the mother are her attempt to transcend the miseries of present reality, to withdraw into the twinkling, enchanted memories of her European childhood. The mother is described sitting "on the other side of the room, in her rocking chair, reading or, with her open book face down on her lap, listening attentively to some sound that I could not hear" (p. 28), and she is prone to romantic, rather than practical-empirical pronouncements, such as "Anyone who loves isn't a traitor." As she utters these words, her dreamy, pensive gaze is turned to a nail in the kitchen wall "that served no particular purpose" (p. 6). That purposeless, redundant nail seems to pierce the pages of the novel like a sharp pin and linger throughout like a sustained, reverberating note.

Proffy resembles his mother in his ability to distance himself from the oppressive here and now, from humdrum, mundane reality. He confesses his fascination with expressions such as "the darkness of the valley of the shadow of death." Such words titillate him with their mysterious, gothic overtones:

> I loved the words "darkness" and "valley," because they immediately conjured up a valley shrouded in darkness, with monasteries and cellars. And I loved the shadow of death because I didn't understand it. If I whispered "shadow of death," I could almost hear a kind of deep, muffled sound like the note that comes from the last key, the lowest one on the piano, a sound that draws after it a trail of dim echoes, as though a disaster has happened and now there is no going back. (pp. 10–11)

Being thus lured by the dark, enchanting mystique of romance, Proffy immerses himself in the tomes of encyclopedias that fire and excite his imagination:

> All that morning, I sailed on the vast sea of the encyclopedia, all the way to the savage war-painted tribes in Papua, strange craters on distant stars blazing with infernal volcanic fire or, the opposite, frozen and shrouded in eternal darkness (is that where the shadow of death lurks?), landing on islands, losing my way in primeval swamps, encountering cannibals and cave dwelling hermits, godforsaken black-skinned Jews from the days of the Queen of Sheba, and I read about the continents drifting away from each other at a rate of half a millimeter a year. . . . At noon, hunger drove me from the origins of the universe to the kitchen. Without even sitting down, I scarfed the food my mother had left for me in the icebox. . . . I didn't even heat it up; I couldn't spare the time. I was in a hurry to finish and get back to the mystic galaxies. (pp. 15–16)

Behind the intellectual curiosity lurks a strong romantic tendency, a desire to flee reality and to find refuge in a colorful, exotic, magical realm. The same romantic streak manifests itself in grandiose plans made by Proffy, whose naivete often elicits benevolent smiles from his audience. Such is his plot to launch a sneak attack on the Goverment House and take the High Commissioner prisoner (p. 21); or his plan for a "surprise attack by the Underground on key government positions in Jerusalem" (p. 27); or "By the middle of the summer I was making plans to build a Hebrew Armada, with destroyers, submarines, frigates, and aircraft carriers. I was planning to investigate the possibility of a coordinated sneak attack on the British naval bases all around the Mediterranean" (p. 32). In addition, Proffy and his comrades in the "Freedom or Death" Underground are in the process of building a rocket calculated to hit Buckingham Palace, no less (p. 27). In sum, Proffy's character is an amalgam of both his parents' personality traits, a fusion of two antithetical, contradictory attitudes. This not only reflects the binary formula of Oz's fiction as a whole but determines the thematic structure and progression of the plot in the novel. Thus the brief introductory chapter telescopes and foreshadows all later developments. It is that "window to the ark" that Noah was instructed to build (Genesis 6, 16), a tiny peephole that affords a panoramic view of the novel and of Oz's entire oeuvre.

A Panther in the Basement as a Quarry Containing All the Ores Found in Oz's Fiction

> . . . *On your mountain tops and in the depth of your mines.*
> —Shaul Tchernihovsky,
> *Not in Moments of Nature's Slumber*

A Panther in the Basement opens with what amounts to a false pretense: it is written in the genre of young adults' literature, but it does not take long for the reader to realize that the target audience of the novel is not limited to teenagers. The novel, in fact, dons a mask, deliberately and consciously camouflaging itself as a story for young adults. It is a pretense, a ruse, a stratagem.

Why does the novel use this surprising, almost sneaky technique? What is gained by adopting an aesthetic strategy that first misleads and deceives, then reveals and exposes? This question will be discussed in this section. The real surprise is not only in the fact that, rhetorically and thematically, the novel is not meant just for youngsters but in the materials that make up the novel and their direct relation to motifs, themes, and patterns encountered in Oz's fiction in general. *A Panther in the Basement* is a quarry that contains all of the ores, minerals, and building materials of Oz's other works, and they are found here in their pristine, unalloyed condition.

As we have seen earlier, Proffy, the narrator and protagonist, is in a perpetual state of flux between two opposing poles. He has a passion for words, books, soft and tender people, awkward and forlorn, like Sergeant Dunlop, for instance, whom he befriends for two reasons: his love of words and the brotherhood of the misfits. But on the other hand, Proffy is attracted to the hardy, brazen types, those who control their feelings and flaunt their machismo, people he calls "thirsty," who despise words and spurn books. Like Ben Hur, for example, who "used words like someone throwing gravel at a street lamp" (p. 29). And yet Proffy, "a child of words," is totally subservient to Ben Hur and obeys his every command, even if it is "to remove all the water in the Dead Sea to the Upper Galilee, bucket by bucket" (ibid.). In this, as in other respects, Proffy's personality is a battle ground for the struggle of rival forces, each striving for domination.

The theme of treachery and espionage is central to the novel, as it is to many of Oz's other works. After meeting with Sgt. Dunlop for the first time, the impressionable, excitable Proffy declares, "Henceforth, I was a spy. A mole. A secret agent disguised as a child seeking to master the English language. From this moment on, I would act like a chess player" (p. 47). As we have seen earlier, many characters in Oz's fiction (including Oz himself) define themselves as spies, double agents, Mossad [Israeli Secret Service] operatives, or moles.[2] This theme is especially prominent in stories dealing with the struggle of the Jewish community against the British mandatory regime ("Mr. Levi," "Longing," *The Hill of the Evil Council*, and *Soumchi*). In these texts, set against a historical background, the dominant figures are children.

Proffy and his comrades in arms in the "Freedom or Death" Underground (whose acronym in Hebrew is HUM—meaning brown—perhaps a reference to their "revisionist" ideology) see themselves as heroes, as undercover freedom fighters, as brilliant strategists whose sole aim is to defeat and drive out the British regime. Most of Proffy's actions in the novel revolve around his self-image as a spy or secret agent. His trysts with Sgt. Dunlop, which are at the center of the plot, are presented in terms of espionage, which will enable him to enter the enemy's camp and trail one of its representatives (albeit a Hebrew-loving, Bible-quoting, pro-Zionist one). Thus Proffy monitors the sergeant's movements and tries to interpret and use them for the benefit of the underground's struggle against the British.

Espionage, by definition, involves bridging two opposing sides. The spy is anchored in one territory and spies on another, then reports back. When the agent bears allegiance to both territories, he/she becomes a double agent. This is what happens in Proffy's case.

We noted that one of the manifestations of the binary division in Oz's fiction is the contrast between a dull, stolid, uninspired man (or father) and a pensive, romantic, spiritual woman, forever pining for distant regions. We also noted, however, that the gray, uncharismatic man is quite often a strong and resolute person, marked by inner conviction, and is dependable. This is true about the father in *A Panther in the Basement*. Compared to the romantically inclined mother, he is indeed boring, "clerical," practical, and straight as an arrow, but behind the seemingly faded, lackluster exterior lies great strength and staunchness of character. For example: "Father closed the door. Still standing in the hallway, he said to my mother. 'Please keep out of this.' And quietly he asked me, 'What do you have to say for yourself?'" (p. 50). The father's restrained rhetoric harbors unmistakable strength. There is even a despotic streak in him; his civility and good manners barely mask the fact that he is depriving the mother of her natural right to intervene. Earlier in the novel, the mother accuses the father of being insensitive and imperious, of never listening to others, and of erecting a wall between him and his son. "Instead of insulting him, why don't you try to find out what he's trying to say? You never really listen to him. Or to me. Or to anybody. All you ever listen to is the news on the radio" (p. 12).

Such accusations are leveled by other women against their husbands in earlier works by Oz. (cf. Ivria in *To Know a Woman*, Hava Lifshitz in *A Perfect Peace*, Hannah Gonen in *My Michael*, and to some extent, Noga Harish in *Elsewhere, Perhaps*). The women who yearn for other landscapes and distant horizons refuse to obey the dictates of cool rationality and dull, humdrum reality; they spurn the practical, down-to-earth attitudes that their husbands display.

When discussing male-female relationships in Amos Oz's fiction, one cannot ignore the phenomenon of the "extended family" (i.e., the injection of a third person into the marriage). But the introduction of the other person does not necessarily bring about the disintegration of the family unit. For the most part, the marriage continues to function in one form or another, but it is a new structure, a tripartite one. And it is a preferred and salutary solution, because the additional man brings into the structure—which has almost collapsed—a missing element or quality. Paradoxically, it is the deviation from accepted social norms that preserves the marriage and saves it from disintegration. But there is a price to be paid; the formal husband has to play by the new rules and share his wife with the new partner. Thus the cuckolded husband's rival also proves to be his benefactor, preserving the marriage. In *A Perfect Peace*, Azaria Gitlin, the stranger who hails from the Diaspora, invades the crumbling marital setup of Yoni and Rimona. Yoni retreats, gives in to his wanderlust, and disappears to regions unknown (to his wife and the other man). But eventually, he returns and accepts the fact that he has to share his spouse with her "other husband." Azaria brings to the crumbling marriage the sensitivity and attentiveness it hitherto lacked. This beneficial and supportive "dowry" makes him a welcome and an equal partner. Similarly, Ilana, in *Black Box*, sees herself married to both Professor Alex Gideon (her ex-husband) and to Michel Somo, her legal second husband. "You [Alex] have been and always will be my husband, my master. Forever. And in the life to come, Michel will take me by the hand and will lead me to a wedding ceremony with you" (p. 34). The simultaneous presence of both husbands in her life exposes her to the two opposing qualities she craves: the aggressive, destructive machismo of Alex Gideon, and the solicitous consideration of Michel Somo (which he displays at least at the beginning of their married life).

Hannah Gonen, in *My Michael*, is married to practical, restrainted, devoted Michael, who serves as an anchor and a ballast for her volatile, tempestuous spirit. His presence in her life helps preserve her sanity and prevents her descent into an abyss. But Michael fails to fulfill her yearnings for erotic adventure, to quell the raging fire in her soul, so Hannah finds compensation in wild, erotic fantasies that involve twin Arab boys. The twins function as a virtual second husband. Hannah's frustration calls to mind an image that recurs in *A Perfect Peace*: it is a picture of a bird with an open beak, as though arrested in eternal thirst. This thirst is a metaphor for the unfulfilled yearnings of Yoni and Rimona, both trapped in a dull, monotonous, kibbutz existence. It also can describe Hannah's desperate yearning for a passionate, dramatic life, away from the staid and stolid husband who cannot respond to her needs. The torrid, erotic fantasies with the Arab twins enable her to be married simultaneously to two husbands: the concrete and the romantic, the realistic and the virtual, each answering a different need in her psyche.

A couple turned threesome also can be found in *To Know a Woman*, where the narrator insinuates that Ivria, Yoel's wife, has a lover, her elderly neighbor, a Bible-loving, guitar-playing truck driver, who is a clone of Ezra Berger in *Elsewhere, Perhaps*, Noa Harish's lover. On several occasions, Yoel mentions an imaginary Eskimo mistress, "submissive as a dog," who would fulfill his heart's desire, thus turning the monogamous marriage into a triangle. This desire, incidentally, is met with facetious enthusiasm by Ivria, who proclaims it a good idea. The jocularity masks the incontestable truth that each spouse feels a deficiency and a lack in the marriage. The third party may infuse the marriage with a new life and ensure its continuity. It is a fact that Yoel refrains from investigating his wife's relations with her supposed lover, despite the fact that he is a secret agent inured to spying, snooping, and probing. Yoel realizes that this addition to their married life, in fact, prevents its disintegration and shores it up. Once again, paradoxically, a deviation from the norm, from the conventional structure of marriage, is seen as an effective strategy for saving the marriage.

To Know a Woman contains yet another love triangle: Annemarie, Yoel's neighbor in Ramat Lotan, and his lover also has (so the narrator intimates on several occasions) an incestuous relationship with her brother Ralph. It is Ralph who initiates the liaison between his sister and Yoel, but he also is an active observer in their lovemaking. His function as a voyeur confirms his role as the third side of the romantic triangle. Here, too, each man supplies the woman with something the other man cannot: Ralph brings with him stability and dependability, while Yoel brings a certain mystique, an undecipherable enigma that excites Annemarie. The secondary plot in the novel thus reflects the theme of the main plot, in the manner of Shakespeare's and Moliere's comedies.

Touch the Water, Touch the Wind provides the example of Ernst, the secretary of the kibbutz, and his "two mistresses" (p. 110). And so does the story "Late Love," in which aged lecturer Shraga Unger suggests to Lyuba that they form a ménage à trois (with her other husband). Noga Harish, in *Elsewhere, Perhaps*, is pregnant with Ezra Berger's child, but she chooses to form a family with another man, Rami Rimon, who will help her raise the other man's daughter, Inbal.

In *A Panther in the Basement*, the romantic triangle of two men and a woman is relegated to the margins of the plot, involving Cheetah Reznik's mother, "the boy with two fathers. (the first one was always away on trips, and the second one would disappear from the house a few hours before the first got back)" (p. 30). Incidentally, this arrangement brings to mind "Mr. Levi," where Uri Kolodny's mother is suspected of sharing the conjugal bed with Froyke, "the crazy electrician" who, like other lovers in Oz's fiction, is unkempt and foul smelling. In the epilogue to *A Panther in the Basement*, we are told that after Cheetah's mother passed away, the two "fathers" continued to live together, another instance of a compromise, a fusion of two opposing forces; the real father represents the stable, homey, "domesticated" aspect, while the "other father" (the lover) represents the darker, more adventurous aspect. The fathers' staying together symbolizes a modus vivendi, a possible reconciliation, a mutual acceptance that allows them to survive.

In an earlier chapter I discussed the significance of the color blue in the depiction of many of Oz's romantic women.[3] In *A Panther in the Basement*, it is a blue shutter that the mother remembers from her childhood. "In the yard of the mill she found a broken shutter painted pale blue and threw it into the stream" (p. 68). She imagined that the shutter would come back with the stream that made its tortuous way through the forest, but the blue shutter did not reappear: "Only ducks came back." The shutter, an object that is meant to protect and hide, is here broken, and eventually lost. In the last paragraph of the book, the narrator mentions the blue shutter once more, commenting wistfully that, "It may be floating on the stream to this day on its circular journey back to the mill." (p. 68).

All of the sentiments and erotic energy the women in Oz's fiction harbor are repressed and stifled by their uninspired husbands, who look at their wives with total incomprehension. Some of the women are driven to despair, while others seethe with venomous anger. For the most part, the husbands are solicitous and condescending toward the women, who seem to them capricious and maudlin, but they cannot begin to fathom their turbulent feelings. The frustrated, erotic energies that find no outlet or relief are bound to erupt.[4] In Oz's fiction, the release of the pent-up emotional and sexual frustrations is carried out in one of three ways.

The first escape route is daydreams and reveries. For instance, Hannah Gonen retreats from a tedious, monotonous reality to a fascinating dreamworld where she makes torrid love to Arab twins. Hannah's addiction to the intoxicating, erotic escapades has a certain Bovary-like quality, even though it is confined to fantasies. Hannah's flirtation with her private student, Yoram Kamitzer, is strongly reminiscent of Emma Bovary's romantic entanglement with a man much younger than herself.[5] Hannah does not consummate her romantic liaison and thus does not bring about the collapse of the marriage. It is quite possible that she stops short, knowing that the demise of her marriage might lead her to insanity or suicide. Hannah finds an additional escape route: disease. Dr. Orbach, the old physician, whose function in the novel is that of a Greek chorus, the voice of reason and wisdom, maintains that Hannah's body wants to heal, but her mind will not let it. In other words, her disease is another means of escape from a dull, tedious marriage. To her, being married to Dr. Gonen is an insurance policy, at best a consolation prize. She cheats on him in her dreams, by being sick and, according to her own testimony, betraying him when she makes love to him; she feels that she is merely using his body, but she is never actually physically unfaithful to him.

The second means of escape is for Oz's women to be unfaithful to their husbands without actually destroying their marital relationships. Lily Danenberg, in "Strange Fire," is an example (though it is a unique case, a category unto itself). Lily betrays her own daughter by seducing her future son-in-law. There is an actual betrayal, but the marriage is not jeopardized. Lily herself, unlike Hannah Gonen, had the courage to leave a husband and a marriage that did not meet her expectations.

Ivria is unfaithful to Yoel (with the elderly neighbor), but the union does not come apart as a result. Uri Kolodny's mother carries on with Ephraim, the "crazy electrician," yet the marriage remains intact ("Mr. Levi"). In *The Hill of the Evil Council*, on the other hand, two betrayals take place, one imaginary, the other concrete. On the one hand, Ruth Kipness expresses her attraction for the lodger, Mitya. "I was willing to come to him in my nightgown, in the middle of the night, all perfumed, come and touch him . . . then hear him groan in my hands, cry out in broken Russian, sing, grunt like a slaughtered ox" (p. 30). The narrator hints that Ruth's hankering for the darker, "repulsive" aspect of sexuality has, in fact, been acted upon in reality. She is unfaithful to her husband, and this turns out to be a humiliating, destructive affair that ends with abandonment.

This is the third, most extreme escape route open to oppressed and frustrated women. Ruth Kipniss leaves her husband Hans behind, deserted, betrayed, despised, and pathetic, and runs away with a one-eyed British naval officer who has "the visage of a ruthless pirate, complete with canine yellowish teeth" (p. 47), a description reminiscent of Isaac Hamburger, with whom Eva Harish runs away from her husband Reuven Harish (*Elsewhere, Perhaps*), another gentle, sensitive, intellectual, cuckolded husband.

Both women, Ruth Kipniss and Eva Harish, when they desert their dull, unexciting husbands, are fatally drawn to the dark, savage, and terrifying aspect of life from which their staid, sober husbands are totally divorced. Both infidelities end with a blatant and an ugly shattering of the marriage. This, then, is the third option for women who cannot content themselves with excursions into daydreams and reveries; feeling besieged and imprisoned, their only solution is to break away from the marriage, leaving behind betrayed, stupefied, and bereaved husbands and children.

In *A Panther in the Basement*, which we termed the quarry in which all of the materials of Oz's other works can be found, the trial and tribulation of love and eroticism do not occupy center stage but are obliquely and marginally presented through the mother's comment: "Anyone who loves isn't a

traitor" (p. 10); in her dreamy, otherworldly look, as she peers through a glass
of tea at the open window; in her jocular comment about the missing rooster,
which elicits a stern rebuke from the father, "Stop, the boy can hear you" (p.
65) (in the same way Hans Kipniss reacts when his wife voices her sexual
frustrations, "That's enough, Ruth, the child hears and understands everything" (*The Hill of the Evil Council*, p. 30); or the wistful yearning that creeps
into the mother's voice when she talks about the enchanted European landscapes she left behind, or when she reminisces about the blue shutter she sent
down the stream in faraway Ukraine, hoping in vain for it to come back. And
perhaps to this day, she is still waiting for it to suddenly land in this tumultuous, sweaty, heat-parched land and carry her back to the dream-shrouded
land of her childhood. Yearnings, desires, dreams, and frustrations are all
present in the novel, but they are muted and restrained. We may ask, therefore, why, in a novel that contains the fundamental themes and motifs of
Oz's fiction, this particular theme (of a woman's anguish and frustration in a
dull, stultifying marriage) is so modestly represented and in such a minor key.
The answer, it would seem, lies in the overall thematic structure of the novel,
in particular, in the hierarchy that determines and governs the characters. In
earlier works by Oz, the characters that dominate the plot and occupy center
stage, are, for the most part, a man and a woman locked in a trenchant
power struggle; the woman represents the dark, savage, and rebellious element, while the man represents the sober, rational, orderly element. Since
the man is incapable of understanding and responding to the woman's turbulent feelings, the woman despises and rejects his orderly, tame world and tries
to subvert and destroy it.

True, not all of the novels and stories follow this paradigm, but a significant number of them do. Here is a partial list: Steffa versus Elisha
Pomerantz, in *Touch the Water, Touch the Wind*; Hannah versus Michael, in
My Michael; Ilana versus Alex, in *Black Box*; Eva versus Reuven, and Noga
versus Rami, in *Elsewhere, Perhaps*; Geula versus the Collective, in "Nomads
and Viper"; Lily Danenberg versus Yosef Yarden and Yair Yarden, in
"Strange Fire"; Rimona versus Yoni, in *A Perfect Peace*; Batya Pinsky versus
the kibbutz society, in "Hollow Stone"; Ruth versus Hans, in *The Hill of the
Evil Council*; the mother versus the father, in "Mr. Levi"; Noa versus Theo,
in *Do Not Call It a Night*; Ivria versus Yoel, in *To Know a Woman*. There are
noticeable variations among the confronting couples: Ivria Ravid, in *To Know
a Woman*, evinces great emotional restraint, something of which Hannah
Gonen and Ruth Kipniss are totally incapable. The storm that rages in the
psyche of silent, timid Rimona, in *A Perfect Peace*, is a far cry from the
fervent hatred that motivates Batya Pinsky, in "Hollow Stone," who shows

more affinity to the introverted, "wintry" women. Fruma, in *Elsewhere, Perhaps*, and Hava, in *A Perfect Peace*, are merely bitter, self-righteous, and resentful, with no trace of the desperate, romantic yearning. Batya Pinsky (in her younger days) had a certain fascinating strangeness that lent her a certain mystique. She is totally different from the practical, efficient, and calculating Steffa Pomerantz in *Touch the Water, Touch the Wind*. And the same applies to the men: despite their common denominator, they seem like different models, possessing markedly different characteristics. Professor Alex Gideon (*Black Box*) is sarcastic, vicious, and destructive, while Michael (*My Michael*) is solicitous, attentive, and considerate; Yoel Ravid (*To Know a Woman*) is cold, cynical, and calculating, while the poet Reuven Harish (*Elsewhere, Perhaps*) show sparks of nobility in his conduct, and so on and so forth. However, despite the variables in the characterization of the men and women, they still fit into the basic formula.

The reason *A Panther in the Basement* does not exhibit the sexual frustration and romantic yearnings we noticed in the earlier novels is due to a significant and dramatic change in the hierarchy that dictates the thematic structure of the novel. Here, for the first time in Oz's fiction, the child is placed at center stage. Except for *Soumchi*, which is a children's novel and therefore a special case, no other work by Oz has a child at the center of the plot playing, as it were, first fiddle in the fictional world. The son in *The Hill of the Evil Council* is quite central to the plot, which is told largely through his eyes. The "formal" narrator of the story is an external, adult figure, not Hillel, but he conveys the story from the child's vantage point. The result is rhetorical tactics of a combined point of view using the child's consciousness as a prism through which the story is presented to the reader. And yet it is the parents, with the characteristic antagonism and power struggle, who are at the center of the plot, not the child, who is just an addendum, a satellite. The story focuses on Ruth Kipniss, who is the epitome of the tormented, romantic, frustrated, Ozian woman. Her restlessness and her erotic, adventurous nature eventually undermine the tame, staid, and orderly world of the father. This conflict, not the child, is at the core of the novella.

In *A Panther in the Basement*, on the other hand, the child occupies most of the territory, while the romantic mother is relegated to the margins of the fictional world (the father is somewhat more prominent). The frustrated sexuality that led to infidelity in earlier works is drastically reduced here (confined to a few oblique comments from the mother). However, since the more blatant eroticism and its corollaries are underplayed, another form of betrayal comes to the fore. The plot of this novel does not hinge on seething desires and unfulfilled feminine yearnings, since its protagonist is a young boy who, as yet, is not concerned with such sentiments. But this deficiency is made up for by other forms of betrayal, with a vengeance. Playing down the erotic theme does not detract from the novel's status as a repository of Oz's fictional themes; it is simply a "transposition of the chessmen" on the narrative board. This dramatic change in the poetic map is marked by a much greater exposure by the "implied author" in a manner hitherto unencountered in Oz's work. The "implied author," a term coined by Booth,[6] is not synonymous with the biographical writer (i.e., the private citizen, Amos Oz).

Who is the implied author of the literary text? He is the repository of all of the textual data that make up the work, the storehouse of its trends and intentions, all of its poetic, thematic, and conceptual manifestations. For instance, if the text uses the poetic tactics of combined narratives, or "plants" literary allusions that refer the reader to other texts, or creates an analogy between two characters, or contrasts two sections of the narrative, and so on, the "responsibility" for these devices falls on the implied author: he is the source of all of the poetic devices, tactics, and strategies used in the text. The narrator of the story is merely an agent of the implied author, a rhetorical tactic, one more device in his arsenal. The biographical writer, the actual person who created the text, must remain outside of the picture, as far implied as the literary scholar is concerned. The subject of analysis is the text, not the person who created it. When dealing with a literary text, the author alone is "the master of the fictional world"; there is no other.

A Panther in the Basement presents not only the quarry, whence all of Oz's materials are mined, but exposes the "principal" implied author of Oz's entire work in an unprecedented manner. True, each literary text fashions its own independent, discrete, implied author, but there are many overlapping areas that enable one to deduce a "principal" or "super" author existing, so to speak, in the bedrock of Oz's fiction which, for this purpose, can be construed as a unified whole. Presenting the implied author in such an exposed, revelatory manner, as is done in *A Panther in the Basement*, is a corollary of the pivotal role the child plays in the plot.

Additional overlapping themes and cross references exist between *A Panther in the Basement* and Oz's earlier texts. We mentioned earlier eroticism and its relative absence from the novel. Sexuality is introduced rather obliquely and suggestively through the mother and Proffy, but, more explicitly, through the character of Yardena, who seems to be a reincarnation of the spunky, sexy student in *My Michael*. This time, she is not a student but the older sister of Ben Hur, however, apart from this "cosmetic" change, there is no mistaking her sexual allure, which makes her the object of Proffy's roman-

tic-erotic fantasies. Yardena's erotic presence figures both at the beginning
and end of the novel, forming a kind of sexual circle around it. At the beginning she strips (albeit unbeknownst to her) in front of the unbelieving and
exultant Proffy (p. 21), an incident he later feels very repentant about. In the
final chapter, "she burst into her radiant laughter, that laugher that belongs
to girls who enjoy being girls" (p. 155). Somewhere toward the end of the
novel, Yardena plays the role of "babysitter" to Proffy, and the two engage in
preparing a "decadent" dinner (Yardena's own droll, sexually charged term).
The description is strongly redolent of lovemaking:

> Seventy-seven years of yearning went past, as slow as torture, beyond
> endurance, and further, to the point of despair, and further still, till the
> heart sobbed, until finally the stock began to bubble and boil, and the
> oil began to hiss and sputter. . . . Then she put the lid on the pan,
> leaving an escape route for the vapors that sent pleasurable shivers
> down my tummy. . . . Mercilessly, she waited until the broth evapo-
> rated, leaving behind a heavenly thick sauce. . . . The whole apartment
> was stunned by the hosts of pungent odors wafting from the kitchen
> that, like incited rioters, invaded every corner. The apartment had
> never known such an aroma since the day it was built. (p. 132)

This metaphoric use of the terminology of lovemaking in the context
of food preparation as it is experienced by the sexually provocative Yardena
and the excitable Proffy (apart from the traditional linkage between eating
and copulating) suggests a literary allusion to Tchernichovsky's poem
"Dumplings" (*Levivot*); the process of preparing and boiling the dumplings,
as it is carried out by Gitl, is a metaphoric reflection on the growing up of
Reizele, Gitl's granddaughter. Since this metaphoric reading of Tchernichovsky's idyll is very familiar and popular, there is reason to believe that
the implied author deliberately included this sequence in order to evoke
Tchernichovsky's text in the reader's mind. Thus, Yardena, who excited Michael Gonen with her unrestrained sexuality, returns in this novel to titillate
the innocent and romantic Proffy.[7]

Other analogies to earlier works abound. Proffy's rounded glasses bring
to mind Hans Kipniss' glasses, in *The Hill of the Evil Council*, and even more
so, Yoel Ravid's glasses, in *To Know a Woman*, who, like Proffy, is a spy, a
secret agent.

Proffy states that he learned from his father how to think rationally
and to analyze reality intelligently and dispassionately (again, like Yoel
Ravid), which reinforces his affinity with Michael Gonen, whose chief traits

are systematic, regimented thinking, emotional restraint, and analytical ratiocination.

Proffy's father's admiration for famous writers and scholars is reminiscent of Hannah Gonen's late father, who "would whisper excitedly that a certain professor who had just vanished into a bookstore was world famous, or was about to acquire an international reputation. And I would see a diminutive old man gingerly feeling his way like a man in a strange city" (p. 11). Compare this to Oz's testimony about himself in "Strange City" (*Under This Blazing Light*, p. 212). However, Hannah's father is humble and self-effacing, whereas Proffy's father is marked by confidence and self-importance, which borders on pomposity. "For an instant, a rare, mischievous glint shone in his eyes, for example, when he told us how he had delivered a crushing reply to some scholar or writer, who had been left 'speechless, as though struck by thunder'" (p. 95). Halfway between prostration before famous people and self-aggrandizing defiance is an attitude described in *The Hill of the Evil Council*. "At a nearby table were seated the philosopher Buber and the writer Agnon. Since they were arguing and could not come to an agreement, Agnon suggested, jokingly, that they ask the boy. Father must have said something witty because both Buber and Agnon burst out laughing and also graciously complimented (Father's) companion. At that moment, Father's blue eyes lit up behind his round glasses and he smiled wistfully" (p. 20). It is interesting to compare this description to a passage in an autobiographical article by Oz. "My father would point out, 'here's somebody of world renown walking in the street.' I wasn't sure what that meant. I figured it must be some disease, because quite often those people he described as 'of world renown' were old people in heavy suits and holding canes, who felt their way gingerly . . ."[8]

Proffy goes on imaginary, adventurous journeys around the world (p. 31 passim), a practice shared by Yair Gonen, in *My Michael*, who is guided and inspired by his father. Netta, in *To Know a Woman*, also shares her father's travels by following them on a map of the world.

Proffy's father resembles Michael Gonen, in that both were unfit for combat duty. *A Panther in the Basement* takes place during the British Mandate, when young men volunteered to serve in the underground and in pre-state paramilitary organizations. But the father is myopic and hence better suited for rifling through books than for loading a Sten, so his job is to write underground leaflets and posters that fearless youths later distribute on the streets of Jerusalem. The scholarly, bookish father was probably a source of disappointment to his son. Similarly, Michael Gonen does his military service in the Signal Corps, "not as a pilot or a paratrooper" (p. 143). Later, we are told, "Michael was released before his time was up . . . because his broken glasses rendered him almost useless at the transmitter" (p. 163). Proffy's father, we are told, "was almost blind in the dark, which is why he never took part in night raids on barricades or fortified police stations. But he had a special task: to compose slogans in English sharply denouncing Perfidious Albion" (p. 81).

Other thematic links exist between this novel and previous works, for instance, Proffy's utopian musing about "the wolf and the lamb feeding together":

> Why couldn't we all get together just once in the back room of the Orient Palace, Sergeant Dunlop, Mother, Father, Ben-Gurion, Ben Hur, Yardena, the Mufti Haj Amin, my teacher Mr. Gihon, the leaders of the Underground, Mr. Lazarus, and the High Commissioner, all of us, even Cheetah and his mother and his two alternate fathers, to chat for a couple of hours, and understand each other at last, make some concessions, be reconciled, and forgive one another? Why couldn't we all go down to the bank of the river to see if the blue shutter had carried back by the stream? (pp. 90–91)

The same sentiment can be found in the letter that Yolek Lifshitz writes to Prime Minister Eshkol, his quondam colleague and political rival:

> Every evening we'll light a candle or two in our tent and have a heart-to-heart talk. And if there's a disagreement, we'll thrash it out between us, and if we get tired, you'll play the harmonica and I'll sit down in my undershirt and write an outline." (p. 172)

It is the same naive, impractical, utopian idea that all conflicts and rifts can be healed by one conciliatory talk.

The description of the intimate family gathering in the kitchen (p. 66) brings to mind similar gatherings in *To Know a Woman*, where Yoel, Ivria, and Netta hold conferences in the kitchen "like delegates of three hostile powers." Sitting erect, keeping their distance, icily civil to one another, they conduct their negotiations efficiently, then bow courteously and disappear, each into their respective rooms. In *A Panther in the Basement*, however, the gatherings are much more cordial, warm, and relaxed. A contributing factor to the amicable atmosphere is the shared interest in stamp collection. They are all engaged in soaking, drying, peeling, and arranging the stamps in the family album. Similar scenes occur in *My Michael*, where father and son indulge in their shared hobby, and in *Black Box*, where Alex and Boaz clip and paste colorful pictures from a foreign geographical magazine. Then there is chess. It is a rare Oz text that does not contain the chess motif. At one point, Proffy declares, "From this moment on I would act as if in a game of chess" (p. 47), meaning, cool, calculating, and methodical, trying to anticipate two or three moves ahead. In the novella "Mr. Levi," Ephraim is such an astute, calculating chess player, as is Michael Gonen, when pitted against his opponent, Mr. Kadishman. In *Elsewhere, Perhaps*, Ezra Berger is pitted in a chess game against his buddy Grisha (p. 290), and here too (as in *My Michael*) the game generates camaraderie and goodwill between the contestants, unlike other Oz stories, in which chess functions as a metaphor for bitter rivalry and an erotic power struggle between males. This is the case in *Black Box*, where Alex's sinister, venomous hatred is described in terms of Death winning a game of chess (pp. 45, 73), evoking Ingmar Bergman's classic movie *The Seventh Seal*. Throughout, Alex is described as a crafty, astute player who can checkmate an opponent in "three brilliant moves" (p. 86). Shimshon Sheinbaum ("The Way of the Wind"), in his perturbing dream, tries to divert his son (whose developing virility threatens the father's status) from a power struggle into a chess game. He acknowledges his son's prowess. "How he has improved in chess. Soon he'll be able to defeat his old father" (p. 48). In *A Perfect Peace*, too, the chess game between Yonatan and Azaria is a metaphor for the sexual rivalry between the two men. Azaria, the interloper, is described as masterminding the repair operation of a defunct tractor. "He presided over the operation from afar, like one of those famous Grandmasters Yonatan had read about in his chess journals" (p. 94). Moreover, Azaria, the triumphant lover, plays chess brilliantly but recklessly, frittering away his advantages (p. 108). Similarly, Ephraim, in "Mr. Levi," is an ingenious yet impatient player who loses to the persevering and plodding father (p. 67). The mother in that story taunts her husband by laughingly telling him that Ephraim Nehemkin came to visit her in the morning to play chess and to install a night lamp by her bed (p. 21). Consequently, an inscription appears one morning on the wall proclaiming (with embarrassing spelling mistakes) "Crazy Ephraim is screwing Uri's mother" (p. 100), an incident strongly reminiscent of the inscription, on the wall of Proffy's house, which accused him too of treachery.

Proffy's mother, who listens to sounds that nobody else can hear, is a kindred soul of Noga Harish, who used "to open her lips in an attempt to receive faraway voices" (*Elsewhere, Perhaps*, p. 27); both women hanker after some magical, savage place beyond the horizon.

An obsession with order and symmetry, meticulous attention to detail, and a compulsive need to fold everything neatly and smooth down imperceptible creases are shared not only by Proffy and his father but by Michael Gonen, Theo (in *Do Not Call It a Night*), and Yoel Ravid (*To Know a Woman*). The thirst that is etched in Ben Hur's face (*A Panther in the Basement*, p. 54) is also reflected in the "thirsty" face of Steffa Pomerantz's general manager (*Touch the Water, Touch the Wind*), the same kind of thirst discerned in the beak of the bird in the picture hanging on the wall of Yonatan's and Rimona's room (*A Perfect Peace*). The boy, Uri Kolodny ("Mr. Levi"), builds himself a fleet of toy battleships, something Proffy also does with great concentration and precision. The idea for an underground rocket, moving like molten lava in the bowels of the earth, which hatches in the febrile brain of Ephraim, the "crazy" electrician, is echoed in the idea that Proffy and his underground buddies have of building a rocket from parts of electric appliances and aiming it at Buckingham Palace.

Above all, *A Panther in the Basement* bears a strong resemblance to *Soumchi*, Oz's earlier (and only) children's book. We noted above that *A Panther in the Basement*'s claim to be a novel for young adults is a mere facade, a poetic ruse, and that the novel is, in fact, targeted to an adult audience. However, there is a great affinity between the two texts; they share themes, structure, and poetic devices, in particular, a child protagonist and twofold narrative point of view. In both novels, the narrator is a young boy who recounts the events from two viewpoints; the reconstructed events as experienced by the child, and the adult's perspective in retrospect. In both novels, the historical background is the struggle against the British regime in Palestine before the establishment of the State (which also figures in "Mr. Levi"). Both protagonists are endowed with vivid imaginations, to which they give free rein. The plot in both stories hinges on a group of kids who taunt and torment the naive and vulnerable protagonist. Both narrators are superior to their peers in knowledge that comes from voracious reading; in both, the protagonist tries in vain to win love and recognition from a hostile society.

Soumchi dreams of going away to scorching, sweltering Africa, perhaps to the source of the Zambezi River. His aching and yearning are of the same order as those of the women in Oz's fiction who feel trapped by their constricting, humdrum environment and who long for an exotic, fascinating existence that seems to beckon them from beyond the blue horizon.

Soumchi, like Proffy, is accused of treason, of fraternizing with the enemy. The accusation is, of course, trumped up. In both cases, the child's defense is that he consorted with the enemy in order to learn English. But in both stories, the accused, at least partially, internalizes the accusation, and while outwardly denying it, feels somehow tainted, because he knows that he is drawn to the British officer not only for linguistic purposes; there is the affinity of the misfits, the outcasts, the "others" rejected and despised by a mediocre "normative" society that feels threatened by their originality and uniqueness.

The similarities between the novels extend to the figure of the father: strict, demanding, pedantic, logical, firmly planted in reality. However, in *Soumchi*, the father is totally insensitive and inattentive toward his spirited and imaginative son (like the father in Bialik's "Aftergrowth"). He slaps him at the least provocation and calls him "crazy." The father in *A Panther in the Basement*, uses no corporal punishment and, from time to time, displays sensitivity and compassion that compensate somewhat for the strict discipline he demands.

In *Soumchi*, too, the color blue is associated with the female element and with an unattainable desire. Here it is linked to Esty, the object of Soumchi's innocent love and hopeless romantic yearnings; "at these evening moments, Esty is probably sitting in her room . . . having drawn the two blue drapes" (pp. 50, 70). Later on, Soumchi's sentiments are requited, but only for six weeks. During these enchanted weeks, blue is associated with joy, eroticism, and love. "For six whole weeks, Esty and I were friends. Those days were warm and blue, and the nights were dark blue. It was a deep and wide summer in Jerusalem when Esty and I were in love" (p. 78).

The motif of the spy or double agent also is prominent in *Soumchi*. "I'll go to London and become a double agent" (p. 61), Soumchi declares, reminding us once more of the link to the author Amos Oz, who defined himself on more than one occasion as a double agent.

Some materials and themes from earlier works do not recur in *A Panther in the Basement*, such as the seething, venomous anger displayed by some of the women in Oz's fiction, for instance, Hava Lifshitz (*A Perfect Peace*), Fruma Rominov (*Elsewhere, Perhaps*) and Batya Pinsky ("Hollow Stone"); or the motif of the stranger who hails from afar, invades the family unit, and undermines it (but not necessarily destroys it), such as: Azaria Gitlin in *A Perfect Peace*, Ephraim in "Mr. Levi," Matityahu Demkov in *Where the Jackals Howl*, and Isaac Hamburger and Zecharia-Ziegfried Berger in *Elsewhere, Perhaps*. Each of these interlopers insinuates himself into an orderly (and seemingly stable) world but does so in his own unique manner, carrying with him the seeds of confusion and havoc. However, since *A Panther in the Basement* has a boy as its center, such themes as a stranger who latches himself onto a couple and joins in the "orgy" are absent, or at least relegated to the margins. But other analogies come to mind. The description of the search by the British secret police is reminiscent of a similar scene in "Mr. Levi," a story that shares with *A Panther in the Basement* a child's perspective.

In choosing to write *A Panther in the Basement* in the genre of "young adult" literature, the author aims at eliciting reactions from the reader that are different from the ones reserved for "regular," grown-up literature. Fiction for young adults is generally conceived as presenting reality without the hypocrisy, cynicism, and cold pragmatism that attend the grown-up world. It is marked by innocence and naivete, and thus, at least briefly, it inspires calm and tranquility. It returns the reader to a basic, pristine state, to a more wholesome and lucid human condition, without the baggage of feelings and weaknesses, pretenses and masks. It is a return to the beginning, to the inception, to square one. Co-opting an aesthetic strategy that is traditionally reserved for young adults' fiction gives *A Panther in the Basement* the quality of a quarry, containing all of the materials, themes, and patterns of Oz's fiction in their primary, elemental condition, as it were, before they were tainted by the adult world.

Finally, the Implied Author Decides to Bare All

I have referred to *A Panther in the Basement* as a quarry, a mine, or a repository of many of the raw materials and unprocessed themes and patterns of Oz's other works. Chronologically, of course, *Panther* is a later novel, a fact that points to a deliberate delay in the exposure of this quarry. It also is unique in its disclosure of the implied author who, for the first time, relinquishes the mask, the camouflage, the pretense that he has hitherto maintained. What emerges is a kind of "super" or "principal" implied author who transcends the confines of the specific novel to encompass Oz's entire oeuvre. Revealed here are sensitivities and sentiments, weaknesses and foibles, embarrassing idiosyncrasies that the implied author (not Oz!) was reluctant to disclose in the past: things hoarded in the attic, swept under the rug, intimate exchanges between parents and children, secrets that are concealed, buried, locked up.

Amos Oz once said (in an interview with Esther Dar, quoted at the end of this book), "It goes back to a hurt one suffered as a boy. Without hurt there is no writer." The hurt can be an insult, a scathing offense, a slap in the face, a false accusation, or a public humiliation. It is a wound that leaves a permanent scar, however small or imperceptible. That ancient wound is the source of creativity, as attested to by Bialik in his poem, "I Didn't Win My

Light in a Windfall": "Sorrow wields huge hammer blows/The rock of endurance cracks/Blinding my eye with flashes/I catch in verse." The wound is ostensibly healed, continues to smart and fester underneath. And it is all the shames (real or imagined) and embarrassments, sensitivities, and vulnerabilities that one tries to repress and conceal. In an attempt to conceal fears, doubts, anxieties, and a brittle self-image, one resorts to camouflage, masks, facades, and protective walls. It requires enormous courage to resolve to emerge from under the layers of concealment, to unmask oneself, to reveal the embarrassing secret. And this is what happens in *A Panther in the Basement*, as far as the implied author is concerned.

The disclosure can be amply rewarding. Exposure may not necessarily result in disgrace and ignominy but rather in finding a robust, indestructible core behind the facade. The implied author, and the "Ur" or Ubiquitous Author of Oz's entire fiction, reveals in this novel fundamental truths that hitherto were wholly or partially concealed.

In earlier texts, shameful, embarrassing, incriminating weaknesses were silenced or muted by being ascribed to certain reprehensible characters, some central, some marginal, who did not enlist the reader's sympathy. They were the shock absorbers, the receptacles for unsavory traits or offensive behavior. And since they contained the reprehensible, embarrassing qualities, the rest of the fictional world remained untainted, decent, blameless. Who are those characters? Azaria Gitlin, for instance (*A Perfect Peace*), Michel Somo (*Black Box*), Matityahu Demkov (*Where the Jackals Howl*), Isaac Hamburger, Zecharia-Siegfiried Berger (*Elsewhere, Perhaps*), Batya Pinsky ("Hollow Stone"), and so on.

If there were manifestations of ugliness or evil in the "likable" characters (such as Hannah Gonen in *My Michael* or Ruth Kipniss in *The Hill of the Evil Council*), the implied author made sure that he offset those less attractive aspects by infusing charm, mystique, or intense and savage passion into the depiction of those characters.

The novel, *Fima* (*The Third Condition*), marks a point of departure in the broader spectrum of Oz's fiction. The protagonist, Fima, is a sort of sad clown, part philosopher, prone to pontification and intellectual ruminations, and part crashing bore, a pathetic ne'er-do-well, squandering his talents, sponging on his friends, and living at the margins of respectable society. Fima can fascinate his listeners with his acuity and verbal wit, but he also can exhaust them with his incessant droning; he is puerile, immature, inept, a total misfit. Fima seems like a later avatar of A. B. Yehoshua's protagonist in "Facing the Forests": pathetic, risible, eccentric, yet intriguing and highly intelligent. The innovation in *Fima* is in creating a central character in whom the negative, unattractive qualities outweigh the positive and appealing ones. The embarrassing, shameful traits are no longer relegated to the outskirts of the plot or attributed to characters of secondary importance. Moreover, the bumbling, long-winded Fima possesses a certain disarming charm; he is not pernicious and does not evoke sinister feelings, as do Azaria Gitlin, Michel Somo or Zecharia Berger.

To Know a Woman (published before *Fima*, hence the progression is not necessarily chronological) marks an escalation in the willingness of the implied author to expose weaknesses and embarrassing frailties of the character who stands at center stage (Yoel Ravid, the spy who refuses to come in from the cold and who insists on denying feelings, sentiments, and passions). Unlike Azaria Gitlin or Michel Somo, Yoel is not an "exilic" type, an outsider in Israeli society, carrying the baggage of misery, distortion, and repulsive behavior that precludes the reader's identification; he is not presented as an interloper, insinuating himself, like a virus, into the wholesome, "blond" mainstream Israeli society.

Yoel is a far cry from Fima, who despite being a "sabra" actually evokes an image of a solitary, rejected, eccentric ghetto type, and whose slovenly, bedraggled appearance and incessant loquacity make him pathetic and obnoxious. Yoel, at least at first appearance, seems like the quintessential "sabra": handsome and virile, with a shock of gray hair, chiseled features, and a robust physique that bespeaks self-confidence, inner strength, and restraint—the image of the mythological, heroic, native Israeli.

Putting Yoel Ravid at the center of the plot and using him to expose shameful weaknesses and embarrassing failings become a huge leap toward exposing and unmasking the implied author. Behind Yoel's attractive exterior lurks a gaping hollow of barrenness, alienation, and life-denying coldness. The facade of the glamorous, intrepid secret agent conceals treachery and betrayal on more than one level.

A Panther in the Basement is the culmination of this process; here, betrayal is not only the center and the instigator of the plot, but it is predicated on a "normative," accepted protagonist who also is the narrator of the tale. Proffy is tainted by betrayal, which is the epitome of human depravity and disgrace. The theme of betrayal is ramified throughout the entire novel, invading every corner and recess. The imputation of treachery is compounded by Proffy's own self-doubt and sense of betrayal. It is fraught with guilt, shame, and embarrassment, now out of the attic, in the public eye, exposed. It is as though the implied author has made a conscious decision once and for all to air all of the dirty little secrets, to wash the soiled linen in public. And he imputes the disgrace of treachery to the protagonist, an exemplary

youth who dreams of heroic exploits, who sees himself as a modern Mac-
cabee, a boy who loves words and writes poetry, a sensitive, spirited, romantic
boy, a seeker of truth and justice. By so doing, the implied author widens the
tunnel that leads to the "shame in the attic," to the final exposure of the
embarrassing secret.

The implied author does not spare his protagonist when it comes to
enumerating and documenting his betrayals and the guilt and shame that
they engender in him. As when Proffy trains his binoculars on Ben Hur's
apartment and inadvertently catches sight of Yardena undressing, "And it was
precisely because of this shadow knowledge that I had a feeling that I was a
despicable traitor" (pp. 29–30). The shadow motif, incidentally, recurs in the
novel, especially at the beginning (p. 13) and at the end (p. 154). It is the
shameful, odious shadow of treachery that haunts Proffy, even though he is
not really culpable. After his first encounter with Sergeant Dunlop, "I said,
'Goodbye. Thank you.' My heart rebuked me: 'Shame on you, Hellenizer,
slave, coward, bootlicker, louse, why the hell are you saying thank you to
him?'" (p. 49). Almost choking with shame and guilt, and in a desperate
attempt to salvage some of his lost self-respect, Proffy refuses to shake hands
with the British officer who has escorted him home during the curfew. But it
is to no avail. The disgrace, the infamy, and the taint of the putative treachery cling to him, continue to haunt him. "So why did I feel once again that
taste of treachery in my mouth, as though I had been chewing soap?" he
wonders. And later, after the kangaroo court his underground buddies carried
out on him—a kind of children's version of the Dreyfus trial—where they
accuse him of aiding and abetting the enemy—Proffy shouts at his departing
comrades, "You're crazy! You're nuts! I hate that Dunlop, that medusa face! I
hate him! I loathe him! I despise him!" (p. 76). But his friends refuse to
believe him. What is worse, he feels that now he has switched from being a
double agent to being a double traitor: he has betrayed his friends by be-
friending Dunlop, and he also has betrayed Dunlop, for whom he feels great
affinity, which both excites and repels him. No wonder, then, that the accusations hurled at him take hold of his mind and continue to haunt him
relentlessly. "Traitor, liar, louse" (p. 76). And soon afterwards, "Pine trees
whispered and cypresses rustled: Shut up, despicable traitor" (ibid.). The
novel concludes with the narrator's realization that he is hopelessly enmeshed
in a web of treachery, and no matter what he does, he cannot extricate himself from the moral dilemma or exonerate himself. "And what about the story
itself? Have I betrayed them all again by telling the story? Or is it the other
way around: would I have betrayed them if I had not told it?" (p. 155). The
end. Curtain. Cut.

The novel ends with the narrator's conviction that treachery has become part of his personality, second nature, that the infamy of the betrayal is forever stamped on his brow, like the mark of Cain. Yet the narrator has no hesitation in acknowledging his shame and the pain it engendered. There is almost alacrity in his willingness to admit it. From the point of view of textual analysis, the narrator is not merely a rhetorical presence anchored in the text and in the plot (and here, as often happens, he also is the main protagonist), not only a conduit for conveying information to the reader. The narrator also is the product of a conscious decision on the part of the implied author. It is the latter who fashions and molds the narrator in response to aesthetic and conceptual needs. In other words, the narrator, too, like the other materials and patterns that make up the text, is a reflection of the implied author who uses the narrator to transmit his poetic predilections, his ideas and purpose. So when the narrator decides to reveal his innermost secrets, to expose his vulnerability, to open his private Pandora's box, it is, in fact, the implied author who does all that; he is the one putting himself on the stage in plain view, baring his chest, putting an end to the pretense, and this requires a great deal of courage.

Whatever the implied authors in Oz's earlier fiction tried to hide, or revealed only in small measure, the implied author in *A Panther in the Basement* discloses without reservation. The spy has resolved to come in from the cold, to emerge from the dark and to face the music.

The implied author is willing to share with the reader personal frailties, sensitivities, vulnerabilities, festering wounds, shame, and ignominy, everything that in earlier texts was concealed, clandestine, hushed. There is a clear progression in the willingness to admit shame and to call a spade a spade. It began with *Fima* through *To Know a Woman* and on to *A Panther in the Basement*. It is interesting to note, that in *The Same Sea*, the lyrical book that Oz published in 1999, the implied author takes further steps toward self-revelation, and yet he retains one veil, the poetic genre, which creates a buffer between the readers and the information revealed by the implied author.

What are the poetic tactics used by the implied author in the gradual divestment of veils and masks that culminate in *A Panther in the Basement*? There is a complex poetic mechanism imbedded in the novel that directs and guides the aesthetic strategy by which the process of divestment is carried out. This poetic apparatus is based on a simultaneous operation of two systems working both in conjunction with and in opposition to each other. The rivalry that exists between the two does not vitiate the smooth operation of the poetic mechanism; rather, it enhances the sophistication and intricacy of the text. One thing is clear: the exposure and divestment are mostly a function of the protagonist-narrator's willingness to share with the reader his guilt feelings, his shame and disgrace (caused by his supposed "despicable treachery") that haunt and torment him. One should, of course, bear in mind that this narrator is not necessarily reliable or trustworthy; he is, after all, a mere boy.

And yet it is clear from the way things are presented in the novel that there is no real separation between the narrator and the implied author, at least not when it comes to Proffy's guilt feelings and his putative betrayal. The implied author identifies with the narrator's feelings of sympathy and affinity for the soft, "fluffy" personality of Sgt. Dunlop, who is formally, at least, an enemy, a political opponent, a representative of the occupying British regime that Proffy and his underground buddies are fighting with such fervor and dedication (see, e.g., p. 85). Although Proffy's betrayal is not real (at least, in my opinion), his own conviction that he is a traitor is not totally groundless. It is an authentic feeling emanating from the split in his own personality, a split that is reflected in the fact that he resembles both his pedantic, self-righteous, pragmatic father and his romantic mother, who yearns to transcend the reality that she finds oppressive and tedious. The very fact that he is pulled toward two opposing poles makes betrayal almost inevitable, since acceptance of one side is a rejection and a betrayal of the other. This duality is particularly conspicuous in Proffy's attitude toward Ben Hur and his moral values. On the one hand, Proffy is well aware of Ben Hur's superficiality and the hollow nature of his worldview, but on the other hand, he yearns to be part of Ben Hur's system of values, to be accepted and approved by it, despite its shallowness and worthlessness. When he fails to gain the desired recognition, he interprets his failure as a betrayal of those values. Thus Proffy's simultaneous attraction to two contrasting systems of values dooms him to a sequence of betrayals; whichever way he turns, he is bound to trip and fall and betray one set of values.

Proffy's determination to expose the guilt and shame of his "double treachery" is a result of the mechanism of disclosure and exposure that the implied author puts in place. He introduces two poetic systems which, despite their opposition and contradiction, maintain close cooperation and dialogue. One poetic system operates on the constant link between past and present. The child-narrator's version is interspersed with the grown-up Proffy's account as he looks back on the events. Even though it is one and the same person at different points in his life, there is a marked distinction in the point of view, the reflecting consciousness, the intellectual and emotional maturity of the two narrators. The younger Proffy is naturally naive and childlike—though not without self-awareness and insight; the older narrator often reflects on the child's account, comparing it to his present, adult experiences and perceptions from a more mature and comprehending—often wryly amused—point of view.

The two points of view are not necessarily contradictory, but rhetorically, poetically, and intellectually there is a distinct split between them. The interpolations of the adult-narrator into the plot's "present tense," in fact, turn the boy's story into a "past," and yet, the adult narrator's comments corroborate and validate the boy's perceptions, his consciousness, and his insights. The adult narrator says repeatedly, "True, this is how I felt then, as a boy, and this is how I still feel today, as an adult." The implied author embraces and reaffirms the boy's point of view, his sensitivity, and his judgment. Thus the self-exposure—with the concomitant guilt and shame of "double treachery"—is affirmed and sanctioned by the implied author, lending it intensity and irrefutable validity.

Some examples follow of the adult narrator's "eruptions" into the boy's narrative, which turn his "present" into his "past":

[T]he nickname Proffy . . . was short for Professor, which they called me because of my obsession with checking words. (I still love words: I like collecting, arranging, shuffling, reversing, combining them (p. 7). Sitting in my father's chair at his desk, I took down the big dictionary and the encyclopedia . . . (to this day I dare not open an encyclopedia or a dictionary when I am working. If I do—half the day is lost) (pp. 14–15). We would take down the big map of Eretz Israel and its surroundings off the hallway wall, lay it on the mat, and plan how to drive the British out and how to repel the Arab armies. Ben Hur was the commanding officer and I was the brain. Incidentally, even now as I write, I have a wall in my home that is covered with maps. Sometimes I stand in front of these maps, put on my glasses (which are not at all like my father's round ones), and follow the military movements in Bosnia, for example (p. 32). Ben Hur had an unquenchable thirst, in his face, in his movements, in his voice. . . . Not long ago I ran into him while waiting for an El Al flight; he was wearing a dark business suit. . . . He still looked thirsty. . . . Just as I was when I was a child, to this day I am fascinated by such people. But with the passage of the years, I have learned to beware of them. Or, rather, not so much to beware of them as to beware of being fascinated by them (p. 54). I should gird myself with cast-iron patience and keep my eyes open (I still give myself advice like this. I don't take it, though) (p. 77). Both at that time and now as I write, I have always found something affecting and endearing about lost people" (p. 85). Yardena said, "Why don't you have any olives in the house? I don't mean those olives from a jar, silly, not vegetarian olives. Why don't you have any decadent olives, the kind that make you a little tipsy? When you find such olives, bring me some. You can wake me up in the middle of the night for this" (I did find some. Years later. But I was too shy to bring her olives in the middle of the night) (p. 131). "What have I got left? Only a little Bible in Hebrew and English that he gave me. I still have it. . . . Where in the world are you, Stephen Dunlop, my shy enemy?" (p. 145). One of these days I'll get up, pack a small bag and set off for Canterbury myself. I'll look in old telephone directories. I'll check in the churches. I'll rummage in municipal archives. Stephen Dunlop, asthmatic, fond of gossip, a pink cotton-wool Goliath. . . . If, by some miracle, Stephen, this book finds its way into your hands, please drop me a line (p. 146). And what is the obverse side of what has really happened? My mother used to say, "Once, when we bumped into each other in a little fish restaurant in Tiberias, on the shore of the Sea of Galilee, some fourteen years later, I asked Yardena." (pp. 154–55)

These examples of the adult-narrator's incursions into the boy's narrative stratum help reinforce the authenticity and authority of the boy's perceptions and insights. At a distance of three decades or more, the adult narrator endorses the boy's point of view. The two narrators are and are not the same person. By injecting himself into the boy's story, the implied author signals to the reader that it is he who stands behind the exposure of frailties and embarrassments, and, in fact, it is he, the implied author, who is thus exposed. The dialogue between the adult's commentary and the child's account serves a broader aesthetic strategy: revealing his own innermost secrets. And this time, as we have noted, he is willing to bare all.

On the other hand, this poetic strategy also has an additional purpose that works in the opposite direction; it creates the impression that the exposure of betrayal, shame, and vulnerability exhibited by the implied author need not be taken at face value or be seen as proven fact, since it is conveyed through the eyes of a boy-narrator, a confused, frightened youngster, torn between two rival forces. His tender age and naivete (constructing a rocket from defunct appliances to be launched at Buckingham Palace) render his point of view suspect and unreliable, so his self-accusations and his eagerness to assume blame and dishonor should be taken with a grain of salt.

Thus the two points of view employed in the novel seem to work at cross purposes. But, as we shall see, this is not a blunder or a poetic failure; it stems from the implied author's intent to create a compensatory mechanism. And here I would like to address once more the issue of the generic classification of this novel as literature for young adults. It has been argued that using this genre to address an adult readership is confusing and misleading, and that, as a result, the novel is "neither here nor there," in short, a blunder, an error, an embarrassment. But it is none of these. The poetic tactics of using the young adults genre are, in fact, a sophisticated, clever, and success-ful aesthetic device.

In this novel, the designation of young adults literature is achieved mainly through the character of the narrator and some plot elements (a group of kids forming a secret society and indulging in imaginary adven-tures). The reason for this choice of genre is that it fosters a particular view of reality, one that does not correspond very faithfully to the empirical world of the target audience, and hence need not be taken "too seriously." True, every literary text is by nature fictional, but in "regular" realistic fiction (i.e., fiction for adults), there is an attempt to suspend disbelief and accept the reality depicted in the plot as a true and concrete representation that abides by the laws of extra-fictional reality. However, literature for young adults (such as *A Panther in the Basement*) seems to signal to an adult reader from the start that the plot does not necessarily adhere to the laws of extra-fic-tional reality. This literary convention that declares a priori that the reality it portrays is shaken and unreliable serves the purpose of the implied author here, since he sets out to expose shameful and embarrassing truths. Adopting an aesthetic genre that signals the reader to be skeptical about the realism and veracity of the account enables the implied author to disclose and expose more betrayal, guilt, and humiliation on his part. The adult reader, cognizant of the limitations of the genre (and of the unreliability of the young narra-tor), assumes a priori that the account is not absolutely factual or realistic. The young adult genre supplies the implied author with yet another mask, while he is in the process of divesting himself of all other masks and dis-guises. And herein lies the paradox mentioned earlier—the device of using the young adults genre and the presentation of the plot through an unreliable narrator, while allowing the implied author to take off his mask, which at the same time achieves the reverse effect, donning another mask. The two trends find themselves at loggerheads here. Primarily, there is a desire to take off one's mask and mitts, to roll up one's sleeves, to air one's dirty linen and expose the skeleton in one's closet, the painful truth behind the facade. This difficult, excruciating task is mediated by the paradox of the aesthetic strat-egy that the implied author adopts, which provides him with a compensatory mechanism that helps soften the impact of the painful exposure. Hence, it is no blunder or poetic misstep but a conscious and an effective ruse by the implied author.

A Panther in the Basement thus proves not only a quarry and repository of many materials, patterns, and themes of Oz's earlier work, but it also is a bold and fascinating evolutionary stage in the continuum of Oz's fiction, a stage in which he goes further toward revealing the reality behind the mask and exposing its seamy underside.

Add to this the poetic sophistication. First is the utilization of the genre of young adult fiction for two different uses: a recapitulation of earlier materials and themes, on the one hand, and a rhetorical device that tones down the amount of exposure demanded of the implied author, on the other hand. Signaling to the reader that this genre offers less adherence to fact and realism allows the implied author to shed more masks and disguises. Second is the simultaneous use of two poetic mechanisms that contradict each other; while the interpolation of the adult narrator into the narrative of the younger narrator reinforces the veracity and realism of the plot, the use of the genre of young adults literature does exactly the opposite, suggesting to the reader that the created reality is somewhat suspect.

The implied author in *A Panther in the Basement* exhibits not only rare courage in his willingness to expose himself but also considerable poetic sophistication. We should not begrudge him the final ruse, the last mask he dons before he bares all. He has gone far enough, exceedingly far, showing both personal valor and literary sophistication.

However, Oz's recently published book, *The Same Sea*, an astonishing combination of prose-fiction and poetry, proves that the master is capable of going even farther, much farther. His woods are lovely, dark, and deep. And although he has no promises to keep, he certainly has many more miles to go before he sleeps, and miles to go before I sleep.

CHAPTER 6

Essays Are Sometimes Masked Aesthetics:
A Discussion of *Under This Blazing Light*

> *Authors write their books*
> *Which are the essence of their deeds,*
> *Thou shalt not perform other deeds*
> *God commanded the authors*
> *Thus preventing them from committing follies*
> *Such as liberating nations and destroying countries,*
> *Or just acting out of distress*
> *Against the rulers or the I.R.S.*
>   —Nathan Zach, "Books and Deeds,"
>   from *Since I'm in the Neighborhood*

In the introduction, I mention Amos Oz's comment about writing essays on politics and social issues, as well as his thoughts about literary, stylistic, and linguistic matters. I took issue with Oz's claim that his essays were not written by a thinker with a systematic, methodical, and well-formulated theory but rather by a sentimental, easily excitable person reacting tempestuously to events, ideas, and opinions, a Dostoyevskian type who, when he does not contradict himself, repeats his own arguments or trips on his own logic, ending up "treating theoretical issues in a non-theoretical manner" (from the Introduction to *Under This Blazing Light*). Oz concludes his Preface with the following confession. "Perhaps most of the essays in this book are substitutes for stories that I have not managed to write."

Since this chapter deals with that collection of essays, I would like to revisit these claims and testimonies by Oz, since they seem to be of special importance to him. I would, however, like to take issue with some of his statements. I query Oz's assertion that he is too sentimental and easily excitable to be a theoretical, scientific analyst. I maintain that his disclaimer is exaggerated, unjustly censorious, and, frankly, does not hold water. I suspect that Oz himself is aware of the untenability of his assertion. His claim, after all, is uttered not by Amos Oz, the objective polemicist, the keen and careful essayist, but by Amos Oz, the author, by Oz the Wizard of Words, who is both a manipulator and a captive of language, who knows the power of rhetorical tactics to affect the realm of poetry but who also knows how to enlist aesthetic strategies for use in the realm of polemics and essays.

When Oz addresses social and political issues—which may include literature, critiques of other authors, and his own autobiography—he is not given to gushing sentimentality or unbridled enthusiasm. Quite the reverse; when Oz sits down to pen a polemical essay about society, politics, or literature, he shuts off, in fact, every sentiment that may cloud his lucid, rational reasoning. He prevents the fervent "black devilish fire" that inhabits his literary-aesthetic writing from entering the regimented, disciplined territory of his essays. What he does in his polemic writing (to borrow Oz's own terminology) is behave like "a cool, sane, and precise pilot" who is in perfect control of his craft. While engaging in polemic writing, he takes aerial photographs of the situation from a clear, well-lighted, rational observation point and analyzes it with the surgical precision of a lab scientist, drawing incontrovertible conclusions. However, Oz is not oblivious to other avenues and possibilities; he knows that question marks are preferable to exclamation marks, and that reality is complex, often contradictory, and consequently, the solutions too cannot be simple or one-sided. The solutions must take into account the simultaneous presence of incompatible, conflicting interests. But while solutions must be flexible and accommodating, they also must be clear, cogent, and well founded. They must provide for a peaceful, viable coexistence between inveterate rivals, because compromise is always preferable to strife and conflict, more welcome than extremism and fanatical entrenchment. The proper, wise approach to reality is always one of sober rationality and levelheadedness, one that recognizes emotion and sentiment yet does not allow them to take over.

There is, then, a marked difference between Oz's polemical-theoretical essays (see his books *Heaven's Silence: Agnon Wonders about God*, and *A Story Begins*, both literary studies) and his aesthetic, poetic, "purely" literary writing, where the black devilish fire rages, emotions run high, and hatred, animosity, rampant eroticism, and frustrated, shameful sexuality are the themes and material of the texts.

Oz's stories and novels, however, are not made up only of gushing emotions, agony, shame, and guilt that know no moderation; his poetic writing also contains a measure of restraint and sober rationality, an attempt to tame and control the rebellious, tumultuous element. Here are some of the more conspicuous representatives of reason and rationality in Oz's works: Michael Gonen, in *My Michael*; Srulik, the kibbutz secretary, in *A Perfect Peace*; Etkin, the spokesman of the pioneers' generation, in "Nomads and Viper"; Dr. Hans Kipniss, in *The Hill of the Evil Council*; Dr. Nussbaum, in "Yearnings"; Yossef Yarden, in "Strange Fire"; the father, in *A Panther in the Basement*; and Theo, in *Do Not Call it a Night*. These and other rational characters shy away from romanticism and wayward sentimentality, and yet they are incapable of contending with the strange fire, with the "panting, hairy element" (as Dr. Nussbaum calls it in the story "Yearnings"), with the tenebrous desires that lurk underneath the surface.

And here we return to Oz's polemic, philosophical writing. Here the door is barred against the black, murky devilish fire. Here the howling of rampant desire is not heard. The writing style is restrained, tempered, refined. The author seems to don a white lab jacket and examine the issue (whether political, social, ideological, or aesthetic) in a cool and calculated manner, with concentration, objectivity, and a touch of healthy skepticism. The tone is crisp, fluent, and unimpassioned, and the reasoning always takes into account the complex, intricate nature of the reality under examination.

Thus various possible avenues are examined and followed to their inevitable corollaries. But one thing is always borne in mind: that absolute justice, though theoretically much desired, is not viable in reality. The only acceptable option is compromise, tolerant, considerate, accommodating coexistence reached through negotiation, detente, and mutual concessions. This conciliatory, sane, and sober approach is consistently applied by Oz throughout his essays.

In *Under This Blazing Light*, Oz addresses four intellectual topics: politics, society, literature, and autobiography. In the first section, which deals with literature, authors, criticism, and literary scholarship, Oz discusses the relationship between the world of literature and the reality that serves as a breeding ground for it. In that chapter, he also deals with the Hebrew language, both high-flown and colloquial, and with the different literary styles that go with each usage. He also talks about the passionate energy of Berdichevsky's fiction, an author with whom Oz has had a long, enthusiastic "correspondence" (which proves, by the way, how fruitful and seminal poetic influence can be when it is carried out conscientiously and in the right proportion; it is by no means "servile imitation," as Achad Ha'am [Zionist thinker Asher Zvi Ginzberg] phrased it). The same chapter also includes Oz's commentary on pioneering Hebrew novelist Yosef Hayyim Brenner, and on the agonized, tormented truths that his stories reveal, as well as the complexity and twisted irony that characterize S. Y. Agnon's fiction. Oz also distinguishes between the fervent jingoistic ideology and the rich aesthetic quality of Uri Zvi Grinberg's poetry. Other essays discuss the first volume of Gershon Shaked's survey of literary history, *Hebrew Fiction 1880–1970*, the intricate and intriguing narrative technique of Emily Bronte's *Wuthering Heights*, and finally, the way in which first-rate literature transforms ugliness, pain, and madness into refined, subtle, poetic beauty.

The second section of the book is entitled "The Israeli Situation 1967– 1987." Most of the essays here deal with the social and political dilemma, both tortuous and painful, in which Israel has found itself since June 5, 1967 (perhaps, to some extent, even before that date): occupation versus with- drawal; Israelis versus Palestinians; the possible establishment of a sovereign Palestinian state; domination of another people; ancient fear, hatred, and hope; chances and risks of peace; the economic, cultural, and ethnic polariza- tion inside Israeli society, and its link to the protracted occupation, messianic sentiments, and "Holy" sites; the need to empathize with the other's suffer- ing, "Us" versus "Them," and the inane slogan, "The whole world is against us," and the isolation it engenders; our just claims versus their just claims; how to put an end to the cycle of iniquity and retaliation and bring about hope and prosperity to the region; and reexamination of the concept of "the chosen people" with its exclusionary and racial implications.

Oz does not shy away from controversial, contentious questions and often calls for a reevaluation the old, nationalistic, Zionist slogans and for the slaughter of sacred cows. His analysis is always marked by cogent, rational thinking and by tolerance, humanity, and acknowledgment of the simul- taneous existence of contradictory forces within society. He strives to reach a compromise, a reconciliation, a common ground that will allow one side's just claim to coexist with the other's equally just claim. Oz recognizes the legitimacy of the Jewish demand for an ancestral home and the right of the Jewish people to live securely and peacefully in that part of the world. But that demand and that right does not negate or eliminate the right of the Palestinian people to live independently on their land, in the shade of their fig and olive trees. As in the Talmudic tractate dealing with two people claiming ownership of one prayer shawl, the solution should be: partition. Only a compromise can guarantee peaceful existence in the Middle East.

The third section of the book is entitled, "Socialism, Socialists, Kib- butz, and Kibbutz Members." If one couples this title with Oz's fundamental belief in tolerance, moderation, and compromise (which should not, however, come at the expense of principles), one will find, in a nutshell, the contents of the entire section, its trend of thought and conclusions. Oz's basic approach to socialism and to the kibbutz as its existential manifestation reflects his general philosophy, which always takes into account the complexity of reality, the need for rationality and flexibility, and the knowledge that demands for absolute justice can lead to iniquity and death. The only viable, tenable socialism is a flexible, adaptable socialism that eschews naive, simplistic, and facile solutions, a socialism that strives for—and is capable of—rectifying social and human wrongs better than any other social and human systems, such as unchecked capitalism or dictatorship. Socialism as perceived here is a social and human structure that has the potential to cause less damage and societal ills than rival systems that purport to accord rights and opportunities to one and all yet cater essentially to the strong, able, and aggressive, abandoning the weak, the backward, and the underprivileged. Humanistic, adaptable socialism has no room for such discrimination and is, therefore, the preferred social system.

The kibbutz as a human and social form of living realizes this preferred social system. It provides shelter, security, and hope for the future. Thus the kibbutz accords well with Amos Oz's taste and temperament. The fact that, for certain reasons, he has elected to live outside of the kibbutz in recent years is not relevant. The kibbutz is a decent, honest way of life, but not because it has eradicated evil, ugliness, and human suffering. That it has certainly not. But for all its imperfections and failings, the kibbutz—in Oz's opinion—is still the favored way of life, because it is more attentive to the individual's need, distress, and suffering. On the kibbutz, there are no homeless individuals rummaging for food in garbage pails; members are cared for even when they are old and decrepit, hence, the kibbutz and socialism. It has been said that a socialist is someone who is not a villain. Amos Oz is such a socialist.

The fourth section of the book is entitled "Where I Come From." Here Amos Oz presents his calling card and provides a biographical sketch, marked by restraint and moderation and not overly revelatory. The account is sensitive, moving, and above all witty. It is a snapshot—not too colorful at that—for an identity card, a peek into the reservoir of Oz's personal feelings, into a couple of corners of the cupboard where his memories are stored. But it also is a polite and kind invitation to a rendezvous with Amos Oz's aesthetic portrait, with his artistic credo, with the poetic mechanism at the core of his writing. In short, a few personal things that Amos Oz permits Amos Oz to say in public about Amos Oz. But before he opens the door, before the curtain rises, he takes a few security measures, modest but efficient. Amos Oz invites us in, and he is a gracious host, allowing us into the living room and the kitchen and perhaps into the little porch, but never beyond. The rest is out of bounds. Our host is courteous and civil, but he also keeps his distance. The guests may be welcome but only for a brief, cursory visit.

What can one glimpse through a door partially open reveal? A few fleeting pictures from Oz's childhood, a childhood replete with thrilling action movies populated by treacherous villains, on the one hand, and heroic, handsome, generous men, on the other hand. In those movies, the heroes always triumph over the marauding hordes that threaten to annihilate them. In the universe dominated by Tarzan and Flash Gordon (very familiar to me from my own childhood), justice always prevails in the end. The courageous few always have the upper hand.

What else can we see through the chink that Amos Oz opens for us with such calculated restraint? His memories of the British Mandate in Palestine, the struggle of the Zionist underground, or the adventure-filled games that took their inspiration from action films and from the struggle against "perfidious Albion"? These memories were later translated into some of Oz's literary texts, such as *Soumchi*, *A Panther in the Basement*, *The Hill of the Evil Council*, "Mr. Levi," "Yearnings," and to some extent, *My Michael*. These fleeting snapshots from Oz's childhood seem like a copy of one single picture, repeatedly replicated and used over and over again, a picture depicting a clear, well-lighted, and very sane world, a fair, just, and orderly world fighting for its survival against the forces of darkness, hatred, and iniquity. The good and happy few are locked in a mortal battle against savage, evil, marauding hordes. This basic dichotomy can be descried across the landscape of Oz's fiction with the rival forces vying for supremacy but also quite often migrating, merging, and hesitantly inching their way toward reconciliation.

What else of Oz's biography can be espied through this narrow peephole? The figure of Oz's father, the ardent lover of seventeen languages and literatures, whose sensitive and moving reflection can be found in the character of the father in *A Panther in the Basement*. To be sure, it is only a partial, stylized, highly polished rendition of the father's image. Only Amos Oz can know how the portrait of the real father relates to the fictional one.

In this section of the book, one also sees glimpses of Jerusalem several decades later, after the occupation, and it is a very different city—still cherished, shrouded in darkness, redolent of ancient secrets and otherworldly mystique, and yet different, alienated, minatory, conniving, deceptive, and hostile.

Through a door that is ajar, we are allowed to peek into Amos Oz's writing laboratory, into the "womb" where his stories germinate, where they begin to develop from an embryonic spark, a mere gleam. We get a glimpse of the milieu where Oz walks gingerly, guardedly, alert, and circumspect, like (his phrase) a gangster on a night of long knives. But he also walks with eyes half shut, as if in a reverie.

Through all of these pictures that Oz briefly invites us to glance at, one can discern that same fundamental theme that runs like a mother lode at the basis of all of Oz's fiction, that vein that touches the black devilish fire of turbulent desire, on the one hand, and cool, sober rationality, on the other hand. Much of the tension generated by Oz's fiction stems from the eternal confrontation between fire and ice, between savage and sinister forces, and between sane and sober reason.

Ostensibly, the four sections that comprise the book are discrete and unrelated, randomly put together in one volume. But, in fact, these various and disparate sections reflect the very complex portrait of Amos Oz, the writer, the essayist, the artist, and the thinker, a man of keen political sense, well anchored in reality, sensitive and attentive to social complaints, a cautious socialist, a chronicler of powerful impulses and desires, a seeker of tolerance and rational solutions, a man who loves his country passionately and unconditionally yet would not let his love deprive others of freedom and happiness, a man who recognizes that fiction cannot provide a recipe for living, since in real life a clash of just causes leads to great misery. In reality, it is important to put out the black devilish fire and quell the evil spirits, to build a bridge between the warring sides, to find a middle ground and accept the other's right to exist.

Oz concludes the Preface (which, in the Hebrew edition, also is printed on the back of the book) by saying, "Perhaps most of the essays in this book are substitutes for stories that I have not managed to write." Well, as I said earlier, I beg to differ. This is not true. The matters discussed in this book of essays are not substitutes for unwritten stories. They are stories that are written again and again. The essays are the excellent and intelligent stories that have been written and are still being written by an author who also is a philosopher, an intellectual, and a thinker who knows full well that when one migrates from one literary republic to another—let alone from the poetic domain to actual reality—one must not only write differently but think differently. And one has to act differently: to avoid extremism at all costs; to enlist all of the powers of reason, patience, and tolerance; to reject all claims to absolute justice; and to strive for reconciliation and coexistence. Oz's sensitive and intelligent story in his book of essays should, perhaps, be read by all of those who dictate our lives—they certainly could learn a thing or two.

CHAPTER 7

Some Rest at Last. Tracing a Literary Motif: The Motif of the Picture in *A Perfect Peace* and Beyond

True ease in writing comes from art, not chance,
And those move easiest who have learned to dance.
—Alexander Pope, *An Essay on Criticism,*

And your hands sing from the wall like the murmur of greenish moss.
—David Avidan, *The Streets Soar Slowly*

T he term *motif* has many connotations and uses. It is borrowed from music, but in literary discussions it has acquired several different meanings. A motif can be "a simple plot structure, often archetypal, found in various works and creating a thematic link between those works and the national literature that gave rise to them. The motif of 'Noah's Ark' or 'Sibling Rivalry,' for example, appears in legends that are far apart both in time and place. The study of such motifs is mostly the task of folklorists and scholars of folk tales."[1]

However, literary scholar Boris Tomashevsky, one of the founders of Russian formalism, though accepting the folklorists' usage of the term, defines motif differently, as a poetic-textual phenomenon. To him, motif is the theme embedded in the smallest textual-semantic unit, thus each sentence, as well as each discrete syntactical unit, has a motif.[2]

The more accepted definition of motif, however, is the one that sees it as a textual element or a textual pattern—word, idea, picture, and so on—which recurs throughout a given literary text, whether a novel, a novella, a drama, a poem, or an essay—easily recognizable and traceable.[3] Examples include the motif of the key in S. Y. Agnon's *A Guest for the Night* or the motif of the tree, with all of its metonymic ramifications—trunk, branch, bough, fruit, and so on—in Bialik's poem "A Falling Twig."

The multiple meanings and uses of the term *motif* can be confusing and misleading, especially when used technically by scholars and scientists. And literature is a science, a systematic investigation that makes use of methodology and discipline and derives from a theory that must be either substantiated or refuted. As Plato and Aristotle stated thousands of years ago, a science, whether biology, physics, history, or literature, may be considered so if it satisfies the principal condition of disciplinary, regimented, systematic inquiry. The humanities should therefore be accorded their rightful place in the pantheon of science.[4]

We mentioned the confusion surrounding the term *motif*. As far as Tomashevsly's definition is concerned, it was mostly in use by the Russian formalists, whereas the folklorists tended to use the term in a denotative and an unambiguous manner when it came to their field of investigation. Thus the definition of "motif" cited earlier is generally accepted in literary studies. Accordingly, a motif is any element, or pattern (a pattern is based on at least two textual elements having a reciprocal relationship), that is repeatedly used in the text to create a "comprehensive" significance that goes beyond the constituent components. A motif, then, is a reservoir of disparate components strewn along the continuum of a given text, each of which reflects, in its unique way, the pattern and basic ideas of the overall motif. Take, for instance, the father motif in *My Michael*. One component of the motif relates to Hannah's father, another to Michael's father, and yet another points to an analogy between Michael Gonen and Hannah's late father (coupled with an allusion to Mazal, the husband in S. Y. Agnon's story "In the Prime of Her Life"). Then there is a further evocation of the father image in Bialik's poem "Orphanhood." Each element represents a unique facet of the father image, while the father, as a distinct motif, as a semantic-symbolic concept, is lifted from the continuous progression of the text to assume a more comprehensive significance and identity; the sum total is greater and more meaningful than the cumulative volume of the individual components.[5]

A motif is a system of textual signs coalescing around a fundamental significance, and as in every system, here too are two aspects determined and dictated by the point of view used for observing the entire system. From a synchronic point of view, all of the elements are considered simultaneously, *en bloc*, thus yielding a comprehensive, complete meaning of the motif. From a diachronic point of view, all of the elements of the motif are examined successively, as they are dynamically distributed through the text. In fact, these are two kinds of dynamics: thematic dynamics, which records the thematic changes in the components of the motif while they are deployed throughout the text (e.g., the transition from one representation of the father image to another that reflects an analogy between Michael and Hannah's late father, and then the allusion to the father in Bialik's poem, etc.), and compositional dynamics, which is an examination of the deployment of the components throughout the text: Are they crowded together, or few and far between? Do they come singly or in clusters? Where in the text do they aggregate, and where is their presence scarcer?

Motifs can be found in all literary genres: poetry, fiction, drama, and essays. They are not confined to any particular form, nor are they more prevalent. Yet it is commonly supposed that motifs are rifer in fiction, due to its textual volume and narrative scope, which allow easier deployment and distribution of the components of the motif throughout the text. But there is something in the aesthetic pattern of the motif that is more natural to poetry, at least as it is traditionally perceived. Here it is not just a question of absorption and "storage" of motifs but of the fundamental aesthetic quality of poetry—which is made up of a continuum of components, each possessing a unique significance; it is the cumulative effect that endows a motif with an unmistakable semantic-aesthetic quality.

Moreover, the fact that the poetic import of a motif is produced simultaneously—diachronically and synchronically—contributes to the semantic-aesthetic density exhibited in the poetic motif, for the poetic text is, by nature, concise, compact, and highly charged. Call it a high-protein literary diet.

In modern Western literature, which includes Israeli–Hebrew literature, the quondam differences between poetry and fiction—that were generally accepted until the 1920s—are no longer distinct and clear-cut. Fiction has seen the introduction of the "stream of consciousness" technique, which contains a strong element of aesthetic-semantic density, metaphoric complexity, and rich, multifarious poetic volume, in short, properties traditionally associated with poetry and its concomitant aesthetic patterns. A few examples that come to mind in this context are James Joyce, William Faulkner, Virginia Woolf, Marcel Proust, and Dorothy Richardson; and, in Hebrew literature, U. N. Gnessin, certain sections of the work of S. Yizhar and, to some extent, Amalia Kahana-Carmon.

On the other hand, the second and third decades of the twentieth century gave rise to the Anglo-American imagistic movement, with poets such as the early Ezra Pound, Amy Lowell, Richard Aldington, Hilda Doolittle, and e. e. cummings, as well as to the Russian-Acmeist school that includes Osip Mandelstam, Anna Akhmatova, and Nikolai Gumilev. These two schools of poetic aesthetics, each in its own way, strove for minimalism in poetry, for the creation of a simple, sometimes simplistic, concise, emaciated poetic language. Even the themes of imagistic poetry are marked by restraint, moderation, and rhetorical stylization. These schools of poetry followed the model of the Japanese Haiku, with its polished, compact simplicity. Thus the traditional demarcation lines that used to separate prose from poetry became blurred, and the two previously distinct modes were assimilated.

To be sure, some poetry and some prose still adhered to traditional aesthetic patterns, but there were other developments as well, such as postmodernism, which opted for an austere linguistic mode and did not shy away from colloquial, substandard language and deliberate, slipshod syntax. Conversely, poetry has proven itself capable of shedding its traditional semantic-aesthetic density, and it makes do with narrower, leaner, single-layered language.

Still, poetry has retained some of its old reputation for high density and richness of semantic-aesthetic and linguistic patterns. Even during years when eminent poets adopted an austere, monastic style, dense and "high-protein" poems were still being written. And, to this day, semantic-aesthetic density is perceived as the hallmark of traditional poetry, as well as of the literary motif, and the use of motifs in a literary text is associated with poetic properties. Hence, filling a text with a thick network of motifs lends it an aura of denseness, a multiplicity of layers, and complexity.

And here we return to Amos Oz's fiction and to the concentration of motifs that characterizes his texts. To be sure, clusters or strata of motifs are not a monopoly of Amos Oz's fiction. The writings of A. B. Yehoshua, Aharon Appelfeld, and Amalia Kahana-Carmon, as well as Agnon, Gnessin, and Berdichevsky, are replete with exquisite and elaborate motifs. But here we deal exclusively with Oz's fiction.

Now I would like to discuss not abstract generalization, but one particular text by Amos Oz; even this analysis will be far from exhaustive but, rather like a peephole, will allow us to glimpse the most prominent components of the text. I will trace one particular motif in one work by Oz and, while delving into the text, I will examine some of its strata and perhaps other aspects of their immediate environment.

In earlier chapters, I discussed some of the salient motifs of Oz's texts, such as the motif of eyes, sight, and the figurine of the blind predator in *To Know a Woman*; the motif of betrayal in *A Panther in the Basement*, and in many other Oz texts; the motif of the blue dress, or blue drape, or shutter, identified with frustrated, agonizing women; the espionage motif, identified and associated with many male protagonists in Oz's fiction; and the recurrent motif of clear, sane rationality as it clashes with the "panting, hairy element," which is the destructive, rebellious force of darkness. This dichotomy often is translated into a bitter battle between a rational, reality-based man and a romantic, frustrated, anguished woman who feels trapped and confined in the man's reality and therefore tries to escape to a world of reverie, dream, and fantasy.

I will not catalogue the many motifs that populate Oz's fiction. My focus is rather a minor, secondary motif, a seemingly marginal, insignificant one, yet a closer analysis will reveal its cardinal importance to the understanding of the work. Peeping through this keyhole affords an unexpected, unimagined vista.

I am talking about the motif of the picture in *A Perfect Peace*. I have already remarked that the novel concludes on a much more conciliatory note than it opens. True, there are no perfect solutions, but the questions are less pressing than they appeared to be at the beginning. The raging storms have subsided and no longer threaten to shatter the world. In the words of Srulik, the new secretary of the kibbutz and a representative of the intermediary generation that supplanted the pioneers and "conquerors of Canaan,"

Pain is an existential fact, but in spite of all this, it is clear to me that we can still accomplish a couple of things here. (p. 381)

The novel that opens with a thirst for change, for transformation— "One day a man may just pick up and walk out. What he leaves behind stays behind. What's left behind has nothing to stare at but his back" (p. 7)—ends with a sane and sober compromise, in a conciliatory, minor key. Even though some of the reasons and motives for this compromise will forever remain inscrutable and unexplained, it is still a much-desired compromise, a hard-earned peace. As Srulik notes in his journal, "There is certainly room for this too, though why I'm not sure" (p. 381).

There is a slow transformation in the novel from a state of sharp polarity to a state of detente or hesitant rapprochement. We see, on the one hand, the decline of Yolek Lifshitz, the old secretary of the kibbutz, a representative of the old pioneering generation, whose temperament and personality bespeak *sturm und drang*, truculence, and implacability. And, on the other hand, the parallel ascendency of Srulik, the new secretary who represents the second generation, whose modus operandi is marked by moderation, reasoned consideration, patience, and tolerance. True, Srulik's personality lacks the wit, keen intellect, zest, and ardor of his predecessor, but he ushers in a new era of appeasement, peace, and compromise.

This seesaw motion, from one pole to the other, can be discerned also in the character of Hava, Yolek Lifshitz's morose and bitter wife, who is strongly reminiscent of Fruma Rominov, the venomous, spiteful wife in the novel *Elsewhere, Perhaps*. Toward the end of *A Perfect Peace*, Hava no longer refers to her daughter-in-law as "retarded," but begins to see in her a likeable "absent-mindedness," something she can view favorably and sympathetically.

Other changes and transformations take place toward the denouement of the novel, all attesting to a movement away from the tempestuous, restless, haunted sentiments of the outset and toward an attempt at accommodation and reconciliation. There is an evolutionary progression throughout the novel that corresponds to the thematic and conceptual development. This basic movement that dictates the direction and progression of the novel finds its correlative in the thematic and compositional dynamics of the motif of the picture. The motif of the picture or the painting in *A Perfect Peace* is based on a widespread system of components that is ramified throughout the novel. One of the clusters of images that make up this motif centers around several allusions to a picture hanging on the wall of Rimona Vogel (her maiden name, which means "bird") and Yonatan Lifshitz:

> [E]ven the sole picture in the room was quiet: in it a dark bird was seen perched on a red brick fence. A diagonal shaft of sunlight shamelessly pierced the surrounding fog and shadow like a golden spear, creating a nimbus of light far away from the weary looking bird whose bill, he discovered upon further examination, was slightly, thirstily agape, its eyes closed. (p. 102)

The fact that this picture recurs several times throughout the text draws the reader's attention to it and points to the unifying significance of this cluster that forms one single motif.

Another fact should be noted in this context; the first allusion and the second allusion to the picture—comprising the first two components of the painting—are given from Azaria Gitlin's point of view, as he observes the bird, its eyes closed and its bill thirstily agape. This fact is significant because of Azaria's important function in the plot as the "other," the stranger, the interloper—an exilic Jew, who hails from afar, from the darkness of the Diaspora— but it also is important because of the symbolic, metaphoric elements exhibited in the motif. There is a conspicuous, blatant sexual element in the picture; the diagonal shaft of sunlight is not only compared to a piercing spear—an obvious phallic symbol—it also is associated with shame—"shamelessly pierced"; the sexual context harks back to the story of Adam and Eve in *Genesis*, where it is written that before they ate the fruit of the tree of knowledge, they were naked "and were not ashamed." But when they acquired knowledge (in the erotic sense as well) and were aware of their sexuality, they were ashamed of their nakedness. The shaft of light that pierces the air like an erotic spear brings to mind Rimona's daydreams about darkest Africa, where a spear pierces the muscular body of a gnu. Similarly, the use of the verb "nakav" (pierced, penetrated with its close association to "nekeva," meaning female) reinforces the sexual connotation of the picture. The same effect is achieved by the open bill of the bird, which affirms the traditional metaphoric link between eating and copulation. In addition, the closed eyes of the bird seem to emphasize the passive role of the female during lovemaking.

The fact that the image evokes profound and painful sexual frustration is a comment on the crisis in the marriage of Rimona and Yonatan. Profound sexual frustration also is the unhappy lot of Azaria Gitlin at the time when he lives alone on the kibbutz, before he insinuated himself into Yonatan's and Rimona's life and became the third side in that triangle. Azaria is analogous to Benjamin Trotsky, who was in love with Yolek's wife, Hava, and in all probability, also was her lover, perhaps even Yonatan's real father. This is a repetition of the same pattern we have encountered before: a family unit comprising two men and a woman. When Azaria goes back to his solitary room after visiting Rimona's and Yoni's room with its pretense of cozy, fulfilled, conjugal bliss, the memory of that picture on the wall lingers with him:

> On his way back to his shack, Azaria thought of the picture that hung in Yonatan and Rimona's room, the dark, thirsty bird on the brick wall, the fog and the shadows, the diagonal shaft of sunlight, and the flaming wound in one of the bricks in the lower corner of the picture. So I'm invited back some other day to chat and play music and chess. (p. 112)

Again, the blatant sexuality is unmistakable. Added to this is the mention of chess which, in Oz's fiction, as discussed earlier, often is a symbol of an erotic power struggle between two males. Thus the sexual overtones of the painting function as a metaphoric crossroads of several paths of plot and theme: the sexual deprivation experienced by both Yonatan and Azaria (as well as by Rimona), Yonatan's departure, which is motivated, at least partially, by that sense of deprivation (and in this respect the bird symbolizes flight and wandering), and Azaria's injection into Yoni's and Rimona's family unit, which is analogous to the piercing shaft of sunlight depicted in the picture.

Moreover, the dreary, autumnal atmosphere of the picture, the thwarted attempt of the bird to flee its predicament, and the obvious yearning for salvation can aptly describe the yearning and agony that grip both Yoni and Rimona at the beginning of the novel. Yonatan dreams of extricating himself from the constricting provincial environment of the kibbutz, of leaving behind the dullness, the insipidity and monotony that is the bane of his existence there, and of going off to faraway places, to foreign cities that beckon him from beyond the horizon. Those anonymous, alien cities remind him that he who is left behind is abandoned, and he who is late will miss everything.

Rimona, too, trapped as she is in her domestic, banal existence, indulges in fantasies of a distant, darkest Africa. She is fascinated by the magic of sun-baked Chad, whose mystic call she seems to hear, and whose wondrous beaches promise her the fulfillment of her heart's desire.

It is not surprising that it is Azaria, the intruding stranger, through whose consciousness we first observe the picture on the wall of Yoni's and Rimona's kibbutz room, a picture replete with symbols of their frustration, deprivation, yearning, and craving.

As for Azaria himself, he is like that shaft of sunlight in the picture that pierces and penetrates and cuts like a jagged arrow, destroying the ostensible peace that surrounds the bird with the fervidly shut eyes. Azaria's incursion into the life of the kibbutz and his simultaneous intrusion into Yoni's and Rimona's married life demonstrate the flimsy and deceptive atmosphere of smugness and somnolence, the misleading, specious sense of security, peace, and serenity that prevailed in those two environments.

Azaria's first appearance on the kibbutz is an act of circumspection, a gingerly, sneaky infiltration. It later gathers momentum, becoming forceful, strident, and obtrusive. His very presence in the kibbutz causes unrest, discomfort, and nervous spasms. His garish, cheap, foreign clothes, his gushing, compulsive volubility, ridiculous and pathetic at the same time, especially in a place where heavy, brooding silence is a badge of honor, and above all, his exaggerated manners, which smack of cheap comedy and vulgarity, all elicit reactions of derision and amazement that are soon translated into disgust.

Azaria, who hails from the Diaspora and injects himself into the brightly lit, summery kibbutz environment, is redolent of that musty, moldy odor that native-born Israelis used to find repulsive and objectionable; his personality projects a certain furtive abjectness, a smarmy, conniving, insincere courtesy that makes him look pathetic and ludicrous and barely masks an innate crassness and vulgarity. In sum, from a Sabra's point of view, Azaria Gitlin embodies the stereotype of the exilic, ghetto Jew, the one who is always out to trick and bamboozle the gentiles. He is reminiscent of Zacharia-Siegfried Berger in *Elsewhere, Perhaps* and evokes the image of the Jew in anti-Semitic and Nazi propaganda.

True, the spear that pierces the picture in Rimona's and Yoni's room is a shaft of light, in other words quite the opposite of the intruding dark force represented by Azaria. But a perfect analogy is not required here, only a parallel between the characters and their actions and reflections in the motif under discussion. Just as the frustrations and yearnings of Yoni and Rimona are metaphorically expressed by the languorous bird with its mouth thirstily open and its eyes closed, so the incursion of Azaria Gitlin into the world of Yoni and Rimona—and the kibbutz—is metaphorically reflected in the ray of light that pierces the picture like a spear.

In her daydreams, Rimona travels to sun-baked Africa, surrendering to the mystique of Chad, where she envisages "a spear piercing a gnu" (p. 176). Thus Azaria's intrusion into her world, represented by the metaphor of the spear in the picture, seems to be a fulfillment of Rimona's desire for the penetrating spear in her African fantasy. And here we encounter another component of the picture motif that runs through the text of *A Perfect Peace*. Here too the dominant image is incursion, a forceful invasion, an entry of a foreign element from outside:

> On the shelf stood a framed gray snapshot of Rimona and Yoni on their honeymoon in the Judean Desert. . . . It's odd, he thought, but I never noticed that there's someone else in that photograph: behind Rimona is a hairy leg in shorts and paratrooper boots. (p. 365)

This is not a painting but a photograph, which makes the motif of the picture even more complex and intricate. This image too—the photograph—is represented from Azaria's point of view. Here too we have a foreign element invading a serene, self-contained world and upsetting its surface tranquility. Like the "diagonal shaft of sunlight" piercing the picture, the crude, hairy leg encroaches on Yoni's and Rimona's honeymoon photograph, threatening to undermine their union.

Azaria's invasion into the sunny, summery world of the kibbutz later finds a metaphoric echo in another element of the picture motif. When he begins to settle in the kibbutz territory (not as a full-fledged member as yet, only as a temporary worker—but his presence is undeniable and strongly felt), after having achieved a certain success with the repair of a disabled tractor, Azaria decides to decorate the walls of the rundown garage where he works:

> In the end, he clipped a large, colored photograph of the Minister of Welfare from an illustrated magazine and hung it on the garage wall. From that morning on, plump-cheeked and jovial, Dr. Burg would look down on Yonatan and Azaria at their work, with benevolent self-satisfaction. (p. 113)

Dr. Joseph Burg, Minister of Welfare at the time (and before that, Minister of Religious Affairs), is the most typical exemplar of "exilic" Jewry so foreign and antagonistic to the Sabra, kibbutz-grown Israelis. Dr. Burg, with his vast erudition, his cultural and linguistic versatility, and his Judaic scholarship, could not be further from the kibbutz members, in their undershirts and shorts, who spend their days in alfalfa and barley fields, or rummaging in the innards of heavy agricultural machinery. For Azaria to pin the picture of Dr. Burg on the wall of the garage is to underscore his foreignness and alienation from the environment in which he wishes to strike roots.

However, it is Azaria's injection into kibbutz society that is the prime mover of the plot; it dictates the main direction and progression of the action. The components of the picture motif serve as metaphors for the main characters—Rimona and Yonatan—and for the main theme: the changes that take place in the kibbutz society as a result of their tolerant acceptance of that strange bird that nestles in their midst. Through the analysis of the picture motif, we can identify the most significant aspects of theme and plot in the novel.

In *A Perfect Peace*, as in other Oz stories, there is a gradual progression from a bitter enmity between warring forces toward a hesitant truce, perhaps even a reconciliation. This moderating trend on the plot level is reflected also in some of the elements in the picture motif. The portrait of Dr. Burg, which Azaria hangs in the garage, is described as "plump-cheeked, jovial, and self-satisfied"—not exactly the traditional, exilic Jew's characteristics as perceived by the Israeli Sabra. (In fact, many of the kibbutz members hail from the same Diaspora; people like Yolek Lifshitz are not ignorant of Jewish lore but, by coming to live in Israel and by building the kibbutz society, they have turned their backs on stereotypical Jewish traits.)

The "exileness" embodied in Dr. Burg's jovial countenance is different from the "exileness" that Azaria Gitlin exudes at the beginning of the novel.

It is less foreign and less inimical to the "blazing sun" of the kibbutz environment. Thus the slow progression from sharp contrasts and rivalry toward acceptance and coexistence is, metaphorically, conveyed through one of the elements of the picture motif.

The gradual movement toward moderation that takes place on two levels simultaneously—in the characters and in the plot—reaches its climax toward the denouement: Yoni comes back from afar (just as Azaria came on the scene from afar) and resumes his place in kibbutz society (just as Azaria has, in the meantime, found his niche in kibbutz society); Yoni returns to conjugal life with Rimona, a setup that now includes Azaria as well. This matrimonial triangle proves stable and satisfactory, just like the rotund, contented, benevolent face of Dr. Burg. Each partner in the triangle finds his or her fulfillment in the arrangement: Rimona finds in Yoni the rough-hewn virility that excites and rouses her, and from Azaria she receives the consideration, attentiveness, and gentleness that responds to the shy, introverted, and enigmatic side of her personality. Azaria, in the meantime, has bolstered his status in the kibbutz through his familial connection to Rimona and Yoni. His self-image has improved considerably, and he has found sexual gratification. And what about Yoni? What does he gain from the transition from couple to triad? He too benefits from this unorthodox arrangement. To his disappointment and chagrin, he has come to the conclusion that his dreams were several sizes too large for him. Migration to large cities that beckoned to him from the dark, with their suave and elegant people who disappear discreetly into the elevators of high-rises, all of this is simply not for him. His thirst for adventure takes him only as far as the army camp in the southern Sinai, to a desert camp situated in the middle of a windswept, desiccated wasteland, where bundles of dried thorns are swept by dust devils. Even legendary Petra is out of reach for him. A return to the familiar circles of kibbutz and married life—in a modified, unconventional framework within the "square" kibbutz environment—is what does it for Yoni. Thus he is able to effect a rebellion on a modest, limited scale. His initial wanderlust and thirst for adventure end with a recognition of his limitations.

The novel ends with a modus vivendi, with a hesitant accommodation, with an acceptance of rival forces. This trend, strangely enough, is conveyed through an analogy between Yoni and Azaria. Azaria, it will be remembered, "with great zeal and energy, undertook to reorganize the tool shed by arranging the work tools in logical order (p. 12). Toward the end of the novel, we see Yoni doing the same thing when he stays with the eccentric geologist-philosopher Tlalim at the edge of the army camp in Sinai. "[Yoni] cleaned up the trailer. He scrubbed the theodolites" (p. 350). It also is said about

Yoni that he has become the old man's "armor-bearer," a function that Azaria fulfilled earlier with Yoni and Udi.

In fact, the analogy between Yoni and Azaria should not come as a surprise; it prepares the way—and the heart—for the tripartite marriage that epitomizes the mutual assimilation of opposites. At the end of the novel, the kibbutz society, that quintessential representative of Israeliness, extends a hand to Azaria, the alien, exilic Other, and it is willing to gather him into its ranks. In his essay, "The Kibbutz at the Present Time," Amos Oz addresses this subtle transformation that has taken place in kibbutz society:

> I am pleased to see how the kibbutz has learned to react calmly, pa-
> tiently, almost surreptitiously, to exceptions and oddities, to altered
> norms, to changing times and tastes, as if it has whispered to itself, "So
> be it for the time being; now let's wait and see." (*Under This Blazing
> Light*, p. 182)

The metaphor Oz uses in this context is of a splinter that pierces the flesh, and the flesh does not reject it but rather grows back over it and covers it up. This is, in a nutshell, what happens in *A Perfect Peace*, and this is the essence of the metaphoric significance of the picture motif: the secret of accommodation, acceptance, and tolerance; the wisdom of embracing the Other, the different; the survival instinct that mandates the rejection of extremes and the movement toward wholeness and unity.

The kibbutz society that has expelled Benjamin Trotsky—Hava Lifshitz's rejected lover, who later became a hotel magnate in Miami and may or may not have been Yoni's biological father—is now capable of absorbing the interloper and misfit Azaria. Perhaps the difference between Trotsky and Azaria lies in the fact that the former elected to use a gun—that missed its target—while the latter preferred a more sneaky, insidious method of penetration, like a worm that eats its way through the flesh of a fruit. But it is more likely that the real difference lies in the changes that have taken place in the kibbutz, that over the years, it has shed some of its extremist, implacable positions and has learned the virtues of compromise and flexibility. *A Perfect Peace*, at any rate, concludes with a tone of acquiescence and appeasement; although Azaria is not totally assimilated in the kibbutz environment, nor wholeheartedly embraced by its membership, he is no longer haughtily and disdainfully rejected. Increased tolerance, understanding, and attentiveness are exhibited vis-à-vis the newcomer or the odd man out.

As in the Bible, where a change of name is always significant and indicative of change in status or orientation (Abram becomes Abraham, Sarai becomes Sarah, Jacob becomes Israel), here too Azaria becomes Zaro which, unlike the exilic, stale, old-fashioned Azaria, sounds more informal, folksy, and with it. It is a badge of acceptance, indicating that Azaria is now one of the gang, that he belongs in the kibbutz society.

And here we return to the motif of the picture, one of whose components best embodies this change. It is a metaphor that reflects the changes in the themes and characters as well as in the plot:

> [I]t occurred to him [to Azaria] to climb up and remove the picture of the Minister of Welfare that he had clipped from a magazine during the winter. In place of Dr. Burg, he put up a colorful picture of the sea; the sea had been much on his mind as the summer heat grew more intense. (p. 357)

The conjunction of summer and sea certainly typifies the Israeli experience, suggesting a mentality, an approach to life. It is the essence of the "blazing light" that is the antithesis of the dark, wintry, claustrophobic world that Azaria came from. Replacing Dr. Burg's portrait with a picture of the sea in summer is the measure of Azaria's integration into the Israeli kibbutz milieu. It also is the culmination of the evolutionary progression from polarity to reconciliation, a progression also reflected in the changing seasons. When the novel opens, it is "the end of fall" (p. 10); it continues through winter—"at four or four-fifteen in the afternoon, the winter light would recede behind the darkening clouds" (p. 19); "how desolate the garden looks on a winter day just before sunrise. . . . The dripping of the pines in the fog as in some Chinese painting. And not a living soul around" (p. 304); then on to spring: "At last winter came to an end. The rains had stopped. The clouds were gone. Harsh winds gave way to soft sea breezes. . . . It was a late spring" (p. 351); then to high summer: "The agricultural season was at its height. The days were long and hot, and the nights were short" (p. 376); then winter again: "Indifferent to the commotion, oblivious to the two men, impervious to the winter storm, Rimona would sit and nurse Na'ama" (p. 379); and spring again: "At the end of May, both Yoni and Azaria were mobilized" (p. 380); then summer: "Soon after, the war predicted by Azaria broke out. We won the war [the Six Day War that broke out on June 6] and pushed forward the front lines" (p. 380).

Thus the seasons change over a year-and-a-half span that frames the plot of the novel. But the passage of time is not a mechanical, indifferent framework that merely encompasses the events of the plot. The passage from year to year has a metaphoric, symbolic dimension: a transition from a "wintry," sullen, lugubrious nature, that is associated with exilic, European, musty existence, into the height of Israeli summer with its white scorching light that is associated with golden Mediterranean beaches, refreshing sea breezes, and the rustling of waves crashing against limestone rocks.

A similar progression can be seen in the details of the picture motif. The first description contains the following component:

> [E]ven the sole picture in the room was quiet; in it a dark bird was perched on a red brick fence; through the shadows and fog in the picture. (p. 102)

And later, an additional component of the motif:

> A bird on a fence. The fence is made of red bricks. . . . The picture is shrouded in fog; a kind of wintry dampness. (p. 362).

The picture motif is first introduced as a wintry, grayish, dreary scene, whereas toward the end, the dominant tone is summery, bright, and cheery:

> In place of Dr. Burg, Azaria put up a colorful picture of the sea, because the sea had been much on his mind as the summer heat grew more intense. (p. 367)

It is never said explicitly that Azaria is foreign born, a product of the Diaspora, but his clothes, his manner, and his accent point clearly to the fact that he is not a Sabra. Moreover, he often quotes maxims and proverbs that are translated from a foreign language. Azaria favors the old guard, the founding fathers who, like him, came from the Diaspora and therefore embody the wisdom of generations of Judaism, over the younger, native-born leadership whom he considers rash, brazen, overconfident, and irresponsible.

The gradual progression toward moderation and compromise that is observed in the plotline is expressed also in a seemingly casual phrase that Srulik, the new secretary and Yolek's successor, writes in his journal: "as the water covers the sea," which is an allusion to the verse in *Isaiah* (11, 9), "for the earth shall be full of the knowledge of the Lord, as the water covers the sea." The subject here is wisdom, intelligence, and universal understanding. But the phrase goes beyond the biblical allusion; it often is quoted by Bolognesi, the convicted murderer who somehow ended up on the kibbutz after being pardoned by the president. For twenty years, Bolognesi has existed on the margins of the kibbutz, "quiet, well-behaved, and useful, a man who had not harmed a fly since the day of his arrival . . . and devoted himself to the art of fine knitting, which he must have learned in prison" (p. 214). This eccentric, somewhat deranged loner lives in a dilapidated shack at the far edge of the kibbutz, the same shack previously inhabited by Binny Trotsky, who in a fit of madness, brought on by his unrequited love for Hava, fired his gun in all directions. Later it becomes the abode of Azaria Gitlin, who somehow found his way to the kibbitz. The oddball blacksmith Bolognesi speaks a kind of gibberish that is composed of mangled, mauled quotations from Scripture, among them, "Horror overwhelm me like water off'a da sea. Selah" (p. 214), an echo of secretary Srulik's phrase. Bolognesi, the local "village madman," is like the Shakespearean fool or Greek chorus who, from a farther perspective, comments on the unadorned truth of the events in the plot. The verse used by Srulik in his journal, and warped and mangled by the "village idiot," speaks of the wisdom of patience, tolerance, and universal acceptance as subsumed by the notion of ocean water covering everything equally, without bias or discrimination.

Three interlopers successively occupy the ramshackle hut at the edge of the kibbutz: Trotsky, Bolognesi, and Azaria, three incursions of strangers coming out of the blue and settling in. Binny Trotsky was the first to come and then to leave. Then came ex-con Bolognesi, who stayed, though completely isolated and alienated from the communal life, his eccentricity eliciting amazement, derision, and vague fear in the members. Then came Azaria Gitlin, and he too stayed. From the rickety shack at the edge of the kibbutz he moves to Rimona's and Yoni's cozy, homey flat. He ascends the ladder, almost assimilated in kibbutz society—almost, but not completely. The difference between Azaria's and Trotsky's lots can be partly explained by the historical, social, and ideological changes that have taken place in kibbutz society in the intervening years, which have made the kibbutz a more open, tolerant environment. But apart from this extratextual explanation, the novel's own thematic rationale should account for it. The fate of the three strangers can attest to this process.

It should further be noted that the unconventional arrangement of Yoni, Rimona, and Azaria is not unique in the novel. There is the failed attempt of Yolek, Hava, and Trotsky, and then there is Eitan R., who lives with two women: Smadar (the Sabra) and Diana (the foreigner)—a miniature reflection in reverse of the main action. When Eitan is killed on the Golan Heights, "his two girlfriends went on living in his room by the swimming pool" (p. 389), just like the two fathers of Cheetah Resnik (in *A Panther in the Basement*), who continued to live in the same apartment after the death of the woman whom they both had shared. Thus the same patterns recur.

The picture motif contains several other components associated with different thematic threads in the novel. For instance:

> Yet small wonders continued to occur. It was said that Paula Levin, one of the founding members of the kibbutz and a longtime kindergarten teacher who headed the young children's committee, had received an album of Durer reproductions from Srulik out of the blue. What was the meaning of this gesture? Some people said one thing, and other people said another. (p. 361)

The concluding sentence, with its ironic tone, has a distinct Agnonian flavor, echoing the phrase "God in heaven only knows" in Agnon's *A Simple Story*, with its implication of "And you, perceptive and shrewd reader, probably know, too." This affinity is not surprising, given Agnon's influence on Oz's writing. However, in the matter of Srulik's gift to Paula Levin, one should note that the restrained, polished, understated style of Durer's paintings and engravings, which combine Gothic, formalistic austerity with Italian Renaissance harmony, is a metaphoric reflection of Srulik's restrained, undeclared feelings, of the control he has imposed on himself for so many years, and of his ability to be so close to his beloved yet so distant from her. His choice of Durer's pictures is, therefore, an apt comment on his own cautious, controlled, surreptitious manner.

Perhaps here too the motif of the picture indicates a certain willingness to relent, to compromise. When Srulik sends his paramour an album of reproductions, he divulges at least some of his hitherto well-kept secret. The narrator hints as much when he reports that the gift caused some tongues to wag, which means that Srulik is aware of the fact that the gift may betray his mistress' secret. This happens at the conclusion of the novel, when Yoni, the prodigal son, comes back from his wanderings, ready to reintegrate himself into kibbutz society and to be part of an unconventional ménage à trois. At the same time, Azaria Gitlin, the outsider, the misfit, the stranger from abroad—who, in this respect, is analogous to the returning Yoni—is also integrated (at least partially) into the Israeli, Sabra milieu. Srulik's willingness to expose his clandestine love also is a departure, a token of acceptance, accommodation, and adjustment to new realities. In sending Paula the pictures—which is, of course, another component of the picture motif—Srulik is seen to relax some of the rigid rules by which he has lived until now.

A Perfect Peace contains another allusion to a famous painting. This allusion surfaces at the picnic attended by Rimona, Yoni, Azaria, Udi, and Einat:

Yonatan took no part in the argument that soon broke out between Udi and Azaria. He remembered a picture he had once seen in Rimona's album that showed a group of picnickers in a clearing in a thick oak forest, bathed in chiaroscuro light. All the men were fully dressed, and among them was one woman, naked as the day she was born, who in his mind he dubbed Azuva, daughter of Shilhi. (p. 145)

The painting in question is, in all probability, Edouard Manet's *"Dejeuner sur l'herbe,"* which hangs in the Louvre in Paris (having originally been turned down by the official salon and later exhibited in the *Salon des Refuses*). The painting, with the provocative, erotic dialectic created by the meticulously dressed men surrounding the naked woman, echoes the classical, idyllic motif familiar from, among others, Raphael's "The Judgment of Paris" and, much later, Picasso's *"Les Demoiselles d'Avignon"* (1907), from his early Cubist period. At the time, Manet's picture elicited mixed reactions; admiration and excitement, on the one hand, and condemnation and hostility, on the other hand. Many considered the picture provocative, vulgar, depraved, and deliberately scandalous. For Yonatan, at the picnic, it is only natural that this particular picture would come to mind. The picnic triggers his subconscious. At the picnic, Yonatan experiences intense, ferocious sexual jealousy when he sees Rimona wiping Azaria's neck with her handkerchief. "I'll break every bone in your body, you little grasshopper, Yonatan thought" (p. 136). The erotic triangle of two men and a woman is taking shape in Yonatan's life, just as it is reflected in Manet's painting. Thus the picture becomes a metaphoric conduit for the events in Yonatan's life, and this upsets him and fills him with jealousy and resentment. These feelings are compounded with a deep sense of frustration; he could defeat his rival, chase him out of his life, yet he does not do so; instead, he lets him invade his bedroom and take possession of his wife. No wonder that, in this connection, Yonatan's thoughts turn to Benjamin Trotsky:

That joker, the old-timers used to say, he couldn't hit it from three feet away, they snickered. And a bull isn't a matchbox! It's a huge target! (p. 145)

The present state of affairs brings to mind Hava's old lover, who is, perhaps, Yonatan's biological father. Trotsky's unrequited love, his desperation and sexual frustration, prompted him to fire his pistol (a sexual symbol!) and shoot in all directions. He eventually aimed his pistol at a bull—another symbol of sexuality and potency—but missed. In the power struggle with Yolek, Trotsky is the loser and is therefore abandoned and banished from the kibbutz. But, in Azaria's case, it is just the reverse; Azaria, with his survival instinct and shrewd, animal sense, realizes that slow infiltration is better than a gunshot. He strikes root and remains in the kibbutz. And it is Yoni who feels defeated, beaten and bested in battle. The blue-eyed Sabra, member of an elite army unit and victorious warrior, is now obliged to share his bed with an outsider, a risible, ludicrous figure who smacks of foreignness and Jewish inferiority. Whereas Yolek, the father, proved triumphant, driving away his wife's lover, Yonatan, the son, is defeated. This is Freud's *Totem and Tabu* in a nutshell: the aging father overpowers his young son for fear that the latter might rise against him, usurp him, and supplant him in the seat of power.

Small wonder then that at the picnic Yonatan's thoughts turn to Manet's provocative painting, where two men vie for the favors of one woman, and from there, they turn to his father, Yolek, representative of the tyrannical older generation, mustering all of his physical and mental powers to smite the younger generation that rises to pit itself against him:

> They stayed there for another half hour or so. Udi and then Azarha took off his shirt and undershirt to soak in the sun. Yonatan kept silent. When a mild dispute broke out whether the three jets roaring overhead on their way South were Mysteres or Supermysteres, Yonatan broke his silence and remarked that his father had once voted in the cabinet against the Franco-Israeli love affair, or perhaps, he had merely abstained. Now, though, his father admitted that he had been wrong and that Ben-Gurion had been right. They've spent their entire lives being right, these old folks of ours. Whatever my father says, even if it's admitting that he was wrong and Ben-Gurion was right, comes out sounding like he's the one who's right and you're the one who's wrong, because you're still young. Only they have rigorously logical minds and sharp instincts and all that, while you're too confused, or too spoiled, or too lazy, or too superficial. It doesn't matter if you're thirty years old. They still talk to you like a grown-up being patient with a child who's only being treated like a grown-up for pedagogical reasons, in order to make him feel good. Just ask them what time it is, and you get a lengthy answer full of explanations, point by point, A, B, C, D, and they constantly remind you that there's another side to every coin, and that one must be guided by past experience. They smile and ask you what you think, but before you open your mouth, they give you the answer. What you think makes no difference, because you belong to a superficial generation. You can't get a word in edgewise. It's like being checkmated by someone who's playing both sides of the board, because you have no pieces of your own, just your psychological problems and your emotional hangups. Then, at the end, they tell you that you have a lot to learn, because you are not mature enough. (pp. 148–49)

Thus themes are linked, and one thing leads to another. Yolek is the father, the aging prototype of the authoritarian founding fathers, who sees in the younger generation rebels who are out to dispossess him. Yolek was victorious in the power struggle with Benjamin Trotsky who, having lost Hava, was condemned to banishment. Azaria is analogous to Yolek who, like him, is a product of the Diaspora, with its overtones of craftiness and devious practices. They are both endowed with linguistic glibness and rhetorical skill that tend to stun and silence the stammering, inarticulate Sabra. They both thrive and triumph in the kibbutz environment, under the blazing sun.

Azaria, like Yolek, comes out the winner in the erotic arena. True, Yonatan is not eliminated from the triangle, but he has to accept Azaria's place in his wife's affections. The sexual frustration and the sense of bitter defeat that Yonatan experiences vis-à-vis Azaria and Yolek, his father and rival, act as a trigger that awakens his remembrance of Manet's painting, with its provocative, highly erotic content. Once more, a component of the picture motif serves as a metaphoric conduit, exposing the most profound themes of the novel. It is like a brief snapshot that captures a crossroad of many convoluted paths: deep-seated feelings of deprivation and mental anguish, a sense of shameful failure and gnawing dissatisfaction, and seething anger, resentment, envy, and sexual frustration.

Amos Oz's fiction is noted for its attractive and effective use of motifs. In a variation on the familiar dictum about a Chekhov play—that a gun displayed in the first act is bound to go off in the final act—one might say that in an Oz story, the motif is a bullet shot from a well-aimed gun at a precise, calculated range, and the shot takes place at a specific point in the development of the plot. From that moment on, the bullet will pierce the various planes and layers of the novel, and in its trajectory, it will gather momentum, semantic density, and poetic volume. These elements coalesce and crystallize and become one solid, lustrous aggregate that reflects, metaphorically, the basic patterns of the work: characters, themes, concepts, and changes in the plotline.

Or, to use another image, the various components that make up the motif can be likened to a train with many cars that crosses the landscape of the work from one end to the other. The locomotive leads the way confidently and resolutely, while through the window can be seen the most spectacular and significant vistas that the novel offers.

Whether a bullet or a moving train, one thing is certain: Amos Oz's fiction knows the meaning of the word "motif," just as it knows the meaning of "aesthetic complexity" and "poetic beauty"; it knows these concepts and demonstrates this knowledge amply and to great effect.

CHAPTER 8

Amos Oz Talks about Amos Oz:
"Being I, Plus Being Myself"—An Interview
with Hillit Yeshourun

J ust an introductory comment, since I do not intend my own few sentences
to encroach on a chapter that is totally Amos Oz's. This chapter is shared by
an important collaborator, the interviewer, Hillit Yeshourun, and yet it is
entirely Oz's. Through Ms. Yeshourun's leading questions, in an interview
that she conducted with Amos Oz in 1989 and later published in *Hadarim*
(Rooms), a literary magazine, of which she is the editor, Oz, in fact, becomes
the author of this chapter. The interviewer here serves as a launching pad, a
trigger or a catalyst, eliciting another story from the author. And here Amoz
Oz speaks directly about Amos Oz and, as always, the story is intelligent,
sensitive, attentive, and moving. He does not, however, shed many masks in
the telling of this story; exaggerated expectations in this respect are bound to
be frustrated, but that is just fine, since a mask is better than a good story.
Well, the mask is still there. It has not been removed, even though, at times,
it seems otherwise. Behind every mask there is always another mask.

The relevance of this additional "good story" by Oz to the book is
indisputable, because here he discusses his writing, the process of creation,
and his own place in that process and beyond. What he shares with the
interviewer is relevant to all of the chapters of this book, because they too
have to do with his writing, with mapping, interpreting, and documenting
the process. Thus a dialogue is created between the author and the scholar
studying his fiction; the author's perspective sheds light on the scholar's perspective, and vice versa.

At the request of both Amoz Oz and Hillit Yeshourun—as far as I
know, this was not discussed between them—the interview is given here in
its entirety, verbatim, as it first appeared in print, including the pithy title.

Even though the inclusion of the interview was not what I had in mind when I first approached Oz with a request that he participate in the book, I gradually warmed up to the idea, realizing that the interview preserves Oz's story in its most authentic context, thus investing the dialogue between us with a more heightened dramatic quality.

And so, as Doctor Michael Gonen in Oz's novel *My Michael* is wont to say to his son Yair, "I'm done." Well, I am done, at least for now. From now on, it is Amos Oz talking about Amos Oz, through the intelligent mediation of Hillit Yeshourun, to whom I am greatly indebted.

"Being I, Plus Being Myself"

Let's try to conduct an open, uninhibited interview.

AMOS OZ: I am neither open nor uninhibited.

Well, let's try. You have just received the Femina Award for Black Box. *How did this affect you?*

AMOS OZ: I was happy. Period. I don't feel as if my book, which had been convicted in a district court, won on appeal in the Supreme Court. This is not what happened. I still care more about what's written in our local "Holon News" [Holon—a dormitory town near Tel Aviv—au.] than in "Le Monde." Because I live here, and a book belongs to a specific place, not to the entire world. And if the book were condemned here in Israel, in its native place—well, not by everyone, to be sure—that judgment would not be rescinded by the fact that the book was awarded a prize in Paris. It is still a book that most critics in Israel excoriated. I deplore this. Still, I was glad that the book was favorably received overseas, but not because they have a better understanding there than this or that Israeli critic.

Once, when discussing your early years in kibbutz Hulda, you said, "I used to talk in high-flown language and that irritated people somewhat." Do you think your language still irritates the critics today?

AMOS OZ: That too. Some people get upset when you touch their exposed nerves. Besides, I do not toe anybody's line. Some critics have been saying for years that we should stop writing this kind of literature and, instead, create meta-realistic fiction; but I don't listen to them because

I can't do that. Perhaps it is time to extol and glorify the State of Israel, but I can't do that either! It is not my nature to answer my attackers, and this, too, annoys some people. "He's condescending, he puts on airs," they say. All these years I have kept my distance from literary circles because of the aggression they generate. Well, if they tell me, "This is not good enough," I respond a priori by saying they are right! There could always be something better. If tomorrow someone wrote that *To Know a Woman* is nowhere near Faulkner, he or she will be right a priori. If they ask why the protagonist does not soar to more tragic heights, they will be justified. I can't do it any other way. I do what I can.

By all accepted criteria, you are a successful writer. How important is success in your world? Does it come at a price?

AMOS OZ: Look, when I was young, I craved respect. Money was not important to me, because I had to give all of it to the kibbutz anyway. Now, I won't say I have no use for respect, but I don't want so much of it. Things that used to excite me now do so to a much lesser degree. I deplore it to some extent. I would have liked this enjoyment to endure. It reminds me of what my grandpa used to say about women. "When you crave them, you can't get them; and when you finally learn how to get them, and they're there, you are satiated, and then you're not as enthusiastic." When I was thirty-seven and already had two daughters, he called me to his study, sat me next to him, and said, "Listen, Amos—Amosele, he used to call me—it's time you and I had a man to man talk about women." He was a Russian type, elegant, with a folded handkerchief in his pocket and golden cufflinks; I guess he was a throwback to fin-de-siecle gallantry. At eighty, he became a widower, and at once he began to blossom. So he seated me next to him on the sofa and said, "Look, Amosele, in some respects, women are just like us, but in others, they're a world apart. But in what things they are like us, and in what they differ—that I'm still working on." He must have been ninety-five at the time.

Malcolm Lowry once said that success is a disaster, worse than a fire that destroys the entire house, because fame consumes the soul. Does this sound romantic to you?

AMOS OZ: No, but it sounds partly valid to me. This may be true about people who have an obsessive need to be loved all the time. Not me. I am willing to announce arrogantly, proudly: I don't need to be loved all the time. Money I do need now, though, and respect I don't reject. I know people who were corrupted and silenced by these trappings. Not me. I don't think about such things when I'm working.

What do you have in mind when you say "respect" or "honor"?

AMOS OZ: That race that decides who's in third place and who's in first. But now I can laugh at it; I know it is not important. I am less and less able to enjoy it, anyway. What is important to me when I write is to hear the right phrase, or to capture a certain scent. If I can capture smell in words, that makes me happy, but if my book sells so many copies, that's an abstraction. It's too vague. To a poet, the difference between a readership of ten and 100 is enormous, but to a person writing fiction that is read by 1,000 or 100,000 people, the difference is only in the royalties. I know authors whose work is read by 200 people, and they write better than I.

I read somewhere that Cervantes wrote to someone from jail. I don't remember to whom. I wish I could find that text and read it again, because at the time I didn't realize its importance for me. If anybody locates that passage, please let me know. At any rate, he wrote something like this, "I don't mind dying in jail, and I don't mind the fact that I wrote a lot of junk, because there is one book I wrote that the world will remember as long as the rock of Gibraltar stands. And that book is *Galatea*." Now, I once had a chance to read *Galatea* in English, and it really wasn't much; it's a piece of garbage. And yet, he didn't even count *Don Quixote* among his books! So what kind of "honor" do you garner when a book pleases or does not please, or when so many copies of it are sold? My greatest joy is when I find the right words to express something that I want to convey. This does not happen very often. For the most part, I have to compromise. I can hear what I want to write, but I end up writing less than that. I search, I try, I erase ten times, and then I have to compromise.

Which one of your books, do you think, will endure?

AMOZ OZ: Frankly, I'm afraid to say. But as of today (December 5, isn't it?), it is my latest book, which is not yet out; I'm sure that's the one, because here I'm closest to what I set out to do. It's entitled *To Know a Woman*. It has nothing to do with the story about my grandfather. It's a book about a man who, for many years, worked for the Secret Service and who has a bit of an obsession with finding the truth. So if you ask me which book is closest to what I wanted to say, I'd have to say, *To Know a Woman*. But perhaps this is Cervante's *Galatea* all over again (and by someone who did not write *Don Quixote*). I'm not sure. Whatever.

Does this book mark a new direction for you, different from Black Box?

AMOS OZ: Every time I wrote a book, I was sure I was doing something I'd never done before. But, as the years pass, I realize that there are similarities, that it is the same person who is writing. I still want to learn about life, death, jealousy, and hatred. I don't want to repeat what I have already done. It's a waste of time. I want to see things differently, to present them differently. I know it will come out the same, though, but I'd like it to be different.

They say a writer writes the same story all his life.

AMOS OZ: I hope it is not true. But I'm afraid it is.

It seems to me, that whatever you wrote after Where the Jackals Howl *is already contained in that novel. That the nucleus is there. Is the story of Yiftach in* On This Bad Land *autobiographical?*

AMOS OZ: Every story is autobiographical. Not everything is a confession, but everything is autobiographical. I agree with your comment on *Where the Jackals Howl.* It was there that I drew my borders. Like a map of Africa—first it was delineated from the outside, with a lot of blank areas. I know I won't have time to fill in all the spaces, it is too ambitious and the terrain is too vast. I think that the new book, *To Know a Woman,* is closer to me than anything I have ever written. And yet not close enough; it is not everything I meant to write. Every book, in fact, contains three books: the one I wrote; the one you read; and a third, the book I would have liked to write but didn't because I lacked the strength. That third book is known only to me. And it is the reason that I am never really pleased with the final product. My latest book is the one closest to the book I would have liked to write, and so I feel good about it.

A. B. Yehoshua said in an interview that he was grateful to the critics because in each review he found something worthwhile. Do you share this perception?

AMOS OZ: This is nice. I wish I could learn from my critics. But I don't think I really can. They are mistaken in assuming that you have more liberty than you actually have. They often say to you, why did you write this and not that? As if one could write differently. To them, you are a little god, sitting at your desk writing. And if only you listened to them, you would do it a little differently, veer a little to the right, shift a little to the left, magnify one character, reduce another. But the author has less latitude than they imagine. There were times when I resented the critics. Why are they giving me a hard time, I protested. What do they want from me? After all, I'm doing the best I can. Then I realized that it was not quite true. There were things they pointed out that I wished I could accomplish. Except I couldn't. I am much less free than people assume. When I write a story about two women and a man, or two men and a woman, after a few pages, they start doing what they want. You can only moderate their behavior a little bit. You are like the head of an exuberant Italian family in a Fellini movie: everyone has opinions, and everyone insists on being heard. All I can do is make sure one of them does not monopolize the entire novel. I can only say, "That's enough!" but I cannot change the characters, nor can I decide who will live and who will die or who will do what to whom.

They dictate to you what to write?

AMOS OZ: There is a certain point where if they don't start to lead an independent life, I discard the manuscript; it is not alive, it is Plasticine. The characters are alive only when they tell me, "You keep quiet now, sit down and write, don't interfere!" When I wrote *The Hill of the Evil Council*," two characters posed a problem. They suddenly meet in an olive grove in the Judean mountains. I tried to reason with them, "This is not the right place for you. You should meet in a cafe on Mount Carmel. After all, you are both 'Yekkes' [German Jews], and this isn't right.

"My story," I argued, "will lack verisimilitude." But they said, "Don't tell us what to do. Keep quiet and write." So all I can do is restrain my characters. I can tell them, "If you want me to write, you must compromise, you must show a little consideration. Or else, go find another writer." In *My Michael*, there were numerous times when I had to tell Hannah, "Go find a female writer. I can't describe how a woman feels in a first-person narrative!" I told her, "Leave me alone." But she wouldn't. I had to write the book in order to get rid of her. But we quarreled all the time: all she wanted was to feel sorry for herself, kvetch about her life, but I wouldn't let her. In the end we reached a compromise.

What you say amazes me. I always thought that the author holds all the reins, that he/she is a creator of worlds.

AMOS OZ: This is a romantic view. My responsibility, my domain, is the words. Deciding which words to use, where to put a comma, when to use an adjective or an adverb—this is my responsibility. Sometimes I fail miserably, sometimes I have a resounding success. Quite often, I sit like a watchmaker, tweezers in hand, magnifying glass in my eye, deliberating whether I should put a comma or use an extra adjective. This is my responsibility. It's a cold, unromantic preoccupation.

And you don't ask yourself what the protagonist is going to do?

AMOS OZ: And if I do ask, it is going to help me? In the end, the protagonists do whatever they want to do. Well, this is not entirely true either. It is not that they do what they want; they pull in their direction, and when I think that they have gone overboard, I try to restrain them. But I cannot tell them, "Do this instead of that." I cannot tell a man or a woman in my story, "Look, you two are going to get married." They will say, "Who asked you anyway." I cannot tell them, "Go sleep together, or don't sleep together." I can only tell them, when they are in bed together, "I am not going to put these or those words in my story; this is going too far." Because those words are either too hackneyed or too sentimental or too pompous.

Are you telling me that it is not you who decides the plot, the progression of the story?

AMOS OZ: Hardly ever. I control the brakes, not the gas. This is not like architecture, but rather like botany. A story is not built, it grows. I know that the theory of literature is all about patterns, structures, fundamentals, passages, infrastructures, compartments—all terms borrowed from the field of architecture. But if I were to write a book about the theory of the novel, I would borrow from another discipline, botany. I'd use terms like: grows, ramifies, blooms, comes to fruition. I would use an analogy that has to do with women. Writing has something womanly about it. If I don't feel it kicking inside me, involuntary kicks, it means the thing is not alive. Only when there is kicking inside do I know that the thing is alive. I may still give birth to a monster. There are more miscarriages and abortions than live births. I often begin a story and never finish it. Sometimes it is too easy, sometimes it is too difficult, sometimes it is too big for me. It happened more than once that I started writing and then told myself, "With all due respect, I must hand this over to Dostoyevsky or to Faulkner. This is not for me, I can't lift it." Like a dung beetle pushing a piece of dung which is way too big for its powers, I may be happy with the dung, but I can't use it. It's too big for me.

Has something like this happened to you?

AMOS OZ: Yes, but I'm not going to tell you about it.

And if this happens again, will you try to grapple with it?

AMOS OZ: I don't want to grapple with anything while I'm writing. It's not a question of wrestling. There are a couple of things I would kill to be able to write, if only I could, if only I had the strength.

The "strength," or the courage?

AMOS OZ: I don't know. I would not swear to it. I am talking like a carpenter now. There is no mystique here. It's enough to glance at another writer's work and say, "I could never write this!" It's not for lack of courage, it's not for want of trying; it's simply beyond me. Like a weightlifter seeing a heavy barbell and realizing he should not even try to lift it. It is not for me. I don't have the strength for it. It's a gut feeling. I'm not sure I can explain it.

It is not a question of "I can't muster enough courage to do it now"?

AMOS OZ: I cannot analyze it any further. This is my most basic explanation. Look, if strength is another word for courage, then it is still a question of lack of strength, but I'm not sure. If Dostoyevsky had tried to describe the military unit in S. Yizhar's novel *Days of Ziklag* I am not sure he could have pulled it off. There is a certain diapason, a certain range that should not be exceeded. Sometimes it can be broadened a little, but that's about it.

Does this bother you?

AMOS OZ: It saddens me, so what?

If it bothers, it means it's alive.

AMOS OZ: But it may come out totally different. Your questions should be addressed to God. These are things I don't know and perhaps would rather not know. At any rate, not now. Now I'm asking myself, "Here's an odor I can practically smell. How do I render it in words?" There are few words for smell in Hebrew. How do you describe smell? I search, I dig, I burrow, I rummage, and eventually I compromise. Sometimes I give up a little, sometimes a lot. Prime Minister Levi Eshkol used to say, "When I want something, I compromise. If it's not enough, I make another compromise, and a third and a fourth. In the end, I get exactly what I wanted." I am not Eshkol, so I can't say this about myself.

One tries to capture in language something that the language does not really want to encompass. Language is a constant. Words are supposed to denote constant things. How can you capture what is fluid, changeable, and between states, in a no-man's-land? There is an inherent contradiction that I can't quite resolve. And I find it very difficult. I have nothing but words to work with. If I could write music, I would compose. If I could build bridges—perhaps I would do so. But I only have words. I seek to do with language something which goes against the language. This is the nature of my work. Not what A does to B. How do you write about a person who has not seen someone very dear for twenty-eight years, then sees that person in a dusty alley in Beer Sheva only to realize it is not the same person. I want to convey something very physical: the reaction of his face and his body as he approaches and sees that it is the wrong person. This is my task. What you call inventing a plot is rather easy, because how many plots are there in the world? Not many. Love, hate, jealousy, friendship.

Is it less important?

AMOS OZ: Less interesting to me. It is less intriguing to me than capturing a unique moment, a physical or emotional movement. To reach the world. I think this is what Joyce meant when he spoke of "epiphanies," those moments when, through snatches of words, for a very brief space, the world is revealed to you, as it had been before we were in it. When I was young, I wanted to see the room without my presence in it. Maybe it wasn't there at all. By the same token, you may ask what happens inside other people. If I were you, if I were him, if I were that cat climbing up there, if I were that man in the cafe reading his newspaper. What's his story? What's his secret? I wanted to know these things since I was little. But one can never find out. One can only guess. And then, what are you left with? A profound wish to be precise, exact, accurate. And you work not with the language but against it. Because language is not made for precision. You mention eyeglasses. What eyeglasses? The pacts you make with the language are shaky. Here is a table. But if we were on a trip to the desert, spreading a *keffia* [Arab headgear] on the sand, I could tell you, "Bring the sheets and put them on the table." You would understand me, because even though the pacts with the language are shaky, they are based on momentary understandings that go beyond language. I strive to write something that perhaps comes from a nonverbal stratum in me, that existed before language was formed in me, and may awaken something pre-verbal, nonverbal, or super-verbal in the reader. This is what I like to do: look for ways to connect through language; say with a wink,

"Leave it alone, these may be the words, but there's something above, below, on the side of it." While reading Faulkner's *The Bear* I, as a reader, say to myself: "I was there!" I don't need Faulkner for this, I already know. Without any physical reason, I can be made to freeze while sitting in a heated room, or to feel mortal fear while in a protected house, just because I am reading a book. Imagine this picture: a man sitting alone in an armchair by a lamp, on a rainy winter night. I know the setting is redundant. You can read a book on a bench in the central station, but for my own romantic needs, I want the reader to be alone in a room with the rain beating on the shutters. I want the reader to experience fear, even though there is nothing in the room to inspire fear. Or laugh, or yearn.

Is it important to you to control the reader?

AMOS OZ: Control is not the right term. Communicate. I'll tell you something that I'll erase later, because I'm ashamed of it; it's like making love. I want to evoke in the woman I'm making love to sensations that I myself will never experience, because I am not a woman. But I want to know that I brought about those sensations. It is to desire something impossible. It means coming out of your skin and getting under someone else's. It is, after all, to find yourself, but also to find someone else. John Locke describes a seaman trying to fathom the ocean by throwing down a rope with a weight. If he throws it as far down as it will go, he knows he won't reach the bottom, because it is deeper than the length of the rope, and yet it is beneficial to him, because he may find out the length of the rope he is holding. This describes to some extent what I try to do. I may not attain those moments of epiphany, find the ultimate truth, God's world, but if I'm lucky, I'll find out how far I can go. How far I can travel inside other people and inside myself. Inside other people is inside myself.

Nietzsche said that you don't find in a book anything you don't already know by yourself.

AMOZ OZ: That's true, but you don't always know yourself. Quite often a book helps you recognize what's in you, it reminds you that "even old sights have had a moment of birth." If I were to write a book about the Andes—I would bring "a moment of birth to an old sight," a reminiscence of a place where the reader has never been, or nothing would happen. If the reader is unwilling to participate and share things that he/she has tasted, smelled, suffered—if he/she is not ready to invest in the experience—then there is no partnership, no sharing.

I strew inky characters on a white sheet of paper. When I describe a sunset, the reader must throw in sunsets that he/she has seen, or there won't be anything. I cannot spread smells on the pages. I wish I could. The reader must come to the reading as a co-producer. If the reader does not invest "dollar for dollar," there is no book.

What attracts you to reading? The language?

AMOS OZ: Yes, but not only language. Remembrance: Yes, I have already been there. Yes, I already know. I can't get excited about things that I have not heard, seen, or tasted. Only when a book evokes a dim recollection, not necessarily of something you actually remember, but of something you remember remembering, when you can say: "I've been there," perhaps you slept there, or been there in your dreams. But if it finds no echo in you, there is no partnership, no reading. So much for the reader. As a writer I can only hope to evoke something in the reader, or else there is no partnership, my work is useless. The deal is off after three pages. And I fully respect a person who says after reading three pages, "This isn't for me. It may be a masterpiece, but it does nothing for me."

It works only when I feel that I've been there before. It is a temptation, like an erotic seduction. Go figure why one man succumbs and another doesn't. Stories and poems are erotic objects. A message, an encoded communication, is sent, and you either respond or you don't.

Who are your favorite Hebrew authors?

AMOS OZ: Brenner, Berdichevsky, Agnon, and Yizhar.

Do you go back to your old favorites?

AMOS OZ: Occasionally, but carefully, as with human old flames. Sometimes you revisit, and they are no longer there. Sometimes you revisit and find much more. Sometimes the love is gone, but the warm, deep, wonderful taste still lingers. I must have reached an age when the memory of an old love is no less exciting than that of a new love, maybe even more. Sometimes it is simply there. Take Cervantes, for example. I recently re-read *Don Quixote*. Now I begin to understand what it's about. When I read it as a child, it was thrilling, funny, crazy, hilarious. Now I'm beginning to see that it's about me.

When you work on a book, is your writing affected by what you read?

AMOS OZ: When I write, I try to avoid reading novels or stories. I don't really know what affects my writing. I'm not sure I want to know. I cannot be a lover, a sex expert, and a gynecologist at the same time.

You said you try to get under the characters' skin, but some questions you answer by saying, "I'm not sure I want to know." You want to understand the characters, but not yourself?

AMOS OZ: Look, deciphering a mystery can be a dangerous thing. You drive a scalpel to the deepest, most intimate parts, and the operation may result in loss of life. For me, it's a luxury to figure out the processes that impel me to write. But it is also fraught with danger. The truth is, it interests me less than what the characters do. If you press me, I may end up with a few quotations from Freud. It is important to know where to stop. When I write about people, I play it by ear for as long as I see fit. It's a matter of the right measure, how much and where to stop. When I describe a couple fighting or making love, the question where to stop is not normative or censorial, not how much the public can tolerate without being shocked. It's a question of aesthetics, of music: where should you place the silences between the notes? If you fill up the silences, you end up with a continuous shriek. Musicians, writers, and artists all work on the spaces, on the squares of silence between the sounds. Those are not failures or lacunae, they are part of the work.

Is there a parallel between your stories and your articles?

AMOS OZ: If there is something I am absolutely sure of, I'll publish an article in the newspaper. When I am of two minds about something and I hear two contending voices inside me, when I feel my genes or my parents moving me, or when I ask myself during a debate what would happen if I were the other person, would I speak like him—then there is an embryo of a story right there. But when I speak to myself in one voice, pat myself on the shoulder and say, "Amos, you are absolutely right on this one," it will not result in a story. When I am completely in agreement with myself on an issue, there won't be a story. A story begins with a conflict.

Do you distinguish between these two kinds of writing?

AMOS OZ: I don't make any distinction about anything. In the final analysis, it is the same person who dreads fanaticism yet feels its impact very strongly, who writes a story and writes an article; it is the same person who knows that fanaticism is death, and it spells death. The same person inhabits the stories and the articles. However, there are moments when I feel that I myself could be that fanatic. I know how contagious it is. I am the kind of person who gets up in the morning, has his cup of coffee, and starts getting under other people's skins. This is my line of work. There are two reasons why a writer is allowed to write political essays; one is the language. When do words become accomplices to murder? I can smell the smoke in my sleep. When language becomes an instrument of murder, I hear it and then I scream. Every political article I ever wrote began with a linguistic issue. Since 1967. I responded to "liberated territories" and to "Peace in Galilee Operation." The second reason is my professional habit of getting into other people's minds. How did we get on this subject anyway? Talking about fanaticism. Most of the people I wrote stories about are relatives of mine. We have many things in common, but most of them believe in things that I don't believe in. They believe in happiness. They want eternal love and absolute justice and freedom at all cost. These are things I don't believe in, but I understand very well how others can. There is great seduction in them, and I am easily seduced.

Is it true that Eternal Love *gave rise to* Under This Blazing Light?

AMOS OZ: No. However, it is true that the story about the aging Russian lecturer came out of *A Perfect Peace.* He was a secondary character in *A Perfect Peace.* When I was in Oxford, I began writing something that later developed into the novel *A Perfect Peace.* I started writing a story and later abandoned it. It had to do with an aging lecturer who spoke of galaxies, Russian Jewry, time, the universe, and death. He was supposed to make one appearance in the book, on a Sabbath eve, on the kibbutz, deliver a lecture and then disappear. But he was stubborn and got what he wanted. What can I do? As I told you earlier, my liberty as a writer is much more limited than it seems to those who study my stories or write reviews and want to know why I did thus and not thus.

How do you view Here and There in the Land of Israel *compared to your stories and novels?*

AMOS OZ: Why should I see any connection there? *Here and There in the Land of Israel* is a travel book. That's its genre. It is not a social statement. I did not use a tape recorder. It is not a reflection of the social and political situation. I deliberately sought the margins, the outskirts of society and not the mainstream. I aimed at creating a polyphonic work, and I hope I've been able to create a polyphonic work also in the stories and novels written before and after it. This is what they all have in common. In *Black Box* I focused on how very different people expose, in letter after letter, their innermost, incestuous desires—it is quite clear that the woman wants to be a mother, a daughter, and a lover to her second husband, and a mother, a lover, and a wife to her first husband: everyone there wishes to fill all the female and male roles in the other's life—but more than that: these people want to become one, to fuse and commingle with the other. Somo wishes to be Alex, and Alex wishes to be Somo, and this can be done only through the woman who wishes to become one with both of them. This you do not find in *Here and There in the Land of Israel.*

In A Perfect Peace *you write about Yonatan Lifschitz: "He felt that those men and women were hiding something from him, and that he could not go on making concessions." Would you have written differently had you not spent thirty years in Kibbutz Hulda? Would your writing be different?*

AMOS OZ: Yes. So what? I could not, and would not, use the people of the Kibbutz. Although at some cynical moments I would say to myself: If I described a certain person exactly as he is, he wouldn't even take offense, because he wouldn't recognize himself. I did not describe people as I saw them through the window.

Jerusalem and Kibbutz Hulda appear in your work as two opposing poles. In My Michael, *you write: "I was born in Jerusalem. But I cannot write: Jerusalem is my city." Why?*

AMOS OZ: This is said by Hannah Gonen. I happen to agree with her on this one, although I want to make absolutely clear that I am not to be identified with that woman. She gave me hell. She crawled under my skin and invaded my soul. While I was writing the novel, I wanted to kill her. I could never say, "Jerusalem is my city," certainly not in 1988 [the year this interview was conducted]. When I was a child, Jerusalem was a loose federation of enclaves, most of which were foreign to me. I grew up in an enclave populated by Jewish Agency and National Fund officials, librarians and intellectuals and scholars who did not find their right place in Jerusalem. I was born in the Kerem Avraham neighborhood with its penurious eccentrics, utopian visionaries, and destitute East European immigrants. Walk down three blocks from there, and you're in a foreign world, totally different. A hundred yards from my home, British and Scottish soldiers were drinking beer and singing nostalgic songs in a language I did not understand. This imbued me with an accursed curiosity to become the other person, if only for a brief moment. This feeling stayed with me for life. It is what sustains me.

Several characters in your books repeat the phrase "Judea fell in blood and fire; Judea will rise in blood and fire," which is the motto of the Beitar movement. Hanna Gonen, in My Michael, *says, "This ideology is far from my heart, but the music in these words has touched me." And later in the novel she says, "I don't like the idea of this slogan, but I like its internal order, the precise balance that is indecipherable to me, and yet at night I feel its presence," and in* The Hill of the Evil Council *the child says about this slogan, "Those words captivated me." Do these words still exert a sinister fascination on you?*

AMOS OZ: Sure. By the way, this verse was written by the poet Yakov Kahan. Everything emanates from poems. When I was a child, I was a great devotee of the Herut movement and Revisionist Zionism. But my revisionist world collapsed because of a screw [in Hebrew, the word "ziyyun" means both to supply with weapons and—in slang—to copulate]. When I was eleven or twelve, my grandfather used to take me to the Edison Theater to hear Menachem Begin talk. I admired and worshipped Begin, because he had been the head of the Underground and I found him enormously fascinating. I wanted him to be a giant, to look like Belmondo and Jean Gabin, but he didn't, and I forgave him because he had been the leader of the Underground. So, in 1952, I went to hear him deliver a speech at the Edison Theater. With great pathos he intoned, "Eisenhower is screwing [i.e., arming] Egypt, Guy Mollet is screwing Egypt, Eden is screwing Egypt, but who is screwing the Israeli government? If I were Prime Minister of Israel now, everyone would be screwing us!" I roared with laughter, and Grandpa, who didn't understand why I was laughing, rushed me out and slapped me on the face. Because of those slaps, the Beitar movement lost me forever. Who knows, had I remained loyal, I could have become a right-wing politician. At any rate, slogans and mottoes that have symmetrical balance, such as "crime and punishment," "war and peace," "fathers and sons," "le rouge et le noir," are very appealing. I would like to live in a world where every suffering is compensated and every wrong is righted, but I know it is not so, and I have seen blood and fire, and I lost the taste for them. But I admit that I find the verse you quote seductive. It entices me all the time, so what do I do? I give it to my fictional characters. Let them grapple with it. This is true about many things that I restrain in myself, because I know I mustn't espouse them, because they are lethal.

In your writing, there is a dichotomy between revisionism, messianism, fire and death, on the one hand, and rationalism, sanity and life, on the other. Do you think the opposites are becoming more entrenched, or has there been some reconciliation over the years?

AMOS OZ: There can be no reconciliation. There may be resignation, an acknowledgment that we must live with both poles. I am no knight in shining armor that will conquer fanaticism. To be such a crusading knight, you yourself must be a fanatic. No, there is no reconciliation, just an acceptance that this is how we must live. But there will always be the fascination of blood and fire and death, and the enchantment of something bigger than life that you can melt into, and all your toil and tribulation will be swallowed by it and you'll be consumed in the flames. I always see this enchantment—always from afar. One must not get close.

In a documentary made by Esther Dar, you say, "Zionism is a story of recovery. It is also my own personal story. I have to recover a little." From what?

AMOS OZ: From what we were just talking about. I need to locate the disease within me, and when I detect it in myself, to recognize that it is a disease.

   All my life I have been attracted to crusades, to fire, snow, operatic death, the grand gestures of life. It must be my "revisionist" genes. As long as there's strength in me, I will resist it, condemn it, and fight against it in the political arena. I will also depict it in my stories and show where it leads.

Which side is stronger in you?

AMOS OZ: Depends when. I don't have a simple answer. We are talking about two very strong emotions. In moments of violence, blind rage, revulsion, and longing for death, I also feel the opposite. I don't describe myself as "civil war" (as the poet Yehuda Amichai wrote in one of his poems). I'm just a person capable of a spectrum of emotions, some of which are contradictory. I don't want to sound like a martyred soul, writhing in agony over monumental differences, because such contradictions exist within everyone.

In Unto Death, *you write: "My master, Sir de Touron, if he were for a moment relieved of his activities, would open up to the signs." And the signs are "an insidious potion, destructive and precise." Is this a description of yourself?*

AMOS OZ: Yes.

Yes, and . . . ?

AMOS OZ: Need I add? I said yes. I've already told you plenty. The answer is yes.

What are those signs you mention?

AMOS OZ: What am I, a miracle maker, a magus? I just know they exist. It often happens that the simplest things around me speak to me both in plain language and in code. What exactly they say, who is it that transmits those signs, and whether they really exist in the world and not just in my head, I never know. I only know that there are things, great and small, sometimes ridiculous and trivial, that speak to me between the lines, amid the objects that I see.

Are those signs sometimes terrifying?

AMOS OZ: Sometimes. Not always. When you look outside into the darkness and you see something distorted moving by the window, you should always consider that the sinister figure is not a Nazi or a jackal or a ghost. It may simply be your own reflection in the windowpane, a distorted reflection of your image coming back at you from the darkness. I know this feeling of something ominous and frightening lurking in the dark from early childhood. But you must always assume that it may be you, not someone else standing outside trying to communicate. The poet Nathan Alterman wrote, "You'll hear me in the crackling of the plaster, in the creaking of the floor in the nights." Those are the noises of physical materials, and you must check the walls and the floor first. Then you can attempt to describe as accurately as possible the "crackling of the plaster" and figure out what it is that makes the floor creak. Only then can you ask yourself if that nocturnal creaking sound also constitutes another language. I don't know the answer. There is another dimension to the physical objects such as chair, table, plaster, that are materials of your ordinary, prosaic, well-lighted world. If they signify something else, I would very much like to know. I listen, I strive, but I may never find out. Those are the signs. Suffice it to know that they exist. There is another matter that occupies me: the laws (if they exist) that govern the accidental occurrences in life. This is a theme that features prominently in my latest novel. The verb "to decipher" recurs many times. There are situations when it seems that nothing is accidental. You don't always see that, and then I say to myself, "Hang on! Just because today I can't see or hear it, it doesn't exist?" We have a great need to make connections. We connect a small occurrence with the larger reality, and then a suspicion arises: perhaps this link is nothing but superstition, fear, or silliness.

How does this change or enrich your relation to the world?

AMOS OZ: It has to do with the intensity of the relationship between me and the reality around me, those little links that may be outside or inside me. It does not matter if a leaf fell while I was thinking about death, or that I was thinking about death when the leaf fell, or I was just standing long enough by the window, or because there was another fallen leaf before that I hadn't noticed and that made me think about death. Or maybe there was a light breeze. Or it was the precise second when the leaf was supposed to fall. The more focused I am (and I think focused is the right word), the more I observe these connections, and the more I love the world, and then I feel more alive. I don't agree with the world, but I love it.

In all your books, reality and dream exist side by side, until a certain moment when the two elements merge and the characters of reality become the characters of the dream. Do you view this as a moment of reconciliation or of destruction?

AMOS OZ: Depends what the dream is.

Do you use dreams as counterpoint to reality?

AMOS OZ: No. Everything is reality. Are my fantasies less real than the newspaper I read? Everything that passes through us is reality. Dreams too. As well as all the things that you won't reveal to a soul.

In The Seagull, *Chekhov writes, "Life should be described not as it is and not as it should have been, but as it is seen in our imagination." What would your characters say about this?*

AMOS OZ: If I placed a glass of water on the arm of this armchair, here by the window, at the right time, and a ray of sun fell on the water creating a rainbow of colors, and if I succeeded in describing it—I'm not sure I could depict the refraction because it is so ephemeral: a cloud may pass, I may move, the angle may change—but, if I managed to capture the uniqueness of the experience in the fleeting moment of its occurrence, then I've succeeded. If I were able to capture it in words, then I've succeeded. I'm not sure this is the meaning of "describing life." It is an attempt to capture in words, to fix, something that is forever fleeing. To preserve the memory of the moment. To hold on to it. To be able to call it back and say, "Come," and it will come. To evoke a recollection. To respond to some internal "Hello."

Do you agree with Novalis, who said, "Dreams protect us from the monotony of life"?

AMOZ OZ: Life is not monotonous. Why accord dreams a different status? Just because the Romantics did so? Hannah Gonen [in *My Michael*] is a very romantic woman. Me, I am not a very romantic man. For me, dreams are not a higher sphere of existence. Signs—yes, dreams—no. I do not share Hannah Gonen's view of dreams. I refuse to be identified with that woman. I gave her and many other characters in my stories my own traits and features: gestures, habits, biographical details, including very intimate details, but I refuse to say, with Flaubert, "Hannah Gonen c'est moi."

Was there ever a time when you did say, "Hannah Gonen is me"?

AMOS OZ: Only when I was actually, physically, writing her. And it wasn't a great pleasure, either. As soon as I finished with her, she became autonomous, facing her own destiny.

And she should answer these questions herself.

AMOS OZ: Yes. I do not identify with what she has to say about dreams. She sees in dreams compensation or substitutes for what she lacks. That's her, not me. I can fantasize, I can daydream. And whatever I say is true for my neighbors and anyone else.

You insist on sounding like the neighborhood spokesman.

AMOS OZ: You have given me a compliment. At the moment, I am more preoccupied with getting rid of all manner of romantic myths that surround the act of writing. If I happen to hear or sense any signals— signals are more prosaic than signs—it is because I am more attentive to detail, less preoccupied with running around and arranging things. But it has nothing to do with dreams. And it is not a monopoly of artists. Look, I have thick, stubby fingers, and I never felt the need to present myself as a muse-inspired person, a star-crossed poet. It is important for me to stress that I am not much different than my neighbor, so that if this is read by a young person who wants to become a poet or a writer, he or she needn't think that they have to ride on a purple cloud. And I'm sorry if I didn't give you the answer you were looking for.

Who is your protagonist? How would you describe his basic situation?

AMOS OZ: Which one? In my new book? I've already said that my characters are my relatives.

Your characters, at least to me, are always larger than life. They are not Molcho [the protagonist of A. B.Yehoshua's Four Seasons*]. They are not the same height as the readers.*

AMOS OZ: I don't see what is so large or high about the child in *The Hill of the Evil Council,* or the old man in "Late Love." In what way is he elevated? I once wrote a novel about a Jerusalem housewife who is dissatisfied with her life. I once wrote about a child who lives a political melodrama that is beyond his understanding yet fills him with strange sensations and contributes to his sexual maturation. I once wrote a novel about two men in a kibbutz, one taciturn, the other garrulous, both involved with a self-absorbed woman. None of these seem to me larger than life. If you, as a reader, tend to see them as elevated, in the Aristotelian sense, that's your privilege. I won't say you're wrong. I don't give instruction how to read my books. I wrote the score, you have the instrument. If you want to play my music on a harpsichord or on a harmonica, that's your decision. Sociologically speaking, at least, I never wrote about people larger than life, except once, perhaps, when I wrote about a crusading knight. But he was accompanied by a wicked dwarf. Normally, I write about real estate salesmen, kibbutz members involved in ideological disputes but also burning with ambition to change the world. Nothing is larger than life, except maybe for one thing; some of them experience very intense, highly significant moments, as I sometimes do. If this is what you mean, the answer is yes. Many of my characters experience this kind of moment that is suddenly charged with enormous voltage.

Perhaps this has to do with the language. There's a sense that you waste the moments of life. You deal with the important, momentous occurrences, and not with the small ones. This finds expression in the language. Events assume symbolic meaning, and life is illuminated by the symbol, by the grand moment.

AMOS OZ: It is hard for me to argue, but I do wish to protest. I don't think that a careful analysis of my work will yield fewer moments of housecleaning, ironing, and hair care than any other writer. Perhaps even more. All sorts of people said all sorts of things about the language in my books. Hardly anyone examined it. There are some accepted cliches; it is often claimed, invidiously, that my language is too pretty, ornate, highfalutin. Nobody ever checked this claim. I think, I hope, that what gave you that impression is, in fact, those moments of epiphany, or revelation, that the characters experience. Those moments when a Jerusalem housewife or a retired neighborhood doctor or a kibbutz member in search of self-discovery experiences a moment when the world opens up to them with great intensity and force. Then they return to their preoccupation with gardening, dishwashing, and earning a living. My work is full of such examples. There is a deep, organic connection between epiphany and laundry, cooking, and political discussion. This is the daily routine, the texture of the fabric. Sometimes there is a tear in the fabric and, through it, something else is perceived. I won't say what it is. It is something. The Moment. This is what happens in my books. But when I hear people say that my fiction is bigger than life, I beg to differ. I demand a reexamination. Because this was not my intention. Perhaps those moments of epiphany are so bright and intense that they give off an eerie, extraordinary light. But this is not to say that my writing is divorced from everyday, prosaic life. My characters change socks. They all do. Perhaps the problem is somewhere in the composition, in my partners, that is, the readers. They have been conditioned to look for the elevated, for the larger than life; perhaps they are hungrier for it.

To what extent are your characters modeled on real people?

AMOS OZ: When the comedian Yosef Rivlin wanted to satirize Shimon Peres in a television commercial on the eve of the last election, he kept answering every question with "yes and no." To me this is not so risible, because there are many questions where my answers would be yes and no, like this question. I may borrow from one person the way he scratches his ear, and from another his shirt, and from a third I'll lift a peculiar word where he puts the stress on the wrong syllable. In this respect, I'm a Peeping Tom, a pilferer, a thief. I never say, "Here's a man crossing the street, let me describe him." This doesn't interest me. When I was living on the kibbutz, I even thought it was morally reprehensible to do so. Except once, when I put Prime Minister Eshkol in my book, which was like Tolstoy's use of General Kutuzov and Napoleon in *War and Peace*. I did that again, once or twice more, mentioning people by name. I did not set any models. I am more interested in the process, in the growth; it's like an embryo starting out with a voice, or two voices, then a gesture is added, then a vocabulary, then facial expressions and tics, dress habits, small, idiosyncratic compulsions, food and sex preferences. Thus, slowly, the person develops and grows. And this fascinates me tremendously. I am totally enthralled when this happens. It isn't as if, behind the literary character, stands a real breathing person. Mostly, the characters contain components from my own personality, or from people who have genetic connection to me, and I know them as my own flesh. Well, actually, I'm not sure.

Are we to infer, in some respect, that your characters are an extension of yourself?

AMOS OZ: You may infer, in some respect, that all the characters are an extension of myself—the emphasis being on "in some respect." Because you may also infer that I myself am, in some respect, an extension of all the people that preceded me, from whom I derive, physically, genetically: my parents, my grandparents, people I never met, people who passed away or were murdered by Hitler, as well as people who passed through my life and whom I barely remember like, for instance, a certain primordial kindergarten teacher whom I dimly remember but who molded me like wax and who left an indelible mark on me. Perhaps also people who hurt me. These are things that I cannot trace, because their presence in my writing is not dependent on their fate, their face, or their clothes but consists in something much more fundamental: their insides. I cannot say that the professor in *Black Box* is a reflection of any specific professor I knew at the university, but I can claim that I recognize in him some of my own traits, but even those traits I probably recognize from earlier avatars, from the genetic reservoir, from people who have crossed my path in a very marked and definite way. Mostly wearing boots. Perhaps this sounds a bit hazy and vague, but it really is an ambiguous point. The simple answer is: no. None of the characters is an attempt to replicate a living person in a literary work. And yes, they are all, in some fashion, connected to me. The manner in which they are connected to me also connects them to other people, because I too am connected to others. It's a complicated answer, but then so is the question.

How important is credibility to you? Is there such a concept as "literary credibility," which is different from realistic credibility?

AMOS OZ: Allow me to replace the word "credibility" with "accuracy," and I'll tell you that it is the most important thing in the world to me. I strive to represent a person's speech, gesture, smell, and environment in the most faithful and precise manner the language can attain. And I don't mean the precision of a photograph, because a photograph is not precise either. It depends where you place your camera. Precision is as it were immanent. Within the rules I have set for myself, as soon as I say, "This is the person," or "This is the place," all the elements have to relate to one another with great precision. Not necessarily corresponding to the outside world. If someone told me, "this kind of cat doesn't exist in this country, only in Switzerland," it would be of less importance. This isn't credibility, it is love of order. Precision is something else altogether. It is the interrelation among parts. It's entirely internal. This is what happens inside a hermetically sealed watch, where not a drop of water from the outside world can penetrate, but where inside everything is coordinated. This is the most important thing for me:

how a gesture made by a woman relates to something a man said, and how both relate to the light that comes from outside. This is the stuff the story is made of, not of concepts, not of messages (a word I hate, by the way); it is made of the way one word is put next to another, and if later I want the readers to be partners and invest dollar for dollar, I have at least to give them precise triggers.

Your dialogues are written with extreme precision. Why, then, don't you try your hand at writing dramas?

AMOS OZ: Perhaps I'm spoiled. I need there to be mountains, wadis, a wind in the cypresses. Besides, I cannot work with collaborators. If I ever write a play, for every line of dialogue, there'll be twenty stage directions.

What brings you from time to time to assume the persona of a woman? First Hannah Gonen and recently "The Matches Woman"?

AMOS OZ: How do I know? I can't answer this question. If I knew what made me assume the persona of a man, perhaps I could tell you. Women are an intimate matter. I was born to a woman, I have loved women, and I begot women. It seems so obvious to me, that there's nothing to explain. When I write about women, from a woman's point of view, at least while I'm writing, I do not act, think, or function as a man. My testicles are put on hold, so to speak. The same happens when I write about a very old man, who is out of the erotic race. Women intrigue me. Mothers intrigue me. Nursing intrigues me, as does menstruation and the aging of women. Extremely so. I would give a year of my life to be a woman for one month. To figure out in what ways we differ and in what ways we're the same.

Only one year?

AMOS OZ: I'm stingy. I cherish every minute.

Most of the women in your fiction are dreamy, haunted, yearning women. Once, when asked to draw a portrait of yourself, you said that all your life you had tried to evoke the picture of a female member of Kibbutz Hulda, sitting on a bench at dusk, singing to herself a Polish song that she remembered from her youth. Fifty years earlier, she sat on the bank of a river in Poland singing to herself a Hebrew song from the Land of Israel. Is this also the image of the mother in The Hill of the Evil Council?

AMOZ OZ: Correction: the men I wrote about also yearn and long a lot. The story entitled "Yearnings" has a man as protagonist. Even the child, Soumchi [in Oz's only novel for young adults *Soumchi*—au.], is full of longing. I asked myself lately, having been provoked, whether my female characters aren't too schematic. Are my women merely female stereotypes taken from Greta Garbo movies? I examined myself carefully, as far as it is possible to examine oneself. Never in my books do I say "That woman" or "That man." The women in my stories were all women who were unwilling to take part and realize themselves in the outside world, and that's why many of them fell into the nostalgic trap. I did not mean to make any broad generalization about the female sex. Are my women afflicted by yearning and nostalgia? Very often they are. More than the men? Perhaps. Because those women were not sufficiently prepared to go out into the world. They are not modern women. If you want to ask me why I don't write about modern women, I'll join you in asking the question. I can't answer it.

I think all those women are your mother.

AMOZ OZ: No. I don't think so. I remember my mother. I remember Hannah Gonen, Rimona, and Ilana. They are not similar. It is not that simple. Of course, there are some elements of my mother in every line I've written, and also elements of other people very close to me, but it is not true that they are the stars or have a central function in my writing.

Why are you reluctant to talk about your mother?

AMOS OZ: I'll tell you something far-reaching: I refuse to discuss private matters. In Israeli society, privacy has become a political issue. Defending my privacy is my Maginot line. Our society invades privacy and gnaws it to the bone. Destruction of privacy bedevils our society. This is partly voluntary; people go to the newspapers and sell themselves. If I were a government minister or a member of the Knesset, you would have the right to pose such personal questions to me. But I'm not a civil servant, and so I am not obliged to report to the public about my personal life.

There is no analogy, really. Your sense of deprivation due to your mother's death is relevant to your writing.

AMOS OZ: Not true. Thousands of people in the world experience deprivations of this kind or another, and they don't write books. If you knew everything about the personal aspect of the story behind the story, you would still not understand anything about the story. What I have been through in my life, for better or worse, is not the stuff that colossal tragedies are made of. Many people have lost dear ones, have known orphanhood and bereavement. Nothing in my personal story explains what impelled me to write my books, and I don't want to be an accessory to an offense and mislead people into saying, "Ah, his mother committed suicide, now I understand everything!" This kind of "understanding" is to me the essence of banality and vulgarity.

You said in the interview with Esther Dar: "A person becomes a writer because of some hurt he/she suffered as a child. Without the wound, there is no writing." Hence, my question.

AMOS OZ: So I said it. I still agree with myself. But I don't see why I have to explain what kind of wound.

I give up.

AMOS OZ: You must give up, because I won't give in. You mustn't try to satisfy people's thirst for gossip. It is a bad thing.

This isn't gossip, sorry.

AMOS OZ: Let me die in peace. Then, if people want, they can write my biography. Don't get me wrong; I like gossip. I lick my fingers when I read Henri Troyat. I have no problem with the idea that after my death, medical students will touch my corpse, but right now—no! I'm still alive. I know this is not a typical stance for an author. After all, in the encyclopedia you find after my name: 1939–? There's a hyphen and you know it's waiting for you, and you can see your grave wide open, but I don't want to leap right in.

Milan Kundera said, in an interview, that "the reluctance to talk about yourself is what differentiates the prose writer from the poet. I had hoped to blur this differentiation, but it didn't work out."

AMOZ OZ: Really? I'll help Kundera. Not you. I can tell you this: Perhaps the reason why I refuse to discuss personal matters is also the reason why I don't publish poetry. I sometimes write poems, but I have no urge to publish them; they're too intimate.

You really think that your stories and novels are not intimate?

AMOS OZ: What are you telling me? "You've already taken off your shirt and undershirt, why don't you take off your shorts?"

No, I'm telling you we've already seen you naked.

AMOS OZ: Alright, so you've seen me. But I don't want you to see more than you already have. Isn't it my privilege? I don't have to deliver my life and my dead ones to the public. I "give" enough. More than most people. Why demand more?

    I really think that there is something anti-cultural in this orgy of striptease that goes on all the time. A person has just published a book of poems, or has just been elected deputy-mayor of a town in Upper Galilee and the papers are full of stories about his life and the lives of his aunts. There is also something debasing and corrupting in all this. I'll tell you something that you can erase later; last night, I had an argument with some people because they had referred to politicians by their nicknames: Gandhi, Raful, Arik. And I, an old-fashioned stickler for decorum, insisted on calling them Mr. Zeevi, Mr. Eitan, and Mr. Sharon. I refuse to accept this facile intimacy. In this you can see the fanatic in me. There is an element of fanaticism. I don't want intimacy with the entire world, only with people I select. Okay?

I accept. You often describe the writer as the witch doctor, the magician of the tribe. What is the function of the mask he dons?

AMOZ OZ: Today this sounds a little romantic. I would phrase it differently: the writer is the watchmaker of the tribe, to whom people bring their broken clocks and watches. He makes the slow watches go faster and the fast ones go slower. If the clock is too loud, he modulates its sound. Every creative act involves donning a mask. When you write a novel, you use several personae simultaneously. It is possible that this bad habit stays with you even when you're not writing. I caught myself three or four times in my life maintaining postures that I'm not particularly proud of, that were, possibly, extensions of characters in my fiction. What is the function of the mask? If you divide yourself into three or four personae, then you are both a person and his/her enemy, and yet you're neither. You learn to wear a disguise. Perhaps the right metaphor is neither a witch doctor nor a watchmaker but a secret agent, like the protagonist of my new book. By the way, this is not a universal law; Brenner did not assume any persona. But even that is not definite. I have a suspicion that Brenner, apart from being Brenner, also fashioned Brenner, honed the contours, carved and shaped Brenner's idiosyncratic traits. Or take Agnon's persona as the wise, omniscient, ironic, old man. Well, this is as far as masks are concerned; you use several personae in order to tell a story.

Behind which mask are you hiding?

AMOS OZ: Not behind one particular mask. But don't ask me what I look like without any mask, because I won't tell you.

I wouldn't dream of it.

AMOS OZ: Shalom Aleichem [the famous Yiddish writer] used to say, "A person is like a carpenter. A carpenter lives until he dies, and so does a person." So I'm telling you, a writer is like a person. It is very seldom that an author appears in front of others totally exposed. Most of the time, he assumes a persona. Here, you're sitting in front of me, asking me all sorts of questions, because this is your job. There are other questions you would like to ask, but you know that it does not fall within the scope of this interview. And perhaps there are questions that I would like to ask you. The clerk selling me stamps at the post office also assumes a persona. Sometimes he smiles underneath his mask, and sometimes I smile at him, and those are precious moments when something peeps from underneath. One mustn't squander these moments.

When you describe your protagonist using the third person, do you, in some way, liberate yourself?

AMOS OZ: Yes.

How?

AMOS OZ: You asked, I said yes. That should suffice.

You hide behind your characters. You hardly ever use the first-person narrative.

AMOS OZ: This is simply not true. *My Michael* is written entirely in the first person. So is "Late Love" and half of *A Perfect Peace* and *Black Box.* What else is needed? A confession? When I'm sixty-four, perhaps I'll write one.

You said that you argue with the characters. Do you feel equal to them? What is the relationship between writer and characters?

AMOS OZ: No, they are inside, I am outside. I can erase things, they cannot. The relationship between me and each of them ranges from deep compassion and empathy to revulsion and disgust and everything in between.

Didn't you ever find yourself feeling only empathy toward one of your characters?

AMOS OZ: Yes, on the whole, a lot of empathy. I felt anger and resentment only when they gave me a hard time, when they rampaged and tried to take control of the story. I never wrote in hate. There were writers who wrote very powerful books out of thirst for revenge, to punish others or themselves. I don't think I am capable of writing without forgiveness. If I feel hatred toward a character, I have no interest in writing about it. I can't loathe a person and then put him or her in a story. Only when a character is engulfed in self-pity and sentimentality do I stop feeling compassion. Then they anger me, and I mock them.

If I can't forgive, I can't see. Anger blinds. Many things can blind you: anger, sorrow, the sun. If you want to write about people, you need to be able to see, your eyes have to be clear. When you see clearly, you don't write in anger, revenge, or hatred.

In a monograph she wrote about you, Nurit Gertz observes that over the years, there has been a devaluation in the status of the narrator: the omniscient narrator today does not know much more than the characters in the story. Do you agree?

AMOS OZ: I'm not sure. Look, nobody is going to believe me if I said that I did not think about this issue. My new book, *To Know a Woman*, is told in the third person by an omniscient narrator. But the narrator is not very vocal; on the contrary, he's almost transparent. I assume Gertz is right. She has read my books. I can't look at my books with a literary scholar's eyes. When I open books I wrote twenty years ago, in 80 percent of the cases, I ask myself how could I write such crap, and I feel miserable; in 20 percent of the cases, I say, how lovely! I'll never be able to write like this again, and then I feel miserable again. That's why I refrain from rereading my old books.

And if you could rewrite those 80 percents?

AMOS OZ: I did that once with *Where the Jackals Howl*, ten years after the publication of the first version. There I felt compelled to do so. In the sixties, when I began publishing stories in "Keshet" [*Rainbow*, a literary periodical—au.], it was a time when Hebrew was still considered new; almost everyone who wrote literature felt obliged to dress up, to put on the entire wardrobe. So when I wrote *Where the Jackals Howl*, I put on my bathing trunks, then my winter coat, then my father's jacket, then my grandpa's hat, as well as a raincoat, umbrella, boots, and a tennis racket borrowed from a cousin. Thus I went out into the street to show everyone that I have a lot of clothes. This upset me so much that, ten years later, I took the text and weeded it out. But I can't do that anymore.

Do you write many drafts, many versions of a short story or a novel?

AMOS OZ: Yes, I change words. A banal little dialogue can torment my soul, can exasperate me for days.

What bothers you most, the question of verisimilitude?

AMOS OZ: I can't even begin to describe it to you. I don't use the word verisimilitude when I talk to myself. I could stand here in the room and shout quietly, before I even hear the sound. It's like trying to match something that you hear to something that you utter. And I've already told you that, in the end, I have to compromise. But to be honest, there are also moments of euphoria when I feel that I've come very close, that I made it, and then I feel good.

One hears many voices in your books, a polyphony, and not just in Black Box. *When do we hear your own authentic voice?*

AMOS OZ: Only in the sum total. You can't point to one violin in the orchestra and say, "that's Amos." Only the totality.

In your opinion, what distinguishes the novel from other art forms? What is it that "only the novel can reveal" (as Herman Broch claimed)?

AMOS OZ: There are certain truths about the rhythm of life that only the novel can reveal. Not the lyrical poem, not the epic poem, not even drama, and apparently not even the short story, except for a few exceptions. Something that has to do with the rhythm of repetition, with routine, with minor variations. The tiny deviations from the norm are revealed more clearly in a novel than in a story or a poem, those barely perceptible deviations, which are the marks of all human activity—acts of passion, or fear, or greed. Deviation from what we wanted to achieve. And even if we did turn out exactly as we dreamed of as children—suppose I wanted to be a firefighter, and I actually became a firefighter; I wanted to be a film star, and I really became a film star—

even when everything came true, somehow it isn't exactly what we had in mind. This slight deviation from the course and how it came about is something that the scope of the novel allows you to capture better than any other literary genre, and I find this more and more fascinating. My protagonist in the new novel says it in so many words.

Is there a perfect novel? I can think of Robert Musil, Herman Broch, perhaps Brenner.

AMOS OZ: No, I never thought about it. I think my answer is no. Just as there is no perfect painting. A frame always breaks the world, and every novel creates a frame. Even when the canvas is of Tolstoyan proportions, something is left outside the frame. In this respect, nothing is perfect, except God's novel, and he too probably just wrote a short story that stretches indefinitely.

Only from this point of view or also from the point of view of the language?

AMOS OZ: In some respect, language is the enemy of life; it's like formaldehyde. It can take care of mummies, not of living animals. The price of capturing the moment in words forever is that you take away its soul. If you want to stop time from fleeting, you must also kill its soul. This theme appears in Agnon's *Tmol Shilshom* (Only Yesterday) in the character of Arzaf, the taxidermist.

Do you recognize a need for maintaining a certain unity, musical unity in the polyphony of various characters, or a unity of motifs?

AMOS OZ: No, I play it by ear. It is not a system of architectural decisions, it's more a feeling at the tip of my fingers. An almost rhythmic issue. There is only a musical logic. I know which one of my works corresponds to which musical form: in *A Perfect Peace*, I worked on a cantata and in *Black Box*, I worked on a madrigal.

How do you view the chapters in a novel? What should a chapter include, and what is its function in the totality of the work?

AMOS OZ: If I divide the work into chapters, it is because I want the reader to stop then and there. I can hear the break. It is essentially like punctuation, only on a different scale. It is comparable to movements in a musical composition. I decide where I want the story to stop for a few moments of silence.

Why did you choose to write Black Box *as an epistolary novel? Did it free you from the conventional novelistic technique?*

AMOS OZ: I did not sit down to write *Black Box* as an epistolary novel. I knew it would include letters, as did some of my earlier works. While working on the book, though, it became clear to me that the positions the characters take vis-à-vis one another should be an epistolary one, because they are both distant and very intimate. What could be distant and intimate at the same time? A letter. It is more intimate than a conversation, and yet the people can be light years away; they don't have to look each other in the eye. The characters are all great talkers, but not good listeners. I said to myself: You fool, what are you doing in the age of the telephone? What planet do you come from? But no. It turns out that when you have a man and a woman, one living in Chicago, the other in Jerusalem, who can't live without each other, yet who dare not approach each other for fear of what might happen, then letters are the answer. Suddenly, letters seemed to me the right medium. It evolved while I was working on the novel. I didn't plan it that way. I began with a letter that the woman writes to her husband after seven years of silence. But I didn't see the whole book written in letters. I can't say exactly at what point in the first letter I realized that there would be a reply. Only much later did I understand the technical problems I was getting into. Supplying information in an epistolary novel is one of the most difficult things in the world. After all, a woman is not going to write to her husband, "As you remember, we got married in 1958." And she won't write, "Our apartment had three rooms, and the bed stood over there." But these are facts I want the reader to know. There were complicated technical problems. I'm not sure I found happy solutions for all of them. There is a price to be paid for literary conventions. Just as in the theater. Just as with an omniscient narrator. Here the structure evolved with the book.

Do you need to have a beginning? Have you ever started a novel knowing how it would end?

AMOS OZ: Yes. Sometimes I know how it ends, but eventually there's a different ending. And sometimes when I'm done writing, I go to the beginning and change it entirely.

There is a distinct perception in twentieth-century fiction that the novel is getting away from storytelling, from the fun of spinning a yarn, and aspires to greater sophistication. What do you think brought this about? Where is this trend leading?

AMOS OZ: I'm not sure that you're right in your generalization. This is not true for South American literature; there you see the fun and pleasure of sheer, unabashed storytelling. Sophistication? Let there be sophistication, but it shouldn't be felt. It shouldn't be proclaimed aloud: Look, how clever I am! We have, in contemporary literature, works of fabulous sophistication with elements of breathtaking risks—I know it, because I am a tailor and I see the inner seams of the garment—but the reader doesn't feel them. With a great work of art, the first reaction perhaps should be: How come I didn't do it? What you point out is perhaps a result of the growing presence of academicians in the lives of the authors. They seem to think that if books were more in need of interpretation, there would be more interpretation to be done. I don't believe that the anemic things will last long. Feeble creatures don't survive. There are animals that are bred in the lab, and if you release them back to nature, they perish. The novel is a creature of the living room, the kitchen, and the bedroom. That's where it is born. But many novels of today, if you take them to the kitchen or the bedroom, they die, they can't survive the climate. As a reader I often ask myself: Will the book stand the test of laughter and crying? I want to laugh and to cry when I read a novel. I'm not ashamed to admit it.

A writer is made up of a certain number of basic words. These are sequences of words, like the sequences of notes in a Schoenberg composition. What are your basic words?

AMOS OZ: No. It is not my business to say this.

In "Unto Death," you write: "I love words; I am their master." In your opinion, is the writer the master of the language or its slave?

AMOS OZ: It is not that simple. I have already said the phrase "it is not that simple" several times in this interview. There is a whole scale of variations in this game in which mastery and servitude are only two, and they are often interchangeable. One can play at master and slave or mistress and slave, and there are many other games in between. It is not an "either-or" situation. There are situations where you make yourself totally subservient to the language, and you derive great pleasure from it. And there are other occasions when you take the language in your hands and almost have your way with it. I use a sexual metaphor here advisedly, because my relationship with the language is of a sensual nature. I'll never be able to completely have my way with the language or follow it blindly to the very end, but I can almost do these things, and many other things. I can be a friend, for example, or a lover, and listen to her wishes.

What is the difference between prose and poetry? Today it seems as if prose has embraced poetry.

AMOS OZ: The difference is in the length of the lines. Honestly, it's only the length of the lines. Somebody said that in poetry, the poet decides where the line ends, while in prose, it is the typesetter who does it. This question of the boundary between the genres doesn't really bother me. I would like to cross that boundary without noticing the barrier. I can read a page of prose and say: here's a page of poetry, and read a page of poetry and say: here's an element of prose. I say this approvingly. That's all.

In Under This Blazing Light, *you write: "One can try and capture the time, the place, the displaced refugees as they are: in their elusive, emaciated condition . . . to write like an overexposed camera." And yet your writing is quite the reverse of this. Is this, then, a wish, a desire?*

AMOS OZ: I was thinking about writing prose in a place that is still in the process of developing, that has not yet accumulated assets and real estate. It is difficult. A novel is, in fact, a plant growing in standing water, not in fast-flowing rivers, perhaps in the slow current of a lake. If the novel were a fish, I'd say it should be in a lake, not in a raging river. In the prevailing situation in this country, one should write emaciated prose and shoot pictures into the sun. Some people do just that, and I'm interested, but I have not followed my own advice, and not for the first time. There are many things that I know should be done, but I don't get around to doing them. If a young writer came to me and told me that he's still looking for a voice, I'd say, son, you should do this and that. I'm an old cat. You assume that I have the liberty to change styles, as one changes clothes. But even if people tried to convince me that there are things I ought to be doing, I still couldn't do them. Suppose someone told me, "Amos, the most urgent thing to do now is to write a book about the Intifada [Palestinian uprising] and describe how it looks from an oppressed Arab's point of view." I'll have to say, "You're right, but I can't do it. It's not that I don't want to, or try to avoid the issue, I just can't." It isn't what I'm all about. I would like to write differently in the same way that I would like to build bridges or be a woman for some time, or be a prime minister for a few months and put an end to our conflict with the Arabs. Even you, who are not a teenager, would blush to hear the things that I would like to be. So what? I can't. In our reality, it could be very interesting to write in a lean style and shoot straight into the sun and burn the film. And write quasi-documentary literature. Even when I wrote *Here and There in the Land of Israel,* I wanted to be a reporter, but I wasn't. I wanted to be objective, but I wasn't. My legs led me to the lunatic fringe, to the margins. I didn't talk to anybody from "Peace Now." Why? Why did I visit only the corners that are opposed to what I am? Because.

Unlike poets, prose writers are often more interested in what never happened to them than in what happened to them in reality. They are like people confessing a sin they have not committed. The question is why and how does a writer write about something that never happened to him or her. What feeds their imagination?

AMOS OZ: The same fuel that feeds all our fantasies. All of us. Our appetite for Life is much greater than our capacity to swallow. We come into this world equipped with huge eyes. This is what feeds the imagination. To write about something is not exactly to live it. You mustn't assume that if a writer describes an emerald palace perched on the top of a bare mountain, it means that he has been to such a place. He is the mason and the stonecutter and he carries the glass, but he doesn't live there. Perhaps the reader will live there. To describe a nightmare or a fantasy does not mean to live through them, only to create them. And it's hard work. I'll tell you something you did not ask me. Yakov Shabtai once told Hayyim Be'er [both noted Israeli novelists—au.] that to write a novel is like taking a toothbrush and scrubbing Allenby Street from Magen David Square to the sea. And I'll tell you that it's like taking the range of Edom Mountains over there and grinding it into gravel. This new novel of mine comprises 120,000 words, a quarter of a million decisions. It is not true that to write a fantasy is to live it. It is to work, to create, to fashion, and sometimes to free yourself from it. There are moments of euphoria and moments of despair, but most of the time you sit at your desk with tweezers in your hands holding a verb and asking yourself where that verb will sit. You pick up three or four verbs or adjectives, examine them against the light, turn them around and ask yourself if they will fit in or not.

Do you like to write? Do you enjoy it?

AMOS OZ: I like to finish writing. No, it's not true. There are moments of great pleasure. When I find what I've been looking for, it's a tremendous pleasure.

How much of the book exists in your mind when you sit down to write it?

AMOS OZ: In the mind? In the body? In the groin? In the belly? It's not right to say that it is in the mind. I don't know. Normally, I know what I am going to do, but normally the result is not what I thought I was going to do.

Do you write every morning? Do you impose a discipline on yourself every day?

AMOS OZ: I punch a clock every morning. I don't have to impose a discipline. I am a very disciplined, square person.

How do you begin your daily routine? By reading what you wrote the day before?

AMOS OZ: Not always. This book, *To Know a Woman*, was not written in an orderly fashion. Some days I come in here, and my day begins with me doing nothing. I pace around the room thinking, or sit down thinking. Often, when I have to write a dialogue, I have to voice it aloud. I have to hear it spoken. Here, nobody can hear me, or else they would laugh. When I write a conversation, I first repeat it several times, until I get it right, then I write it down. Sometimes I reread what I've written. Sometimes I don't pick up where I left off the night before but start with another angle, from a different place in the book. In the end, it all ties up. Or it doesn't. I remember that in my first stories (perhaps because of the conditions that prevailed then), I would compose the whole story in my head, and only then sit down for a couple of hours and write it down. Not any more. I write several drafts. Not copying anew the revisions but writing different versions, and when I have five or six versions, I lay them on the desk and look at them, and then I combine them all into one version.

What happens during the period of gestation of a new book?

AMOS OZ: I sit here in my room looking around. In the past, when I lived on the kibbutz, this used to get me into real trouble. I would walk into the dining room at noon, after sitting in my study for five or six hours, writing nothing or erasing two–three lines I had written the day be- fore—so I had a deficit—and I would look at the people coming in from work and ask myself, how dare I come here to eat, to put food on my plate? It was very difficult. Today I see myself as a store owner. My job is to open the store and keep it open for several hours, even if no customer shows up. When there are many customers, I keep the store open after hours too.

How do you regard contemporary Israeli prose? A. B. Yehoshua, Shabtai, Kenaz. Do you find any of the young writers particularly interesting?

AMOS OZ: We live in a very intimate environment. I have a lot to say, and I won't say it in an interview, because I may hurt someone needlessly. There's enough suffering in the world as it is. I'll tell you in general that I find the literature being written in Israel at present, both poetry and prose, exciting and intriguing. Even when the product is mediocre. Nothing that I read seems to me anemic or watery. It doesn't leave me cold. Some things anger me, even disgust me, but nothing leaves me cold.

"I am writing this because people I loved have died. I am writing this because when I was young, I was full of the power of loving, and now that power of loving is dying." This is the beautiful opening of My Michael. *Explain it, please.*

AMOS OZ: Why are you asking me, ask Hannah Gonen. She thinks there is a connection between writing and the dwindling of the power to love, and a connection between the dwindling of the power to love and death. She sees a link between the three things: the power to love, her writing, which is her antidote to the dwindling of the power to love, and the third thing, which is death. In order not to die, you must go on loving, and in order to go on loving, you have to go on writing, and if you've stopped loving—you must write, because it strengthens the power to love.

　　Writing is connected to the forces of life and to the temptations of life, not to death. To the trees and the stones. Whoever writes does not wish to die. In this, Hannah Gonen is not alone. Even a suicide, when leaving a letter, indicates he doesn't really want to die. While writing the letter, he is on the side of the living. The letter is not meant for the dead. But even if he addresses the letter to the dead, even when one talks to the dead, it is in order to make them live a little, not to give in to death. Not to give in to death is to go on loving. If you write about someone who is dead, while you are writing, that person is no longer dead. You don't write to the bones or to the flesh already consumed by worms. You are inviting the dead person to your room, you are calling that person home.

Notes

Chapter 1

1. Cf. Yair Mazor, *The Dynamics of Motifs in S.Y. Agnon's Works* (Tel Aviv: Dekel—Academic Press, 1979), 5–8, 12–21.

2. On the interpretative fringe benefits of comparing literary texts, see Yair Mazor, *The Triple Cord: Agnon, Hamsun, Strindberg: Where Hebrew and Scandinavian Literatures Meet* (Tel Aviv: Papyrus Press—Tel Aviv University, 1987), 31–61.

3. See Joseph Ha'efrati, *Tchernichovsky's Idylls* (Tel Aviv: Sifiryat Po'alim and Hakibbutz Hame'uchad, 1979); see also Yair Mazor, *The Other Tchernichovsky: The Landscape Pattern of His Stories: The Narrative Art of Tchernichovsky* (Tel Aviv: Papyrus Press—Tel Aviv University, 1979).

Chapter 2

1. Julia Kristeva, "The Bounded Text," in *Desire in Language: A Semiotic Approach to Literature and Art*, trans. T. Gora, A. Jardine, and L. S. Roudiez (New York: Columbia University Press, 1980), 36–63.

2. Irena Makaryk, ed., *Encyclopedia of Contemporary Literary Theory* (Toronto: Toronto University Press, 1944), 568.

3. J. A. Cuddon, *Dictionary of Literary Terms and Literary Theories* (New York: Penguin Books, 1991), 222.

4. Ibid.

5. Raman Selden and Peter Widdowson, eds., *Contemporary Literary Theory* (Lexington: Kentucky University Press, 1933), 147.

6. Amos Oz, *Under This Blazing Light* (Tel Aviv: Sifriyat Ha-Po'alim, 1979), 84.

7. Amos Oz, *Here and There in the Land of Israel,* (Tel Aviv: Am Oved, 1983), 126.

Chapter 3

1. Cf. Eliezer Shvaid, *Three Watches in Hebrew Literature* (Tel Aviv: Am Oved, 1967); "The Way of Repentance," pp. 62–70 (on the substitute motif in "In the Prime of Her Life"); Abraham Band, "The Unreliable Narrator in *My Michael* and in 'In the Prime of Her Life," *Hasifrut*, vol. 3, part 1 (1971): 30–34; Yair Mazor, *The Dynamics of Motifs in S. Y. Agnon's Works* (Tel Aviv: Dekel—Academic Press, 1979), 61–62.

2. Cf. Yair Mazor, *From Wooded Meadows to Downtown Tel Aviv: Contemporary Hebrew Poetry* (Tel Aviv: Papyrus Tel Aviv University, 1996), 61–62.

3. Cf. J. E. Cirlot, *A Dictionary of Symbols*, trans. J. Sage (New York: Philosophical Library, 1962), 50. Cf. also 'blue' as indicating cold rationality in the character of Bluma in Agnon's novella "A Simple Story." And see also Yair Mazor, *The Triple Cord: Agnon, Hamsun, Strindberg: Where Hebrew and Scandinavian Literatures Meet* (Tel Aviv: Papyrus Tel Aviv University, 1987), pp. 117–122.

4. *The Triple Cord*, op. cit., 110–14. In *Hunger, Mystery*, and to some extent *Victoria*, Hamsun attaches contradictory meanings to yellow in different contexts: at times positive and pleasant, at others negative and off-putting. On the potential connotations of yellow, see: J. G. Frazer, *The Golden Bough: A Study in Magic and Religion* (New York: Macmillan, 1950), 17–18; Hans and Shulamit Kreitler, *The Psychology of the Arts* (Durham: Duke University Press, 1972), 69.

5. Cf. Northrop Frye, *Anatomy of Criticism* (Princeton: Princeton University Press, 1973); "The Mythos of Spring: Comedy," 163–85.

6. Cf. Nurit Gertz, *Amos Oz: Monography* (Tel Aviv: Sifriyat Po'alim, 1980), 14–43. One should mention here two comprehensive studies of Amos Oz's poetics by Avraham Balaban, *Between God and Beast: A Study of Amos Oz's Fiction* (Tel Aviv: Am Oved, 1986), and *Between Language and Beyond: Language and Reality in Amos Oz's Fiction* (Tel Aviv: Am Oved, 1988).

7. The analogy here is to the biblical Samson in the book of *Judges* who was consecrated as a Nazarite even before his birth. The mention of an altar in that context underlines the fact that this is another instance of sacrificing a son on the altar of the parents' and society's expectations. See also Yair Mazor, *From Medieval Spain to the Land of Cinderella: Studies in Hebrew Poetry*, (Tel Aviv: Tag, 1996), "Samson the Danite or Danny the Hero? Duality and Oxymorons in the Rhetorics of Children's Literature," 115–42. Cf. also Yair Mazor, "Who Is Afraid of Hebrew Children's Poetry and Why, or: The Importance of Being Earnest about Cinderella," *Israel Studies Bulletin*, vol. 12, No. 1 (spring 1996): 4–8; vol. 12, no. 2 (fall 1996): 20–25.

8. Hillel Barzel, *Six Authors* (Tel Aviv: Yachdav, 1972), 221–15.

9. Cf. Edith Hamilton, *Mythology* (Boston: Little, Brown, 1969), 65.

10. Cf. Sigmund Freud, "Dreams of the Death of Beloved Persons," in *Basic Writings of Sigmund Freud*, trans. and ed. A. A. Brill (New York: The Modern Library, 1938), 209.

11. On the eroticism of the female foot and its manifestations in world literature, see Yair Mazor, *The Triple Cord* op. cit., 84–87.

12. Ibid., 181–83.

Chapter 4

1. Cf. Yair Mazor, *The Dynamics of Motifs in S. Y. Agnon's Works* (Tel Aviv: Dekel Academic Press, 1979), 38, 40–41.

2. For a discussion of the analogy between Yoel Ravid and Sophocles' *Oedipus Tyrannus* and *Oedipus in Colonus*—in the trilogy that also includes *Antigone*—see Nitza Ben-Dov "Oedipus in Ramat Lotan: The Link between *To Know a Woman* and Sophocles' Plays," *Haaretz* (October 3, 1990). In the article, Ben-Dov analyzes the dualities in the novel and the allusion to Judas Iscariot.

3. For a discussion of the bird imagery in Dahlia Ravikovitch's poetry, see Yair Mazor, "Besieged Feminism: Contradictory Thematic Trends in the Poetry of Dahlia Ravikovitch," *World Literature Today*, vol. 58, no. 3 (1984): 354–59. A Hebrew translation of the article appeared in Yair Mazor's: *A Sense of Structure: Studies in Modern Hebrew Poetry and Fiction and in Biblical Literature* (Tel Aviv: University Publishing Projects, 1987), 17–25.

4. Cf. Northrop Frye, "The Mythos of Autumn: Tragedy," in *Anatomy of Criticism* (Princeton: Princton University Press, 1957), 206–22.

5. For a discussion of a possible reconciliation between opposing poles, cf. Avner Holtzman, "Fima Waits for a Miracle," *Haaretz* (February 15, 1991). A denouement that hints at a possible reconciliation accords well with Oz's later fiction in which he tends to map and depict situations of disease and recovery. Both kinds of closure evoke compassion, loving-kindness, appeasement, and propitiation. Hannah Naveh addressed this issue in an insightful lecture she gave at the Jewish Theological Seminary in New York in June 1998.

Chapter 5

1. Cf. Yair Mazor, *The Dynamics of Motifs in S. Y. Agnon's Works* (Tel Aviv: Dekel—Academic Press, 1979), 11.

2. Cf. also Avraham Balaban, *Between God and Beast: A Study of Amos Oz's Fiction* (Tel Aviv: Am Oved, 1986), 12–15. Balaban continues his extensive analysis of Oz's fiction in his next book, *Toward Language and Beyond: Language and Reality in the Work of Amos Oz*, (Tel Aviv: Am Oved, 1986).

3. Cf. Juan E. Cirlot, *A Dictionary of Symbols*, trans. J. Sagel (New York: Philosophic Library, 1962), 53; Hans and Schulamit Kreitler, *The Psychology of the Arts* (Durham, N.C.: Duke University Press, 1976), 68.

4. Cf. Yair Mazor, *From Wooded Meadows to Downtown Tel Aviv: Contemporary Hebrew Poetry* (Tel Aviv: Papyrus—Tel-Aviv University, 1996); see the chapter, "The Impossible Difficulty of Women's Poetry and Dahlia Ravikovitch's Poetry," in Yair Mazor, *A Sense of Structure: Studies in Hebrew and Biblical Literature* (Tel Aviv: University Publishing Projects, 1987), 59–67; see also the chapter "Feminism under Siege, or Between Yearning and Wilting: Dialectic Rhetoric in Dahlia Ravikovitch's Poetry," ibid., 17–25.

5. This aspect has been addressed by several other critics.

6. Cf. W. C. Booth, *The Rhetoric of Fiction* (Chicago: University of Chicago Press, 1961).

7. About 1,500 years before Freud discussed the connection between food and sex, the Talmud (Nedarim, 20, 2, 12) quotes a woman's complaint against her husband: "I set a table for him, and he turned it over" (referring to coital position). Employing a "clean language," the woman uses the word table as a metonym for food, which is a metaphor for copulation.

8. Cf. Amos Oz. "Beyond the Mountains of Darkness: Literary Bibliography." *B. Hasofer*. Vol 1 (1994), p. 3.

Chapter 7

1. Yosef (Joseph) Even, *Dictionary of Literary Terms* (Jerusalem: Academon, 1975), 13–14.

2. Boris Tomashevsky, "Thematics," in L. T. Lemon and M. J. Reis, eds. *Russian Formalist Criticism* (Lincoln: Nebraska University Press, 1965), 61–95.

3. Yair Mazor, *The Dynamics of Motifs in S. Y. Agnon's Works* (Tel Aviv: Dekel—Academic Press, 1979), 8–19.

4. As always, I am grateful to my teacher and colleague, Dr. Boaz Shachevitz, scientist *par excellence*, who taught me how to think methodically, logically, and succinctly. I borrow his useful definition of Science.

5. Cf. Yair Mazor, *The Dynamics of Motifs in S. Y. Agnon's Works*, op. cit., 10–12.

Bibliography

List of works of literature and scholarship cited in this book

Primary Sources

Oz, Amos. *Black Box*. Tel Aviv: Am Oved, 1987.

———. *Do Not Call It a Night*. Jerusalem: Keter, 1994.

———. *Elsewhere, Perhaps*. Tel Aviv: Sifriyat Po'alim, 1986.

———. *Fima (The Third Condition)*. Jerusalem: Keter, 1991.

———. *From the Slopes of Lebanon*. Tel Aviv: Am Oved, 1987.

———. *The Hill of the Evil Council*. Tel Aviv: Am Oved, 1976.

———. "Hollow Stone." In *Where The Jackals Howl*, 2d ed. Jerusalem: Keter, 1996, pp. 170–199.

———. *In the Land of Israel*. Tel Aviv: Am Oved, 1983.

———. "Late Love." In *Unto Death*. Tel Aviv: Sifriyat Po'alim, 1971, pp. 7–83. First published in *Keshet*, Vol. 49, 1961.

———. "Mr. Levi." In *The Hill of the Evil Council*. Tel Aviv: Am Oved, 1976, pp. 55–113.

———. *My Michael*. Tel Aviv: Am Oved, 1987.

———. *A Panther in the Basement*. Jerusalem: Keter, 1995.

———. *A Perfect Peace*. Tel Aviv: Am Oved, 1982.

———. *The Same Sea (Let Her)*. Jerusalem: Keter, 1996.

———. *Heaven's Silence: Agnon Wonders about God*. Jerusalem: Keter, 1993.

———. *Soumchi*. Tel Aviv: Am Oved, 1978.

———. *A Story Begins*. Jerusalem: Keter, 1996.

———. "Strange Fire." In *Where The Jackals Howl*. Tel Aviv: Massada, 1965.

———. *To Know a Woman*. Tel Aviv: Am Oved, 1989.

———. *Touch the Water, Touch the Wind*. Tel Aviv: Am Oved, 1973.

———. *Under This Blazing Light*. Tel Aviv: Sifriyat Po'alim, 1979.

———. *Unto Death*. Tel Aviv: Sifriyat Po'alim, 1971.

———. "The Way of the Wind." In *Where The Jackals Howl*, 2d ed. Jerusalem: Keter, 1996, pp. 43–63.

Secondary Sources

Agnon, S. Y. "In the Prime of Her Life." In *On the Door's Handles*. Tel Aviv: Schocken, 1975, pp. 5–54.

———. *Shira*. Tel Aviv: Schocken, 1971.

Alterman, Nathan. "The Mole." In *Poor People's Joy*. Tel Aviv: Hakibbutz Hame'uchad, 1967, pp. 161–163.

Amichai, Yehuda. "Sudden Longing." In *An Hour of Grace*. Tel Aviv: Schocken, p. 71.

———. *Time*. Tel Aviv: Schocken, 1977, poem No. 10, p. 10.

Balaban, Avraham. *Between God and Beast: A Study of Amos Oz's Fiction*. Tel Aviv: Am Oved, 1986.

———. *Between Language and Beyond: Language and Reality in Amos Oz's Fiction*. Tel Aviv: Am Oved, 1988.

Band, Abraham, "The Unreliable Narrator in *My Michael* and in 'In the Prime of Her Life.'" *Hasifrut*, vol. 3, part 1 (1971): 30–34.

Barzel, Hillel. *Six Authors*. Tel Aviv: Yachdav, 1972.

Ben Dov, Nitza. "Oedipus in Ramat Lotan: The Link between *To Know a Woman* and Sophocles' Plays." *Haaretz* (October 3, 1990):

Bialik, H. N. "Aftergrowth." In *The Works of Ch. N. Bialik*. Tel Aviv: Devir, 1956, pp. 125–154.

———. "A Falling Twig." In *The Works of H. N. Bialik*. Tel Aviv: Devir, 1956, p. 50.

———. "I Didn't Win My Light in a Windfall." In *The Works of Ch. N. Bialik*. Tel Aviv: Devir, 1956, pp. 31–32.

———. "My Father." In *The Works of Ch. N. Bialik*. Tel Aviv: Devir, 1956, pp. 55–56.

Booth, W. C. *The Rhetoric of Fiction*. Chicago: University of Chicago Press, 1961.

Campbell, Thomas. "Hohenlinden." In *The Pleasures of Hope*, 1799, p. 92.

Cirlot, J. E. *A Dictionary of Symbols*. Trans. J. Sagel. New York: Philosophical Library, 1962.

Cuddon, J. A. *Dictionary of Literary Terms and Literary Theories*. New York: Penguin Books, 1991.

Emerson, Ralph Waldo. "Considerations by the Way." In *Poems*. Cambridge: 1847, p. 81.

Even, Yosef (Joseph). *Dictionary of Literary Terms*. Jerusalem: Academon, 1975.

Frazer, J. G. *The Golden Bough: A Study in Magic and Religion*. New York: Macmillan, 1950.

Freud, Sigmund. *Basic Writings of Sigmund Freud*. Trans. and ed. A. A. Brill. New York: The Modern Library, 1938.

Frye, Northrop. *Anatomy of Criticism*. Princeton: Princeton University Press, 1973.

Gertz, Nurit. *Amos Oz: Monography*. Tel Aviv: Sifriyat Po'alim, 1980.

Ha'efrati, Joseph. *Tchernichovsky's Idylls*. Tel Aviv: Sifriyat Po'alim and Hakibbutz Hame'uchad, 1979.

Hamilton, Edith. *Mythology*. Boston: Little, Brown, 1969.

Holtzman, Avner. "Fima Waits for a Miracle." *Haaretz* (February 15, 1991):

Kreitler, Hans, and Schulamit. *The Psychology of the Arts*. Durham, N.C.: Duke University Press, 1976.

Kristeva, Julia. "The Bounded Text." Pp. In *Desire in Language: A Semiotic Approach to*

Literature and Art. Trans. T. Gora, A. Jardine, and I. S. Roudiez. New York: Columbia University Press, 1980.

Lessing, Gottfried. *Laoocom.* New York: Moonday, 1957.

Makaryk, Irena, ed. *Encyclopedia of Contemporary Literary Poetry.* Toronto: Toronto University Press, 1994.

Mazor, Yair. "Besieged Feminism: Contradictory Thematic Trends in the Poetry of Daliah Rabikovitch." *World Literature Today,* vol. 58, no. 3 (1984): 354–59.

———. *The Dynamics of Motifs in S. Y. Agnon's Works.* Tel Aviv: Dekel—Academic Press, 1979.

———. *From Medieval Spain to the Land of Cinderella: Studies in Hebrew Poetry.* Tel Aviv: Tag, 1996.

———. *From Wooded Meadows to Downtown Tel Aviv: Contemporary Hebrew Poetry.* Tel Aviv: Papyrus—Tel Aviv University, 1996.

———. *The Other Tchernichovsky: The Landscape Pattern of His Stories: The Narrative Art of Tchernichovsky.* Tel Aviv: Papyrus—Tel Aviv University, 1979.

———. *A Sense of Structure: Studies in Modern Hebrew Poetry and Fiction and in Biblical Literature.* Tel Aviv: University Publishing Projects, 1987.

———. *The Triple Cord: Agnon, Hamsun, Strindberg: Where Hebrew and Scandinavian Literatures Meet.* Tel Aviv: Papyrus—Tel Aviv University Press, 1987.

———. "Who Is Afraid of Hebrew Children's Poetry and Why, or: The Importance of Being Earnest about Cinderella." *Israel Studies Bulletin,* vol. 12, no. 1 (Spring 1996): 4–8; vol. 12, no. 2 (Fall 1996): 20–25.

Pope, Alexander. "An Essay On Criticism." In W. J. Bates, ed. *Criticism: The Major Texts.* New York: Harcourt, Brace, Jovanovich, pp. 174–81.

Rabikovitch, Dalia. "Twenty Five Years." In *Death in the Family.* Tel Aviv: Sifriyat Po'alim, 1976.

Selden, Raman, and Peter Widdowson, eds. *Contemporary Literary Theory.* Lexington: Kentucky University Press, 1933.

Shvaid, Eliezer. *Three Watches in Hebrew Literature.* Tel Aviv: Am Oved, 1967.

Someck, Ronny. "The Sonnet of the Sleeve of the Landscape." In *Rice Paradise.* Tel Aviv: Zemora-Bitan, 1996, p. 101.

Tchernichovsky, Saul. "Dumplings." In *The Works of Saul Tchernichovsky.* Tel Aviv: Am Oved, 1990, Vol. II, pp. 64–67.

———. "Not in Moments of Nature's Slumber." In *The Works of Saul Tchernichovsky.* Tel Aviv: Am Oved, 1990, Vol. I, p. 53.

Tomashevsky, Boris. "Thematics." In L.T. Lemon and M. J. Reis, eds. *Russian Formalist Criticism.* Lincoln: Nebraska University Press, 1965, pp. 61–95.

Wisseltir, Meir. "Over the Mountains and Over the Waves." In *Take.* Tel Aviv: Siman Keri'a, 1973, p. 14.

Yehoshua, A. B. "Facing the Forests." In *Facing the Forests.* Tel Aviv: Hakibbutz Hame'uchad, 1968, pp. 9–55.

Zach, Nathan. "Books and Deeds." In *Since I'm in the Neighborhood.* Tel Aviv: Hakibbutz Hame'uchad, 1996, p. 247.

Index of Literary and Critical Works

203

Index of Authors and Artists